The Vermont
YEAR ROUND
COOKBOOK

Books by Louise Andrews Kent

The Terrace

Paul Revere Square

Mrs. Appleyard's Year

Mrs. Appleyard's Kitchen

Country Mouse

"... with Kitchen Privileges"

The Summer Kitchen
(*with Elizabeth Kent Gay*)

The Winter Kitchen
(*with Elizabeth Kent Gay*)

The Vermont Year Round Cookbook

Stories for Young People

Douglas of Porcupine

The Red Rajah

Two Children of Tyre

He Went with Marco Polo

He Went with Vasco da Gama

He Went with Magellan

He Went with Christopher Columbus

Jo Ann, Tomboy (*with Ellis Parker Butler*)

In Good Old Colony Times
(*with Elizabeth Kent Tarshis*)

The Brookline Trunk

He Went with John Paul Jones

He Went with Champlain

He Went with Drake

He Went with Hannibal

The Vermont
YEAR ROUND
COOKBOOK

Louise Andrews Kent

ILLUSTRATED WITH SIXTEEN PLATES
IN FULL COLOR BY HANSON CARROLL, JOYCE WILSON
AND GRANT HEILMAN

Published in collaboration with *Vermont Life* Magazine,
Montpelier, Vermont

HOUGHTON MIFFLIN COMPANY BOSTON
THE RIVERSIDE PRESS CAMBRIDGE
1965

Foreword

AMERICAN COOKING, including Vermont cooking, is basically English. The original settlers brought it to New England with them and it still persists. The glossary (p. 211) shows how many cooking terms, still in use, originated in England.

What it was like to dine with King Arthur is described in the following verses, written a little after his time and looking back wistfully at those happy days.

> When good King Arthur ruled this land
> He was a goodly king:
> He stole three pecks of barley malt
> To make a bag pudd*ing*.
>
> A bag pudd*ing*, the Queen did make
> And stuffed it full of plums
> And in it put great lumps of fat
> As big as my two thumbs.
>
> The King and Queen did eat thereof,
> And noblemen beside,
> And what they did not eat that night
> The Queen, next morning, fried.

If you have limited your contact with Guinevere to *The Idylls of the King* and *Camelot*, you may now feel better acquainted with her. Apparently she was a domestic character who never harmed anyone except by too much cholesterol in her menus. Loyal to her memory, the English still make suet pudding. Mrs. Appleyard herself, at Christmas time, turns out a rather nourishing plum pudding and the same tradition is being followed in many Vermont kitchens. And out of respect for King Alfred pancakes are scorched on many a griddle.

The difference between English and French cooking is not so much a matter of quality as a point of view. The best English cooking is excellent. England should not be judged by fish and chips shops any more than America should be judged by the average roadside stand. There is plenty of bad cooking in New York City. Mrs. Appleyard hates to believe it but she has heard that it is possible to get bad food in France — in an inexpensive little pension, for instance.

The English point of view about good food is that it must be "honest." A big sirloin of beef is honest, so is a steak perfectly broiled or a brace of mutton chops. It is honest to cook vegetables separately in lots of water. Things should not be mixed up and veiled in sauce. Gravy made in the pan the meat was roasted in and served in a tureen is honest. So is bread sauce. It may seem rather like a poultice but you know what it is and accept or reject it on that basis. The French, however, have what the British regard as an insincere habit of making odds and ends taste better than they really are. The trick is done with loving care, sauces and seasonings.

Is that honest? Of course not and an honest Englishman calls them French kickshaws or gallimaufries. Naturally he speaks contemptuously. Why not? He's been doing it since Shakespeare's time.

There has long been a plan for a tunnel under the Channel between England and France. The idea is apparently practical and since it was first seriously discussed, more than a century ago, the French have been in favor of it. The English, however, when it comes to the point, always find some reason for not doing it at that particular moment. The latest delay was caused by the Profumo scandal.

Mrs. Appleyard wonders if the underlying reason isn't because British wives don't want their husbands running over to Paris for lunch. Suppose you were an American wife confronted by the same menace — would you want your husband coming home to dinner and demanding French kickshaws instead of that honest TV plate, each part of the meal so carefully insulated in its little compartment? Answer honestly, please!

The only possible advantage is that he could not very well say, "I had that for lunch."

Of course you might improve your cooking. In fact this has already happened in America, in Vermont among other places.

Vermont cooking is not static. Every new bride who has come here with a few of her grandmother's best receipts in her notebook has changed it a little and it keeps on changing.

Mrs. Appleyard can remember when the chief items carried in Vermont stores, so far as the main course of a dinner was concerned, were salt fish and salt pork. The modern version of the country store is attractively romanticized. Mrs. Appleyard remembers them as dark, dingy, untidy and smelling of kerosene, a flavor that often pervaded the merchandise. The kerosene can had a potato on the end of its spout. This was to keep the kerosene from spilling. It served its purpose but when the storekeeper had to fill a lard pail one of his customers had brought, he had to remove the potato.

Where did he put it? In the handiest place, naturally — on top of the cracker barrel or the flour barrel or the sugar bin or on a firkin of butter — or most natural of all — in the potato bin.

There was an old Vermont conversation half a century ago that went like this: "When did you have your potatoes?" "We had them at night," or if the main meal was at noon, "We had them at noon."

Potatoes, in fact, with codfish or salt pork, were your pièce de résistance and they were often subtly flavored with kerosene.

Country stores also smelled strongly of tobacco in various forms. The favorite was the chewing variety, so there were plenty of cuspidors. Some of them were Bennington ware — if that makes it any better. Luckily the flavors of tobacco and kerosene were somewhat obscured by that of freshly ground coffee and by woodsmoke from the cast-iron stove.

Mrs. Appleyard is able to do without this flavor blend and she shops with satisfaction in her neighborhood store, which is clean, sunny, well arranged, with a wide variety of foods and with petunias blossoming in the window in January. There was excellent food served in the good old days and there was bad food too, plenty of it. Good food meant then — and still means — good materials cooked by someone who cares, cares about the food and about the people who will eat it. Bad food is produced by cooks whose basic philosophy is "I couldn't care less."

The receipts Mrs. Appleyard gives were cooked by people who aimed at excellence. Some of them come from old cookbooks used in Vermont for more than a century. There is Miss Beecher, who, in 1841, begins her chapter on baking by telling you how to construct a brick oven. There is Mrs. Cornelius who wrote in 1850 that "the happiness of the husband is often abridged by absence of skill, neatness and economy in the wife." His health, she adds gloomily, is often injured by habitually eating bad bread. There is Miss Parloa who, by 1880, had discovered France and that accurate measurements were necessary to good cooking. There are handwritten cookbooks still, after almost a century, smelling faintly of cloves and cinnamon and written neatly in ink now cinnamon colored. Mrs. Appleyard wishes she could thank all these writers and also her own grandmother, whose firm handwriting in ink still black, adds information on extra leaves in the backs of old books.

Mrs. Appleyard can at least thank her daughters and granddaughters for some contemporary ideas and acknowledge the kindness of the friends whose initials appear with some of the receipts. She is grateful to the Brookline Public Library for checking some ancient cooking lore. She thanks Mr. Freeman Walker and Colonel Joseph Bayne for explaining how Vermont wind can make snowballs.

She especially appreciated help from Walter Hard, Jr., for many ideas including the one for the articles that appeared in *Vermont Life* and for suggesting that they might be made into a book. She also thanks the photographers who made the color plates, included here, for the magazine articles. Unlike food in most photographs, this is not synthetic. It's as genuine as granite or dandelions or sugar maples.

Any mistakes in receipts are Mrs. Appleyard's own invention.

Contents

WINTER
IN VERMONT

Winter in Vermont

ALL VERMONTERS and adopted Vermonters have their favorite Vermont season. If conversation ever flags — it does sometimes, though Vermonters are less taciturn than is generally supposed — it can always be brisked up by asking a group which season they like best. A surprising number choose winter. They agree that it's the most beautiful season. Mrs. Appleyard thinks there are other reasons for this choice.

One of them is, she thinks, a sense of achievement. Just to cope with the difficulties of winter and survive is a daily triumph. Before she had spent a winter in Vermont, she took the inhabitants seriously when they groaned about the coming of snow. Some of them begin to do this about June 23rd by announcing in lugubrious tones: "Well, the days are getting shorter!" Others wait till a fine hot day in August. They see a maple hanging out a dying branch, its red flag of danger, and they announce gloomily: "It won't be long now."

Awful details of past winters are dredged up from minds all too well stored with memories of frozen pipes and frozen ears, broken hips, crumpled fenders.

Yet Vermonters really like winter. Partly, Mrs. Appleyard thinks, because there are still farms and farmers in Vermont. Yes, she knows that many farmers have left Vermont. They began to leave early in the nineteenth century. As soon as they saw those steep fields, those determined-looking rocks, those especially adhesive black bogs, they decided that farming must be easier somewhere else. Soon they were on the Erie Canal and writing home describing rich level land as far as you could see. Letters like these — there are still some in an old desk in Mrs. Appleyard's house — made other Vermonters start west. Some stayed in the good farming country but others were homesick and came back, establishing a pattern still being repeated.

3

One young man who went west from Appleyard Center never wrote home. He was too moderate to stand Vermont winters, his father said, so he wasn't much help anyway. His mother, however, worried about him enough so that after some months she wrote to the postmaster of the Iowa town where her son had said he might go.

The Iowa postmaster, a former Vermonter, sent this reply:

> The gentleman you mention
> Was once in our employ.
> The tasks we put upon him,
> They seemed him to annoy.
> To be a hustling Westerner
> Was not to be his fate.
> He hurried-once-and swung aboard
> A fast-bound Eastern freight.

P.S. Try Appleyard Center, Vermont.

The young man returned. Finding farming exhausting, he became a schoolteacher and an authority on the West and on Indians. As the years went on, he remembered more and more about more and more Indians. To listen to him around the hot stove in the store was one of the winter pleasures of Appleyard Center.

For farmers winter is a time of comparative leisure. They merely do twice as much work as most people instead of three times. In between the hours spent in milking forty or fifty cows twice a day, there are moments when they can relax as they cannot do in sugaring or ploughing or haying or harvesting. Vermont farmers have been known to arrange to have their chores done and go to Florida for a vacation. Sometimes they visit Boston or even New York but usually they just enjoy Vermont. They take the children skiing or drive their wives to town for shopping. They saddle horses and ride to the top of hills where they can look off over blue-shadowed white fields, over the dark twisting patterns of brooks and rivers to wooded hills beyond that are deep purple furred over with silver. Higher hills are sharply cut in air-force blue against a pale sky. Higher still the mountains are blue clouds as pale as the sky. They are crested with white that flushes pink at sunset.

If you have your back to the west, you can see the purple shadows of pines and elms and maples racing across the pinkish-gold snow in front of you. As the sun slips swiftly down, the tree shadows are as long as the shadows of cathedral spires. Even as you turn to look at the trees themselves, the last of the sun's red disk vanishes among purple and gold flames. The sky is so clear it is almost green. Trees against it are sharply cut in black.

Of course the farmer can't watch it long — there are still those fifty cows to milk. There are still those bales of hay that looked like shredded wheat in the fields last summer to decompress for the cows' supper. But do you know a family who had a live Shetland pony at their Christmas tree? Mrs. Appleyard does.

She has now almost written herself into thinking winter is her favorite season. Perhaps about seasons she is the same as about her children and grandchildren: her favorite is

the one she is looking at. When she looks at a winter sunset, she conveniently forgets the January thaw when cars skid on ice under melting snow, when wheels spin in mud, when mud comes into the house on overshoes.

She remembers clean crisp air and snow like powdered rainbows. Deer come down the hill before dawn to drink from the brook. Their dotted trail curves from the south across the field. Gray squirrels have jumped across it, brushing snow with their tails, leaving marks like ostrich plumes. Blue jays have left their claw marks. There are even the prints of Mrs. Appleyard's velvet and fur boots, made as she carried some special delicacies to the compost heap. She ought to pick up her feet better, she notes critically, especially the left one. Luckily it is starting to snow again. All tracks will be obliterated.

Snow falls and the hills vanish. When you next see them, they have changed again and are white etched with black under black clouds. If you have never seen snow knocked off an old apple tree by both blue jays and yellow evening grosbeaks at once, you have never seen color.

Another unusual sight — it happens perhaps once in twenty years, the experts tell her — is when the wind makes snowballs, as it did one February morning in 1964. The snow was as light as gossamer and there were clouds of it as dry and fine as freshly sifted flour. The wind came from the northwest across an open field that tilts slightly to the southeast. The snow already on the field had melted a little the day before and then had frozen at night. It looked that morning as if it had been waxed and polished by some careful housewife.

The fresh snow covered it quickly. Then suddenly the wind whirled the new snow into little balls no bigger at first than frozen crab apples. The balls began to roll across the field. As they did so they grew, almost imperceptibly at first, until they were white golf balls rolling across white putting greens. Some stopped — an old stalk of goldenrod, a ripple in the snow might stop them — but others went on. New ones were formed and followed. Now some were the size a small boy likes best to throw but if you touched one, it vanished: it was as much frozen wind as snow. Now they were the size of grapefruit, still moving, still growing, quickly now. They were as light as tumbleweeds. They seemed to blow faster than the wind blows.

Then, as suddenly as their career began, it ended. The largest were perhaps as big as a man's head when they slowed down and stopped. Even a fierce blast no longer moved their weight and the wind had dropped a little now. The falling flakes grew larger. Perhaps they were a little too moist, a little too heavy. Soon the balls were covered. They lost their individuality. Before long the surface of the field was only rather uneven in texture. By the time the sun came out, the whole thing seemed like a dream, half remembered.

It may not happen for another twenty years. Yet it might happen tomorrow. In Vermont it pays to keep watching the weather.

Snow brings out other colors besides the red of barns and the blue of hills. On her trips to town Mrs. Appleyard notices a cheerful amount of scarlet on the streets. Plaid mackinaws and scarlet caps are still worn, though deer season is over, and there are parkas of crimson silk.

Half a century ago silk was a feminine material. Now husky carpenters and plumbers have quilted jackets in pastel shades. Bankers and lawyers have fur hats and fur-collared coats. Bankers used to wear black suits and hats with brims. Underneath their overcoats, they now have jackets subtly plaided with olive and indigo. Sometimes they wear bow ties of harmonious shades. Doctors in hospitals have gowns of sea green or misty mountain blue. Mrs. Appleyard thinks the blue is more becoming to most complexions, but she likes both. She also likes brilliant mufflers and amazing shirts of many colors and handsome waistcoats, especially with gold buttons.

Or does she just like men?

Perhaps that's it. After all, men, especially Vermont men, are woman's best invention.

Who ploughs the roads? Who works thaw rigs upon frozen pipes until water drips again, then trickles, then gushes? Who passes the plate in church with such dignity? Who puts gold on the State House dome? Who raises musk oxen?

You've guessed? What a coincidence!

Of course men have their faults. They love to knock down trees with bulldozers. They'd like the world better if it were covered with concrete. They thought up bookkeeping by double entry and trained women to do it.

Women are also permitted, sometimes even encouraged, to write books. For this Mrs. Appleyard is very grateful. How else would she get through the winter?

Crusty, Fragrant, Golden

"It is about time," Mrs. Appleyard said, "that someone repaired the staff of life. Imagine trying to lean on this!"

She was looking at a loaf of commercial bread made apparently of kapok flavored with plaster of Paris with a large amount of air beaten into it. Mrs. Appleyard felt sure it was not Vermont air, which is bracing and which gives a certain amount of backbone to practically anything. Of course, as proclaimed on the wrapper, the bread contained preservatives to keep it just as limp and tasteless as it was when first baked.

"If I had needed a poultice and not bread and butter for afternoon tea, I would have bought it." Mrs. Appleyard announced.

By one of the happiest of accidents Andrea Morini, one of the neighborhood's best bread-makers, came into the shop at that moment. She looked like a Renaissance princess, and she was carrying two loaves of bread, her donation to the PTA Food Sale. Mrs. Appleyard bought them before they hit the red and white checked tablecloth. Home-baked bread, she notices, always vanishes first at a food sale. Cakes with fluffy frosting cannot compete with it.

"I think this looks like an especially good batch, even for you," she told Andrea.

"That," Andrea told her, "if so, is because your daughter Cicely was with me while I was kneading it. Breadmaking goes much better if you have congenial company than if you thump it morosely alone."

Mrs. Appleyard cannot imagine Andrea doing anything morosely but she agrees that breadmaking is an emotional experience and, as an invention, is more remarkable than anything electronic, as a process magical and mysterious. However, she also thinks a little practical advice does no harm and as Andrea has generously described her method, Mrs. Appleyard takes pleasure in passing on the directions. Her own contribution is the suggestion that beginning bakers had better start with white bread rather than with whole wheat which, under the hands of amateur kneaders, often results in quite a challenge to the family teeth. Use stone-ground flour if possible, or anyway unbleached, enriched flour.

ANDREA MORINI'S WHITE BREAD

FOUR LOAVES

Scald 3½ cups milk and cool to lukewarm.
Measure 1 cup warm water into a warm mixing bowl.
Add 3 packages active dry yeast, stir to dissolve. Add salt to taste.
Stir in the lukewarm milk in which you have dissolved 4 tablespoons butter.
Add half of 14 to 15 cups flour sifted with 6 tablespoons granulated sugar,
    2 tablespoons salt.

Beat with a wooden spoon until smooth. Batter should fall in sheets from the spoon. Mix in enough of the remaining flour with your hand until dough leaves the sides of the bowl. Turn onto a lightly floured board. (I use a marble slab, which requires less flour.) Cover. Let dough rest 10 to 15 minutes. Knead until smooth, pushing dough away from you with the heel of the hand, pulling it back with your fingers. (A cool kitchen makes kneading harder and the grain of the bread finer than a warm one does.) Knead until dough is smooth — 10 to 12 minutes. Make into a ball. Put into a buttered bowl. Turn the ball over so that the whole surface is slightly buttered. Cover with a clean dish towel moistened a little with warm water. Let rise in a warm place (about 85°) until double in bulk (about one hour). If your oven has a pilot light it will be warm enough. If it hasn't, put a pan of warm water in the bottom of the oven. Use a thermometer. Add more hot water occasionally to keep it about 85°. When the dough has risen enough, two fingers pressed into it will leave an indentation. Punch it down with your fist. Let it rise till double again (about 30 minutes).

Divide in 4 parts. Cover. Let it rest 10 minutes. Shape each part into a loaf. Thus: flatten dough into an oblong 9 x 12 inches, pressing out air with your knuckles. Fold dough in half, lengthwise. Flatten to an oblong 15 x 5 inches. Again press out air. Fold in thirds by overlapping the ends, keeping dough the same width as the pan. Press out air. Roll toward you, a third at a time, sealing well with heel of hand, and seal each end by pressing with the edge of hands. Smooth loaf lightly and place sealed side down in well buttered 9 x 5 x 3 tin loaf pan. Brush top with melted butter. Cover. Let rise till dough reaches side of pan and top is rounded (50 to 65 minutes).

Bake at 425° for 25 to 30 minutes. If it browns too quickly reduce heat to 350°. Total baking time may be 45 minutes or more according to number of loaves, kind of pans used. When bread shrinks from pan and sounds hollow when tapped, it is done. Take it out of the pans and place on rack to cool. Brush with butter. Cover with a towel briefly so it can finish cooling out of a draft.

Perhaps the most important piece of equipment is a musical ear, sensitive to the right resonance of a tapped loaf. Andrea does not trust herself. She calls her husband to tap and listen and pronounce that the bread is done.

Mrs. Appleyard says that it satisfies all five senses: sight with its golden brown crustiness, touch with its fine firm texture, smell with the fragrance that makes everyone hungry, hearing with that note of a distant drum, and — last of all — taste.

"And," she adds, "if you can get some loaves into the freezer before the neighbors smell it and come for hot buttered slices, you will be lucky enough to have a staff of life you can lean upon with confidence. I'd better get some yeast myself."

PARKER HOUSE ROLLS
ABOUT FOUR DOZEN

It is possible to make very good rolls from a package of hot roll mix. If they are cut and folded in the proper way they are a good deal more like the original Parker House rolls than any commercial product that now travels under that name. When you have practiced with the mix, you might like to make them the way Mrs. Appleyard's grandmother used to serve them.

1 yeast cake	2 tablespoons sugar
½ cup lukewarm water	1 teaspoon salt
2 cups milk, scalded	6 cups bread flour
4 tablespoons butter	extra butter

Crumble the yeast cake into the water, which should feel just barely warm to your fingers. Bring the milk to the point where small bubbles begin to appear around the edge. Remove from heat. Stir in the butter, sugar, and salt. Let this stand until the mixture is lukewarm and then add the yeast cake, which by now should be dissolved. Sift the flour and add it to the mixture. Flour varies in how much liquid it will absorb so it is possible that you will not need the whole six cups. The dough should be just stiff enough to handle. Grease a large bowl. Knead the dough well on a lightly floured board. Put it in the greased bowl. Brush the top lightly with melted butter. Cover the bowl and set it to rise in a warm place out of the draft. It should double its bulk in about 2 hours. A piece of old patchwork quilt is handy for keeping it at an even temperature. Now flour your hands and make the dough into balls about 2½ inches in diameter. Flatten them slightly. Flour the handle of a wooden spoon and press it gently across the middle of each ball. Brush the half nearest you with butter and fold the other half over it. Put the rolls in dripping pans. Set them to rise covered with clean dish towels in a warm place for about 45 minutes. Brush tops with butter. Bake at 425° for about 15 minutes. Change position of pans in the oven from the upper to the lower shelf after 7 minutes. Serve hot.

This same dough may be shaped into twists or crescents. It can also be made into clover-leaf rolls by putting three small balls of it into well-buttered iron muffin pans. Let them rise in a warm place till they double their bulk. Brush the tops with butter. Bake them at 450° until they are delicately brown — about 20 minutes. If you want a richer roll, add 2 well-beaten eggs to lukewarm milk and butter mixture before you add the flour.

GRAHAM BREAD

The discovery that it is a mistake to throw away the most nourishing part of wheat flour is not a new one. Graham (whole wheat) flour is named for Dr. Sylvester Graham, who was born at the end of the eighteenth century and died in 1851. Most nineteenth century cook-books contain rules for graham bread but they usually assume that you make your own yeast and advise you to use a teacup of it. If they tell you how much flour to use, they tell you to "wet it up" with an unspecified amount of water. If the liquid is accurately measured, the amount of flour is left to your imagination. When bread dough turned sour — as it often did in warm weather — you are told that all will be well if you work in "enough saleratus to sweeten it and then shape it into biscuits." Miss Beecher says that these were so well liked that "some persons allow bread to turn sour for the purpose." Mrs. Appleyard takes this statement with a grain of saleratus (soda).

Miss Parloa is more helpful. The following rule, used by Mrs. Appleyard's grandmother, is based on Miss Parloa's directions.

GRAHAM BREAD
TWO LOAVES

1 yeast cake	2 cups white flour
½ cup lukewarm water	1 teaspoon salt
2 cups scalded milk	½ cup light brown sugar
1 tablespoon butter	2½ cups graham flour

Dissolve crumbled yeast in the lukewarm water. Scald the milk (you may use water if you prefer) and add the butter (or lard if you prefer). Some people say lard and water make a more tender loaf of bread. Cool the liquid to lukewarm. Put the well-sifted white flour into a deep bowl. Make a hole in the center of the flour. Mix the yeast with the liquid and pour it into the flour slowly, beating well all the time until the mixture is smooth. Cover the bowl well and set it in a moderately cool place, about 60°, free from drafts, to rise overnight. In the morning mix salt and sugar with the graham flour and beat this mixture into the risen dough. Beat vigorously. A spoon with holes in it or a pastry blending fork may be used. Grease bread tins with butter. Turn dough on a lightly floured board, knead it, shape it into loaves, put them into the tins. Let bread rise until double in bulk, about one hour at 100°. A barely warm oven with burners off may be used for 45 minutes. (Check temperature with oven thermometer.) Then remove tins, cover them well. Heat oven to 375°. Let bread rise 15 minutes longer. Bake until a loaf sounds hollow when rapped, about one hour. Turn loaves over, tip them up in the pans, turn off oven, open the oven door and leave them in the open oven five or ten minutes longer.

If you can keep the family from eating this while it is hot, it slices well for thin bread and butter and makes good sandwiches. If your bread tins are small you will have enough dough left to make graham gems, baked in oblong shaped iron pans. Butter the pans well, fill two-thirds full. Cover and let rise to top of pans. Brush the tops of the gems with melted butter. Bake at 375° to 400° for about 20 minutes.

Easier and quicker to make than the yeast bread is

SOUR CREAM GRAHAM BREAD
TWO LOAVES

2 cups white flour	2 teaspoons baking powder
2 cups graham flour	2 eggs, well beaten
1 teaspoon salt	½ cup thick sour cream
2 teaspoons baking soda	1½ cups sour milk
	1⅛ cups maple syrup

Sift the dry ingredients together. Beat the eggs well and stir them into the cream, milk, and syrup. (Mrs. Appleyard formerly used cream skimmed off a pan of milk; now uses sour cream from a carton like anyone else.) Beat in the dry ingredients. The batter should be quite stiff. Add a little more graham flour if necessary. Butter bread tins and line them with heavy waxed paper. Fill them two-thirds full with the mixture. Bake in a moderately hot oven (375°) for half an hour. Change position of pans in the oven, reduce heat to 350°, and bake about half an hour longer. Test with a straw. When it comes out clean, the bread is done.

A favorite Vermont dessert used to be slices of this bread buttered, sprinkled with granulated maple sugar, and served with very thick cream cither sweet or sour.

DATE NUT BREAD (MRS. APPLEYARD)

The line between bread and cake is not always very sharply drawn. It would not take much to turn this rather sticky concoction into fruitcake. Mrs. Appleyard's family were not fussy about what it was called. They liked to eat it slightly warm. In fact Mrs. Appleyard can't seem to remember that any was left over to get cold.

2 cups graham flour   1 cup dark molasses
1 cup white flour   1 cup sour cream
½ teaspoon baking soda   2 large eggs
2 teaspoons baking powder   ½ cup nuts, chopped, floured
½ teaspoon salt   1 cup dates, cut in pieces and floured

Sift the dry ingredients. Don't discard the bran from the graham flour. Stir it back into the flour mixture. Mrs. Appleyard hopes you have a triple flour sifter. It's a great time-saver. Stir the molasses and cream together and add the eggs, well beaten. Add the dry ingredients, beating them in well. Heat the oven to 375°. Butter a large bread tin, flour it lightly, line it with heavy waxed paper. Stir floured nuts and dates quickly into the mixture. Pour the mixture into the bread tin. Bake half an hour. Reduce heat to 350°. Bake about half an hour longer.

Mrs. Appleyard used to make this with butternuts but she hasn't seen any lately, uses walnuts or pecans now.

OATMEAL BREAD
THREE SMALL LOAVES

2 cups water   2 tablespoons butter
1 cup regular Quaker oats   ½ cup molasses
1 yeast cake   2 tablespoons wheat germ
⅓ cup lukewarm water   4½–5 cups flour
              1 teaspoon salt

Put water into the top of a double boiler. Bring water to a boil, stir in the oatmeal and cook it over hot water for one hour. Dissolve the yeast cake in the lukewarm water. When the oatmeal is cooked, put it into a large bowl, add the butter and the molasses. When the mixture is lukewarm, add the dissolved yeast cake and stir in the wheat germ. Add 4½ cups of the flour, sifted with the salt, and beat hard with a spoon. Grease another large bowl, put in the dough. Set it to rise in a warm place, well covered, until bulk doubles — about 2 hours. Flour a board lightly, toss bread and knead well. Use the extra half cup of flour on the board and on your hands. Heat the oven to 375°. Grease two large or three small bread tins. Shape dough into loaves, put into tins. Bake half an hour on top shelf of the oven. Reduce heat to 350° and bake on lower shelf half an hour longer. Turn off oven. Turn bread over, tip it up in the pans and let it stand at the open oven door for 5 minutes.

Thirsty Season

COFFEE

IN THE nineteenth century children often enjoyed a delicious sequence of smells: coffee roasting, coffee being ground, coffee boiling. These are the instructions Mrs. Appleyard's grandmother gave her so that she could make a good cup of coffee. A combination of Mocha and Java coffee was the best, she said. To roast it, begin by drying it for an hour or two over low heat. Do this in a round-bottomed iron kettle. There are often, she told her granddaughter, little stones, the same color as the coffee beans, mixed with them. These should be picked out carefully. When the coffee is thoroughly dry, put the kettle over high heat and stir constantly until coffee beans are well browned, about 15 minutes. Put in a bit of butter the size of a chestnut. Constant stirring is indispensable.

Never leave it, even for half a minute, or some kernels will turn black and this will injure all the rest. Not more than two pounds should be roasted at once. The practice of grinding up a quantity for two or three weeks is a poor one. Roast often, grind every time coffee is made.

This is how she said coffee should be made:

Always use an enamelled granite ware tall coffee pot. Tin, pewter and Britannia metal spoil the flavor. To three pints of water use a good coffee cup of freshly ground coffee mixed with one egg crushed — white, yolk and shell. Put this mixture in the coffee pot and pour on hot — not boiling — water. Bring it quickly to the boil and boil it not over 10 minutes. Now pour out a little from the spout to remove any grounds that have boiled into it and pour the coffee back into the pot. Next pour in half a cup of cold water. Set the pot where the coffee will keep hot but not boil for 5 minutes. Then, without shaking the pot, pour off the liquid into a clean pot, leaving the grounds behind.

When eggs are scarce, coffee may be cleared with a fish skin. Take the skin of a salted codfish that has not been soaked. Rinse skin and dry it in a warm oven. Cut it into inch squares. One of these serves for three pints of liquid coffee. Put it in with the grounds. Use egg if possible: it makes a richer coffee.

Wash the coffee pot with strong soap and water, scour with sapolio, rinse several times. Lay it on the table on the back porch, facing the sun with the lid opened.

Mrs. Appleyard remembers seeing it there. She also remembers that a child who had shown special virtue (being seen and not heard, for instance, or sewing squares neatly together for a patchwork pillowcase) was sometimes treated to a "coffee duck" — a lump of sugar dipped rapidly into coffee and placed, before it melted, in the mouth of the model of her sex. Who needs ambrosia?

S. S. Pierce still has Mocha and Java coffee, well roasted, freshly ground. It can be made just as Mrs. Appleyard's grandmother made it. Use a glass or enamel ware pot, never aluminum.

Mrs. Appleyard wonders why men invented instant coffee. Could it be that women scorched coffee beans, ground too much at a time, left stones in it, economized on eggs, left out the fish skin, boiled it till it was bitter, didn't rinse grounds out of the spout? Is it possible that, on the average, instant coffee is better than boiled? She knows hers is. She learned how to make it from TV. You allow a generous teaspoon of coffee to a cup. Make it in a glass pot. Add cold water. Bring it to a boil but don't boil. Let it steep 5 minutes. No egg, no fish skin. People have been known to take a second cup.

TEA

She learned to make tea from her father, an Englishman with an accurate palate and strong opinions.

"Reminds me of someone I've met," said Mrs. Appleyard's daughter Cicely.

Ignoring this remark, Mrs. Appleyard started warming a sturdy brown pottery teapot. Tea, her father told her, must be made in pottery, never in metal. When the pot was warm, you put into it a teaspoon of tea for each person and one for the pot. As soon as the teakettle boiled really hard, you brought the pot to the kettle — never the other way — and poured the boiling water on the tea and covered the pot with a tea cozy. Much art was expended on tea cozies. Apple blossoms, outlined with gold thread, embroidered on velvet made a nice effect. Still, even well-padded Turkey-red cotton would keep the tea warm while it steeped the proper number of minutes — five for a small pot, seven for a large one. At the end of this time, you stirred the tea well with a silver spoon and strained it into another well-warmed pot.

One of the problems about tea is to have enough hot water on hand. There are always weak spirits, Mrs. Appleyard for instance, who like hot water delicately flavored with tea, milk, and sugar. How she can tell whether Earl Grey's mixture has been used is a mystery: she can, though.

She realizes that you are probably going to use a tea bag anyway. Don't feel guilty if you do. The tea thus made is often much better than most nineteenth century tea which was often steeped all day on the back of the stove and as brown as ink. The resulting tea leaves were saved until there were about half a peck. The housemaid dampened them slightly and scattered them over the Brussels carpets and then swept them up again. The idea was that all the dust that had collected since last Wednesday came up with them.

Mrs. Appleyard has tasted tea that makes her think that some frugal housekeepers saved these leaves and again brewed a dark decoction. She thinks a tea bag is preferable only she hopes you'll be generous. She knew one bride who announced that she had made thirty-seven cups from one tea bag. Even Mrs. Appleyard detected a certain feebleness in this infusion.

COCOA SHELLS

A favorite nineteenth century New England drink was made from the shells of the cocoa bean. It was an economical substitute for hot chocolate. Mrs. Appleyard knows how to make it but she intends to keep this information a secret. In her opinion it was worse than parched-wheat coffee cleared with a fish skin. Instead she mentions

HOT CHOCOLATE
FOR TWELVE

6 squares Baker's chocolate	1 tablespoon brandy
1 cup water	or
6 tablespoons sugar	2 teaspoons vanilla,
8 cups rich milk	or
1 cup cream, whipped	2 teaspoons instant coffee

Grate the chocolate. Put it into the top of a large double boiler with the water. When the chocolate has melted and the mixture is smooth, add sugar gradually, stirring all the time. Scald the milk — do not let it boil — and pour it on the chocolate mixture beating well with a wire whisk. Add the flavoring. Keep on beating till it froths. Serve whipped cream separately for those who are not self-conscious about their silhouettes.

HOT BUTTERED RUM
FOR FOUR

One cheering moment at Abdiel Appleyard's crossroads store was when the oxteam arrived from Boston with "West Inja goods." Abdiel made a good profit on the sugar and molasses and also on the rum, which he sold for six cents a pint. If you had six cents you could entertain lavishly with this formula:

4 lumps sugar	hot water
4 teaspoons butter	grating of stick cinnamon
4 ounces rum	grating of nutmeg

Put a lump of sugar and a teaspoon of butter in each glass. (Tablespoons are clearly marked on modern sticks of butter. A teaspoon is ⅓ of a tablespoon.) Add an ounce of rum to each glass. Fill the glass with hot water. Grate a little of the spices into each glass. Whole cloves may be used, two to a glass, or the spices may be omitted entirely. Anyway they should be added with a light hand.

Mrs. Appleyard has reason to believe that materials for all four glasses were often mixed in one tankard, which was put beside the fire to keep warm. She thinks it is quite possible that the maker consumed it all and was economical with the hot water.

POMANDER PUNCH
FOR SIXTEEN

Pomanders are often used in closets. They are made by sticking an orange or an apple full of cloves put so close together that none of the peel shows. People like the spicy smell and moths are supposed not to.

It is less trouble to make pomanders for punch. You need to stick only about 12 cloves into each tart red apple. Six apples is enough for a big bowl of punch. They should be baked a few minutes, just enough to soften them slightly, before you stick in the cloves.

1 gallon of real unpasteurized cider	6 oranges or 6 McIntosh apples (or 3 of each), cloved
1 cup water	2-inch stick cinnamon
1 cup sugar	½ a nutmeg, grated
1 quart Jamaica rum (12 cents worth? Alas!)	

Heat cider almost to boiling point. Make syrup of the water and sugar and boil it 3 minutes. Put the hot fruit and the spices in the bowl. Pour in the rum and the hot syrup. Stir. Add the hot cider. This serves 16 generously.

You can make practically a temperance drink of this by pouring the rum over the fruit and sugar and lighting it. When the flame dies down, you add the hot cider and the spice. Mrs. Appleyard says you can also make a very good punch without any rum at all. Have a bowl of this for children when you serve the other.

VERMONT BROSE

This is a complicated subject (see Glossary). In Scotland brose was made by first mixing oatmeal and water to a thick paste, letting it stand about an hour and then straining all the liquid you could get out of it. You were supposed to extract about ¾ of a cup of this oatmeal water. Next you mixed the oatmeal water with an equal amount of strained honey, poured the mixture into a quart bottle, and filled it with whiskey. You were advised to cork the bottle tightly and shake it well. You used your own judgment about how to apportion it to a shivering world.

Mr. Appleyard's Vermont brose was different. It was a mixture of a cup of maple syrup, a cup of cream, and a cup of whiskey gently stirred together. Mrs. Appleyard was once acquainted with an eleven-months-old baby who was being brought up on beer because he did not care for milk. He could probably have tossed off a schooner of brose with no ill effects. Mrs. Appleyard finds a liqueur glassful is plenty.

SYLLABUB

Syllabub (see Glossary) seems to have been made in about as many versions as there were makers. Here is Miss Beecher's prescription:

> One pint of cream
> Sifted white sugar to your taste (perhaps a cup)
> Half a tumbler of white wine
> The grated rind and juice of one lemon
> Beat all to a froth.

Sometimes the amount of wine was larger. Sometimes sherry was used. There could be brandy in it and beaten egg whites. It could be spiced. It could have almonds in it and port wine. However you mixed it, you served it at evening parties. Mrs. Appleyard would like to find it at one this evening of stars sparkling through the green glare of Northern lights. Oh well — luckily she has some delicious carrot juice on hand!

EGGNOG

FOR TWELVE

Eggnog made with Vermont cream is a rather vibrant drink, not entirely on account of the cream.

12 egg yolks	1 cup Jamaica rum
2 cups granulated sugar	2 quarts heavy cream
1 fifth whiskey (bourbon)	2 cups milk

Make this in the morning of the day you plan to use it. Beat the egg yolks light with a wire whisk. Beat in the sugar. (You may use less sugar if you prefer. Some think a cup is plenty.) Stir in the whiskey and rum and let the mixture stand in a cool place for at least 3 hours. Then stir in the cream and chill the mixture again. Just before you serve the eggnog, stir in the milk. Doing this needs a little judgment. You want the eggnog to be of a drinkable consistency, not too thick, not too thin. Temperature and how strong your beating arm is make a difference to the mixture. Add the milk slowly, stirring rather than beating. Add a little extra if you feel it is needed.

Plan to make meringues with the egg whites. (Rule in *The Summer Kitchen*, p. 41.) They go well with eggnog and the whole project will keep you busy and out of other mischief for quite a while.

Not for Pythagoras

Mrs. Appleyard catches interests in different subjects the way other people catch colds — suddenly and by contact. She got acquainted with Pythagoras because a relative of hers by marriage, one of her daughters in fact, was studying the works of that philosopher. Mrs. Appleyard dipped into them too and could soon tell you that Pythagoras was mathematical, musical, mythical. He invented triangular numbers, figured out musical intervals and may very well — since he had a golden thigh — have been the god Apollo in disguise all the time.

Being good at forgetting almost as quickly as she learns, Mrs. Appleyard would rather not be cross-examined on this subject. She does however remember one thing clearly — Pythagoras used to say firmly to his disciples, "Eat No Beans."

Obviously he would never have been happy in Vermont.

His reason for this prejudice was that Greek beans had a small figure of a man in them. Eating them was, he said, cannibalistic. Mrs. Appleyard likes to think that the soldier beans, often used by Vermont cooks, may be direct descendants of Pythagoras' beans. Perhaps that is a Greek soldier you see in them. Probably a hoplite. Luckily yellow-eyes, which she prefers, do not present these dangers: no cannibal she.

Now the cooking of beans is a somewhat controversial topic in New England. People have discussed it ever since they used to travel in oxcarts with chunks of beans, frozen string and all, hanging from the sides of the carts. Frozen brown bread came along too. When you stopped for dinner, you made a fire, melted a little snow in an iron kettle, added the beans, laid the brown bread over the top, covered the kettle and pretty soon were able to enjoy your wife's cooking though you were almost in Vermont and she was still in Massachusetts. There was already the question whether you liked beans small, slippery and pallid or well browned and rather like a roasted chestnut in consistency and whether you flavored them lightly with maple syrup or liked them swimming in molasses. Later people started deluging them with tomato ketchup, thus arousing the disapproval of the old school, who called tomatoes "love apples" and considered them poisonous.

Mrs. Appleyard likes them the consistency of chestnuts, only lightly sweetened, with a tang of mustard and onion but with no flavor predominating over the subtle one of the beans. She thinks a bean pot is convenient to cook them in but she says she has eaten delicious beans cooked in a graniteware pan, in an enameled iron casserole, in the aluminum kettle of a fireless cooker, and in a dish of Bennington tortoiseshell. What is necessary is long, slow cooking. No doubt a brick oven produced wonderful beans but only if you made a fire in it of the right kind of wood, first "winging out" any ashes with a turkey's wing, shoveled and swept out the fire at exactly the right moment and were adept at balancing a bean pot on a baker's peel.

If you have a brick oven handy, don't hesitate to ask Mrs. Appleyard to let you practice with her peel, which is a long-handled iron shovel. To use it, all you need is determination, the strength of wrist necessary to hit a baseball for a home run, and the balance of any good tightrope walker. A hand as steady as that of a thrower of darts is helpful too, and of course you won't mind getting your cheeks scorched. On the whole, perhaps, a gas or electric oven with thermostatic control is more restful.

VERMONT BAKED BEANS

FOR SIX

4 cups yellow-eye beans	2 small onions
1 pound salt pork	1 teaspoon mustard
4 tablespoons maple syrup	

Soak the beans overnight. In the morning drain them, cover them with cold water and heat them slowly. Keep the water below the boiling point and cook the beans until the skin cracks when you take some out on a spoon and blow on them. This should happen in about 40 minutes.

Drain the beans, saving the water. Cut a thin slice off the pork and put it in the bottom of the bean pot. Put the onions in whole. They will vanish during the cooking and their flavor will be only a memory. Mix the mustard and maple syrup — or brown sugar if you have no syrup on hand — with a cup of boiling water. Put some beans on top of the onions. Make several gashes about an inch deep in the rind of the salt pork. Put it into the bean pot. Surround it with the rest of the beans, letting the rind show on top. Then pour over the water with the seasonings dissolved in it and add enough more water to cover the beans. Put the lid on the bean pot and set it into a slow oven — 300° — for 8 hours. Add a little water occasionally. After 7 hours uncover the beans so the rind of the pork will get brown and crisp.

Mrs. Appleyard usually serves some of her own apple-mint chutney with the beans and also some Boston brown bread. She likes her brown bread made without raisins. She also confides that she likes it sliced (you do it with a string: this is one of the things New Englanders save string for), buttered and run briefly under the broiler.

Whenever she sits down to this combination she feels sorry for Pythagoras. How sad to spend your life in the company of triangular numbers and eat no beans!

BROWN BREAD
GOES WITH SOUP

There is no law that you have to serve brown bread with baked beans. Mrs. Appleyard has seen Vermonters happily eating whole wheat bread or corn muffins or Parker House rolls with baked beans. However, there does seem to be a sort of classic harmony between beans and brown bread. Grandmother Appleyard called it Rye 'n Injun and made it this way:

1 cup rye flour	¾ teaspoon soda
1 cup graham flour	¾ teaspoon salt
1 cup yellow cornmeal	¾ cup molasses
1¾ cups sour milk	

Sift the dry ingredients thoroughly. Do not remove the bran from the graham flour but stir it in well. Put the sifted ingredients in a bowl and make a hollow in the mixture. Your molasses will pour better if you set the bottle into warm water while you are sifting flour and getting cans ready. A real brown bread steamer is of course the best sort of tin but you can manage with any tin that has a tightly fitting cover which overlaps the can. If you have any doubt about the cover fitting properly, seal it with masking tape. The tins should be taller than they are wide. Mrs. Appleyard treasures one that came with English biscuits in it. Brown bread made in it is just the size for sandwiches. Whatever tin you use, grease it, including the cover, thoroughly with butter.

Now mix the milk and the molasses and pour it into the hollow in the flour, beating it in well as you do so. Fill tins not more than ⅔ full. Set them on a rack in a deep kettle. Put in plenty of boiling water: it must come halfway up around the tins. The bread must be steamed for 3 hours. A lot of water can vanish in that time; cover the kettle well so that as little as possible will steam away. The bread will steam more evenly if you do not have to uncover the kettle and replace water during the steaming process. If you do have to add water, be sure it is boiling. At the end of 3 hours, remove tins from the kettle, take off the lids. Set them in a 300° oven to dry out for 5 or 10 minutes.

Add raisins to your brown bread if you like them. The Appleyards don't. About half a cup, floured, ought to be enough, Mrs. Appleyard thinks, but her opinion is not really worth much. She does not always slice brown bread with a string but often uses a Christy knife, warmed and wiped over with the paper off a stick of butter.

It is possible that you had baked beans left over from your Saturday night ritual. It is not necessary to eat them Sunday: they can be frozen for use later. Freezing beans used to be done by spooning some beans out on a pewter plate. Then you pressed a string into them, piled some more beans on top and set the plates in the pantry where the beans quickly froze hard. At serving time you set an iron skillet over the fire, put in some water or snow, which was sometimes handier — and the beans and stirred them until they melted and were steaming hot.

It's a little less trouble to freeze beans now. A well-washed quart size ice cream carton is a good container. Fill it almost full. Label and date it. Set it in the below zero section of your freezer. Reheat the beans when you need them. You don't need to add snow. Put them in the top of a double boiler.

Perhaps, however, you would rather make

BAKED BEAN SOUP
FOR FOUR

If you have this soup on a cold Vermont evening, you don't need much else for supper except some brown bread and cream cheese sandwiches and a dessert.

2 cups baked beans	4 cooked frankfurters
4 cups water	1 lemon, sliced
1 tablespoon minced onion	2 hard-boiled eggs
1 teaspoon instant coffee	2 tablespoons sherry

Mrs. Appleyard makes this in her blender. It can also be made by heating the beans slightly with a cup of the water and pressing them through a fine sieve or a food mill.

If you use the blender, you will have to do this in two batches, a cup of beans and a cup of water and some onion in each batch. Put the purée into a large casserole from which you can serve it. Add the rest of the water, the coffee, and the sliced frankfurters. Heat carefully, stirring well until the mixture starts to bubble. In each soup plate put slices of lemon and of hard-boiled egg. Add sherry to the soup and ladle it into the soup plates.

This is a sort of country cousin of black bean soup. You won't taste the coffee. It just gives the soup color and the flavor blends into the mixture.

Serve brown bread with it.

Another cheering soup for zero weather is

ONION SOUP COUNTRY STYLE
FOR FOUR

garlic butter	French bread, sliced and toasted
3 large onions	2 cups light cream
3 tablespoons butter	pinch of nutmeg
3 tablespoons flour	½ teaspoon pepper from the grinder
2 cups milk	pinch of dried tarragon
1 cup jellied chicken stock	salt to taste

1 cup grated Vermont cheese

Begin by making the garlic butter. Mix ½ teaspoon garlic powder with ¼ pound of creamed butter.

Chop the onions. Cook them in the butter till they are transparent and straw colored, about 5 minutes. Blend in the flour over low heat. Remove pan from the heat and stir in the milk. Add chicken stock. Cook, stirring, over low heat for 5 minutes. Turn off heat and let it stand until serving time. Toast bread, sliced one inch thick on one side. Spread the other side with garlic butter, and brown lightly under the broiler. Have soup plates very hot. Put a slice of the toast on each plate. Add cream and seasonings to the soup, heat to scalding point and pour soup over the toast. Pass the grated cheese and extra slices of toast.

Omit the bread if you like and serve brown bread sandwiches with the soup.

CLAM AND CELERY SOUP
FOR SIX

2 tablespoons butter	2 cups milk
1 small onion, minced	1 bunch celery
2 tablespoons flour	1 cup jellied chicken stock
salt to taste	1 cup cream
¼ teaspoon mace	2 cups clam juice
½ teaspoon paprika	2 tablespoons minced parsley
½ teaspoon pepper	2 tablespoons minced chives

Melt butter. Add onion and cook until it is straw colored. Mix flour and seasonings and blend it smoothly into the butter over very low heat. Remove from fire, add the milk slowly, stirring until it is smooth. Cook over low heat 5 minutes. Into the blender put the celery, washed and cut up. Include the best and crispest of the celery leaves. Add the chicken stock and blend till the mixture is thick and smooth. Add this mixture to the soup, simmer for 5 minutes. Put the soup into the top of a large double boiler and let it stand over hot, not boiling, water till serving time. Then add the cream. Bring the mixture to scalding point. Heat clam juice separately and stir it in. Do not let the soup boil after adding the clam juice or it will curdle. Serve it with minced parsley and chives scattered over it. Serve brown bread with it, or hot popovers if you'd rather.

CHICKEN STOCK

In summer Clam and Celery Soup is good served very cold. Mrs. Appleyard makes the chicken stock by simmering wing tips and necks of chicken and one onion in her electric skillet for several hours, strains it into a bowl, chills it, skims the fat off it, puts it in covered jars in the refrigerator where it keeps well for a week or more.

MULLIGATAWNY SOUP

FOR SIX

This is a New England version of an eighteenth century East Indian soup. It was a favorite cold weather soup, almost a stew. With brown bread and some fruit and cheese for dessert it makes a whole meal. It is most easily made in an electric skillet but it can also be cooked in a big iron frying pan.

3 tablespoons chicken fat or butter	3 tablespoons flour
3 large onions, chopped	extra butter
1 small carrot, sliced thin	8 cups water
4 stalks of celery, cut fine	3-pound frying chicken, cut up
2 pounds veal, in cubes	2 tablespoons curry powder

Try out chicken fat. If there is not enough, add butter to make 3 tablespoons. Cook the onions, carrot, and celery in this over low heat until the onions are straw colored. Put in the veal cubes and toss them 5 minutes. Shove vegetables and meat to one side and make a roux with the flour, adding extra butter first if needed. Over very low heat, add the water and stir until there are no lumps. Put in the pieces of chicken, cover the pan tightly. Simmer until veal and chicken are tender, about 3 hours. Now remove chicken, free it from bones and skin, cut it up in medium pieces. Return these to the soup. Mix curry powder with some of the broth and stir the mixture into the soup. Let it simmer half an hour longer. It will be all the better if you make it in the morning and reheat it at night just before you serve it. Pass boiled brown rice with it.

Any Pearls Tonight?

ONE OF the high points of the winter in Vermont used to be the oyster supper. It may seem hard to believe that in 1880 Vermonters could get better oysters than we can now, yet Mrs. Appleyard is afraid it's true. Oysters came in their shells, packed in ice in barrels. Your oyster man in Boston put the barrels on an early morning train and they were in Montpelier or St. Johnsbury or Burlington in plenty of time to be served that night at the oyster supper.

This was usually a church supper but you might also encounter oysters at other winter gaieties — whist parties, dances, kitchen junkets, quilting bees. Oysters were served in many ways. Men opened them. Women cooked their specialties. It was an honor to be asked to make a dish of scalloped oysters or to preside over the oyster stew.

Such an honor was not lightly conferred. Mrs. Appleyard has occasionally been a member of a committee that is planning a supper and she says that if we want tact, kindness and wisdom in international diplomacy, we should turn our problems over to the Community Supper Committee. Nothing unkind is ever said about anyone's cooking.

When a name is suggested, there will be a slight pause and then someone will say, "Didn't she give us a pound of butter last year?" or "She always does a real nice job taking tickets," or "She has lovely lettuce in her garden. I wouldn't wonder if she couldn't make a good tossed salad. Seems as though."

The right place for her talents, whatever they are, is found.

Mrs. Appleyard has seen young girls start in as waitresses and then move up to kitchen jobs. They fill plates with cakes of many colors. They are at the hatchway passing out baskets of hot rolls. They keep the coffee urn filled. Then, before she knows it, they are carrying in their own casseroles and jellied salads and their daughters are filling the water glasses.

No doubt at the oyster supper the hierarchy was already established. Some gave pounds of butter or quarts of cream. Some, dressed in their best black silks, their bustles, their ornaments of shining jet, acted as hostesses. Others had embroidered silk aprons over their second best dresses and checked cotton aprons over the silk ones. They washed dishes or brisked up the fire at the right moment. This was no task for youth and ignorance.

"Modern cook stoves," as Miss Beecher warns us, "are infinite in their caprices."

Their stoves were modern: they burned coal.

It took brains and experience to dominate them. With this temperamental equipment and their husbands to carry coal and wood and draw water and open the oysters, the ladies cooked and served menus like this:

Oyster on the Half Shell with Lemon and Horseradish

Pickled Oysters   Pigs in Blankets

Oyster Stew, Montpelier Crackers or Oyster Crackers

Escalloped Oysters, Brown bread sandwiches

Oyster Pie   Fried Oysters

Creamed Oysters with Pastry Diamonds

or Oyster Patties

Potato Salad

Apple Pie, hot or cold   Mince Pie, hot or cold

Cheese   Coffee

No one apparently had thought of any way of serving oysters for dessert. Mrs. Appleyard has heard — though she can hardly believe it — that some valiant Vermonters ate some of every dish and survived to go to a sleighing party and kitchen junket the following night. Of course oyster suppers were expensive, they often cost a dollar, so the patrons felt they must get their money's worth. Most suppers were fifty cents — children half price of course.

Mrs. Appleyard does not expect you to duplicate this menu to raise money for the PTA but there are things in it you might like to make for company at home. She does not advise you to try to serve oysters on the half shell. The place to eat those is at an oyster bar in Boston or New York or Baltimore. However, she says you can serve oyster cocktail at home. This is a comparatively modern invention. Up to about 1906, it was customary to serve only quarters of lemon and horseradish with raw oysters. Some adventurous gourmets add a drop of Tabasco sauce to each oyster.

COCKTAIL SAUCE

1 cup Heinz tomato ketchup	1 cup Heinz Cocktail Sauce
1 cup Heinz tomato juice	1 tablespoon Lea & Perrin's
2 tablespoons prepared	Worcestershire sauce
horseradish	2 drops Tabasco sauce
1 small onion, minced fine	thin peel and juice of ½ lemon

Buy frozen oysters. Thaw according to directions. Allow six oysters to a person. Mix the sauce well and chill it thoroughly. Fill cocktail glasses half full of sauce. Stir in the oysters. The glasses can then stand in the refrigerator until serving time.

A combination of half frozen shrimp and half oysters is also good with this sauce.

Sandwiches of Boston brown bread go well with any oyster dish. There is a rule for Brown Bread on p. 19. Excellent brown bread is also made by Friend's near Boston. The can provides slices of just the right size. Get the kind without raisins to serve with oysters. Slice it ⅜ of an inch thick. Spread it thinly with butter and more thickly with cream cheese. Cut the sandwiches in halves.

PICKLED OYSTERS

When they were made for the church supper, the rule called for the opening of 200 oysters. Let us moderate our transports: a quart of frozen oysters will be a treat. Thaw them according to directions. With their liquor mix 1 cup white wine, 1 cup cider vinegar, 1 teaspoon salt, 1 teaspoon whole black peppers, 12 cloves, 1-inch stick cinnamon, a bay leaf, ½ teaspoon grated nutmeg, a red pepper pod. Have sterilized jars ready. Bring the pickle to the boiling point, boil it hard one minute. Strain it while still boiling hot over the oysters. Pack them in the jars. Add enough liquid to cover them. Chill them and keep them in the refrigerator. A good combination is chicken salad, pickled oysters, thinly sliced baked ham and watercress sandwiches.

Even earlier than the eighties of the nineteenth century, oysters used to be carried far inland but not by trains. There weren't any. In the fall an oyster man would pack oysters in a mixture of sand and Injun (cornmeal). If the sand mixture was kept damp by watering it twice a week, the oysters were perfectly happy. Some epicures considered the cornmeal-

fed oysters even better than those fresh out of the water. Peddlers used to load barrels of these oysters on sledges drawn by oxen and journey north, selling them to tavern keepers or bartering them with local storekeepers for maple syrup, country cheese or hand-woven blankets. There is still a building near Appleyard Center that was once a store stocked with goods brought from Boston by oxteam. No doubt an occasional barrel of oysters as well as the standard rum, sugar and molasses found its way to Appleyard Center. Perhaps when it did someone made

PIGS IN BLANKETS

Season large oysters with salt and pepper. Wrap each oyster in a slice of bacon, fastening it with a small wooden toothpick. Heat a frying pan and put in the "pigs." Have small squares of buttered toast ready. Cook the "pigs" until the bacon is crisp, 2 or 3 minutes. Turn them and move them gently in the pan so they will not scorch. Put them on the pieces of toast. Do not remove the toothpicks. Garnish the platter with parsley. Allow three oysters to a serving.

Another way, Mrs. Appleyard remembers, was to wrap each oyster in bacon, put six "pigs" on a silver skewer. Sometimes there were mushrooms on the skewers too. Each guest had a skewer. The skewers were placed over hot charcoal and broiled until the bacon was crisp. The result of this item with chicken salad and toasted oatcake was a distinctly well-nourished feeling.

OYSTER STEW

At the oyster suppers stew was made to order. For six customers:

2 cups milk	pinches of paprika and nutmeg
2 cups cream	(optional)
1 teaspoon salt	4 tablespoons butter
¼ teaspoon pepper	1 quart oysters

Two pans are needed. In one heat the milk and cream with the seasonings. In the other melt the butter. When it starts to froth, put in the oysters and cook them until the edges curl. The milk and cream should be scalded, not boiling. Combine the mixtures. Serve at once in hot soup bowls with oyster crackers or pilot crackers buttered and put under the broiler until they just start to brown.

SCALLOPED OYSTERS
FOR SIX

For this you need a rather shallow baking dish. The important thing about scalloped oysters is that there should be only two layers. If there are more, the oysters on the top and bottom layers will be toughened by overcooking or else the inner layer will be half raw.

1 cup Montpelier cracker crumbs	¼ cup melted butter
2 cups homemade bread buttered and cut in small croutons	½ teaspoon salt
	¼ teaspoon pepper
2 tablespoons thick cream	¼ teaspoon nutmeg
2 tablespoons sherry	1 quart oysters
¼ cup oyster liquor, strained	¼ cup butter (extra)

Roll the crackers into fine crumbs. Butter the bread and cut it into very small cubes. Mix this with the cracker crumbs. Mix cream, sherry, oyster liquor, melted butter and seasonings. Mix with the crumbs. The mixture should not be too wet: oysters supply moisture. Add more cracker crumbs if necessary. Butter your dish. Cover the bottom with a thin layer of the crumb mixture. Add half the oysters, cover with more crumbs, add the other half of the oysters. Top with the rest of the crumbs. Dot with the extra butter. Bake for 10 minutes at 450°. Reduce heat to 400° and bake until the top is well browned, 15 to 20 minutes longer.

OYSTER PIE

This may, if you like, include the white meat of chicken and sliced mushrooms as well as oysters. Begin by making a medium thick

CREAM SAUCE

½ teaspoon dried onion flakes	¼ teaspoon pepper
1 cup milk	½ teaspoon paprika
4 tablespoons flour	4 tablespoons butter
½ teaspoon salt	1 cup cream

Soak the onion flakes in the milk. Combine flour and dry seasonings. Melt the butter. When it bubbles, rub in the flour. Reduce the heat and cook this roux very slowly for 3 minutes. Do not let it brown. It should be a rich ivory color. Stir it carefully, remove pan from heat, then add the milk slowly, a little at a time, rubbing well into the roux with the back of the spoon. When it is a smooth paste, add the rest of the milk and then the cream. Return to low heat.

If you are using chicken in your pie add it to the sauce now. Sauté mushrooms, washed, sliced but not peeled, in some butter. Skim them out and add them to the sauce. Allow a cup of chicken cubes and half a cup of sliced mushrooms to a pint of oysters. Drain the oysters. Dry them on paper towels. Cook them in butter until the edges just start to curl. Add them to the sauce. The filling for your pie is now ready. Put it into a buttered shallow casserole and set it where it will keep warm but not hot. Heat the oven to 450°. If you do not have any of Mrs. Appleyard's pastry on hand, you have her permission to use your favorite mix. Make cross-bar strips and lay them across the pie. Put a twisted ribbon of pastry around the edge. Bake pie at 450° for 10 minutes, then reduce the heat and bake until the pastry is delicately browned, about 20 minutes longer.

This pie can be varied in several ways. You may add shrimp, crabmeat or lobster or a little of each. You may add a little white wine or sherry just before you put on the crust. You may beforehand bake a circular lid of pastry for your casserole. Gash it to allow steam to escape, and put it on the pie. In this case the pie needs to be in the oven only 5 minutes.

A salad of sliced avocado, orange, and grapefruit with watercress goes well with it.

Creamed Oysters with Pastry Diamonds and *Oyster Patties* are simply different ways of serving oysters in a cream sauce with pastry. Both may be varied by the addition of chicken, mushrooms, or seafood as with the pie.

FRIED OYSTERS

Frankly Mrs. Appleyard thinks oysters are too good to fry. They are on her list of things she never makes. However, they were popular at oyster suppers where they were on order. Six were served to each person. They were dried thoroughly between clean towels, rolled first in flour, then in beaten egg, then in a mixture of dry bread crumbs and cracker crumbs rolled very fine. They were fried in deep fat until brown, and drained on brown paper. They were handled with slotted spoons or tongs since with a fork there was danger of piercing them. Coleslaw was served with them and they were garnished with lemon and parsley. The friend Mrs. Appleyard consulted suggested 375° as the correct temperature for the cooking fat. The ladies who presided over the oyster supper judged the heat of the fat by how long it took to brown an inch cube of bread. Some old dim ancestral memory makes Mrs. Appleyard think it was supposed to brown in 40 seconds. On the whole she thinks it's a lot safer to make oyster stew.

Oysters are an acquired taste, but once acquired it's hard to lose. Mrs. Appleyard, when she was a débutante, learned to eat them because she hoped to find pearls in them. She knew a girl who had a rather well-matched pair of pearl earrings for which the pearls had been found at a dinner party. The only pearls Mrs. Appleyard ever found had been scalloped and were a rather moldy shade of charcoal gray. However Mr. Appleyard, hearing her lamenting her hard luck, gave her some pearl earrings when their daughter Cicely was born. So the story has a happy ending. Think of getting the pearls and Cicely too!

Fish in Winter

OF COURSE oysters were only for grand occasions. What you were more likely to find cooking in Vermont kitchens was a salted codfish.

SALT CODFISH DINNER

FOR SIX

Salt cod is a good deal easier to cope with now than it was in 1850 when Mrs. Cornelius wrote *The Young Lady's Friend*. When the young lady planned a codfish dinner, she was advised "to lay the fish into the cellar a few days before it is to be cooked, that it may be softened by the dampness. The afternoon before it is to be boiled, wash it carefully in several waters. It is well to keep a brush on purpose to cleanse salt fish and use it repeatedly while it is soaking."

She is talking about a whole codfish, just the way it came from the fish house. Modern salt fish, clean and neatly packaged, needs less time spent on it. However, the old advice on how to cook it is still good. Soak it overnight. In the morning change the water and put the fish on to cook. As soon as the water reaches the boiling point, reduce the heat and simmer the fish till it is tender. It took four hours or more to cook old-fashioned codfish. Modern fish should be tender in about half an hour.

A salt fish dinner is a sort of ritual. Almost as soon as their honeymoon was over, Mr. Appleyard took his bride to the Parker House in Boston so she could learn the proper way to serve it. She thinks the pleasantest way to have a salt fish dinner is still at the Parker House but — take her word for it — even quite a stupid bride can do it at home.

1½ pounds salt codfish	6 beets
3 cups Egg and Cream Sauce (p. 95)	6 small white turnips
6 onions (medium size)	6 boiled potatoes
6 carrots	½ pound salt pork

parsley

Perhaps you think you have heard of this combination of vegetables before. You have — and if you lived in Vermont in the winter, you would meet it often. They are what were in your root cellar.

Begin by making your sauce. Keep it warm in a double boiler. Put the vegetables and fish on to cook. Each vegetable must be cooked separately. While they are cooking, cut the salt pork into ¼-inch cubes and try them out until the scraps are golden brown and crisp. Do this over very low heat. The pork fat must not scorch. It should be deep amber in color. At serving time, lay the fish, well drained, on a large hot platter. Put the vegetables around in heaps, a variety of vegetables in each heap. Beets and carrots should be sliced, the others left whole. Decorate the platter with sprigs of parsley. Be sure your dinner plates are scorching hot. Serve the hot fat and the pork scraps in one sauceboat and the egg sauce in another.

Each salt fish dinner lover begins by cutting his potato up rather fine. Then he cuts the other vegetables into it, then works in pork fat and scraps. Last of all he tops the whole thing with a generous amount of fish and of egg sauce. The result is a superb mound which fills his plate. The blend of flavors and textures is somehow different from what went into it, for cooking is a happy kind of arithmetic in which the sum of all the parts is not the same as the parts themselves. Part of the enjoyment of a salt fish dinner, Mrs. Appleyard thinks, is because men, like children, love making mud pies. Perhaps this is why pie for dessert seems appropriate. After salt fish, Pumpkin Pie (p. 138) is rather soothing to the palate.

SALT FISH HASH

The experienced housekeeper always cooked extra salt fish and potatoes, for well she knew that as red flannel hash follows a boiled dinner so did her family expect fish hash after a salt fish dinner.

There are two theories about this hash, each with its defenders. One party maintains that only potato and a little onion should be mixed with the fish. The other thinks that it should be a form of red flannel hash with enough beets to give it color and that you may sneak in a little carrot and turnip too. One usually rather tolerant neighbor of Mrs. Appleyard's became quite violent on this subject. In his opinion red flannel hash is just a feminine subterfuge to conceal the fact that there is practically no fish — or meat in the case of corned beef — in the hash. Mrs. Appleyard, who has eaten her share of hash made with this motive, prefers the kind made just with fish, potato, and a small amount of onion. She says if all the pork fat and scraps were used the day before, you must begin by trying out some more pork.

FISH HASH
FOR SIX

¼ pound salt pork, diced	½ cup milk, part cream
1 cup salt fish flaked	¼ teaspoon ground pepper
2 cups potatoes, chopped	1 tablespoon butter
1 small cooked onion	extra milk

sprigs of parsley

Try out the pork. Skim out the cracklings when they are golden brown and crisp. Drain on brown paper. Have fat about ¼ inch deep in a 10-inch black iron frying pan. Chop fish, potatoes, and onion together. Scald milk, add pepper and butter. Stir into the fish mixture, mix well. Have the pan over low heat. Put in the mixture. Smooth it down well. Cover. After 2 minutes, stir mixture again and smooth it down. If it seems too dry, dribble a little more milk if necessary. Cook uncovered till it starts to brown around the edges. Loosen the edges with a spatula. Make a crease across the hash at right angles to the handle of the pan. Fold hash over like an omelet. Turn it out on a hot platter. Garnish it with cracklings and parsley.

Mrs. Appleyard was much gratified recently by a letter saying that the writer, since reading *The Winter Kitchen,* was now turning out delicious prickly fish balls. The rule is on page 32 of that work. She herself has been devoting herself to modernizing a favorite New England dish of the eighties called

MATELOTE OF HADDOCK

½ cup court bouillon	1 tablespoon minced parsley
whole haddock, about 4 pounds	1 cup oysters (frozen)
1 small onion, minced	6 slices salt pork or bacon
2 tablespoons butter	2 tablespoons melted butter, extra
2 cups bread, diced	½ cup white wine
2 tablespoons cream	1 cup frozen shrimp
¼ teaspoon each nutmeg and thyme	1 lemon, sliced
1 egg	sprigs of parsley

If possible buy the fish whole and have the fish man give you the head and the bones. There are still a few shops where they carry fish not, apparently, born and caught in a cellophane bag. Frozen fillets are better than the half-thawed limp things found at the ordinary supermarket fish counter. Begin by making

COURT BOUILLON

Put the bones and head of the fish into a kettle and cover them with cold water, about 2 quarts. Add:

1 onion	2 tablespoons lemon juice
12 peppercorns	1 tablespoon tarragon vinegar
1 bayleaf	3 cloves
1 carrot sliced	pinches of herbs
1 cup white wine	

Cover. Bring to the boil. Simmer for one hour. Strain.

This liquid is good for boiling fish or in chowder as well as in the Matelote. By the way *matelote* means a sailor's fashion of cooking fish. Mrs. Appleyard rather doubts that Yankee sailors ever spent much time making court bouillon. Perhaps French ones did. Anyway it's good.

While the bouillon is cooking, sauté the onion in butter for 3 minutes. Add bread cubes. Sauté 2 minutes. Add cream, seasonings, and egg. Add oysters. Remove pan from heat. Now stuff the fish with the mixture or lay it between frozen fillets. Put the fish on a rack in a rather shallow pan. Lay slices of pork, bacon (or beef suet if you prefer) over it. Heat the oven to 425°.

Mix the ½ cup of court bouillon with the extra butter and white wine and pour it over the fish. Miss Parloa wants you to have a bouquet of herbs in the corner of the pan. Mrs. Appleyard realizes that our age of efficiency has improved away the pleasant habit your market man had of sending you what he called a soup bunch. It contained a stalk of celery, sprigs of parsley, a leaf or two of tarragon, sprigs of basil and marjoram. "Alas!" is about all she can say about this advice.

Use a meat thermometer. Its point must touch fish, not stuffing. Cook the fish at 425° for 10 minutes. Reduce temperature to 350° and bake about 35 minutes longer. Temperature of fish should not be over 155°. Baste it often with the juice in the pan.

At serving time, put the fish on a hot platter. Pour the juice in the pan into a small saucepan. Bring it to the boiling point and poach the shrimp in it for five minutes. Garnish the fish with the shrimp, lemon slices, parsley sprigs and pour the rest of the liquid over it. Sometimes sautéed mushrooms were added to the stuffing. Mrs. Appleyard wonders where even French sailors found them. In the Sargasso sea? Seems unlikely.

Boston brides used to say as a sort of incantation, rapidly, all in one breath: "Miss-Parloa-says-it's-delicious."

Miss Parloa thought it was a nice idea to garnish the Matelote with a ring of fried smelts. Mrs. Appleyard's idea is that just what you don't want to do at this point in the meal is to fry smelts. However, when smelts appear in Lake Champlain, showing that spring may come someday, she likes to serve them as the main dish for supper.

SMELTS WITH TARTARE SAUCE

Allow four smelts for each person to be served. There are several ways of coating them before you cook them. They may be dipped first in melted butter, then in flour. They may be seasoned with lemon juice, olive oil, and pepper, allowed to stand 15 minutes, then dipped in cream and flour. Or (Mrs. Appleyard's way) they can be dipped first in flour, then in beaten egg, then in a mixture of Montpelier cracker crumbs and dry bread crumbs rolled fine. Allow a cup of crumbs and one egg to 12 smelts. Melt butter in a large frying pan. Lay in the smelts. Heat the oven to 450°. Sprinkle a few extra crumbs over them. Bake 5 minutes. Turn the fish very carefully with a spatula and a pancake turner. Scatter a few more crumbs over any bare spots. Dot with butter. Cook about five minutes longer.

Serve with Tartare Sauce — mayonnaise with chopped capers, olives, tarragon, dill pickles. Use half a tablespoon of each to a cup of mayonnaise.

Smelts may also — if your oven is in use — be cooked on top of the stove. This takes your whole attention for about 10 minutes: more if you are serving many people. Use 2 frying pans. Half an hour beforehand dip the fish first in flour, then in egg, then in crumbs. Melt butter in the pans. Lay in the fish. Have a hot stainless steel platter ready. Cook the smelts over medium heat. Keep them moving with a spatula and a pancake turner. Turn them as soon as they brown. Remove to the hot platter when they are brown on both sides. Add uncooked ones. Keep it up until all are done.

See what Mrs. Appleyard means about not garnishing a Matelote with them?

What Miss Parloa would like best to have you do is to make a ring of each smelt. You stick the tail of each in the opening at the gills and fasten it with a wooden toothpick, then you dip them in egg and crumbs and fry them in deep fat. Mrs. Appleyard remembers them done this way, says they really were delicious, plans to live on the memory and cook contemporary smelts in the oven.

BROILED SCALLOPS

The scallops usually offered in inland markets are not scallops at all but skate cut in chunks. If you think you don't like scallops, it is probably because you have been eating skate. You may be able to get real Cape Cod scallops frozen. Properly cooked, they are delicious.

For two people allow:

1 12-ounce package scallops	1 cup dry bread crumbs, rolled fine
2 tablespoons lemon juice	4 tablespoons butter

Remove scallops from package. Sprinkle lemon juice over them. Let them stand until they can be separated easily but are not fully thawed, about 10 minutes. Butter a shallow fireproof pan in which you can serve them. Roll scallops in the crumbs. Put them in the pan. Dot them with half the butter. Put them under the broiler three inches from the flame. They should be golden brown in about 3 minutes. Turn them over with a pancake turner and a spatula. Sprinkle with a few more crumbs. Dot with the rest of the butter. Broil 2 to 3 minutes more.

SCALLOPS IN THE SHELL
FOR SIX

Real scallop shells are the most attractive containers for this dish, but small ramequins will do, or it can be made in one casserole.

2 cups frozen scallops	¼ tablespoon nutmeg
1 cup frozen shrimp	2 cups milk
4 tablespoons butter	1 cup buttered bread crumbs
small onion, minced	extra butter
½ cup sliced mushroom caps	½ cup cream
4 tablespoons flour	1 tablespoon minced parsley
½ teaspoon pepper	1 tablespoon lemon juice
½ teaspoon paprika	2 tablespoons sherry

Lightly butter 6 scallop shells. Open packages of scallops and shrimp and let them stand at room temperature while you prepare the sauce. Melt butter. Sauté onion till straw colored. Sauté mushroom slices until soft. Push onion and mushrooms aside. Remove pan from heat. Mix flour with seasonings and rub it into the butter. Add the milk gradually, stirring well until it is smoothly blended. Let cook over very low heat 3 minutes. In another pan, toss bread crumbs in 2 tablespoons butter (extra) until they are lightly browned. Add cream to the sauce. Cook 2 minutes. Remove pan from fire. Sauce should be quite thick. Add parsley, lemon juice, sherry, scallops, and shrimp. Divide the mixture into six shells. Top with the buttered crumbs. Set shells into a shallow iron dripping pan or on an aluminum cookie sheet. Bake ½ hour. If one shell starts to brown more quickly than others, change its position in the pan. Do not overbake.

Kettle on the Crane

IT WAS a fine crisp winter day and Mrs. Appleyard had all the materials ready for a fish chowder when a tree fell on the power line. A strange silence settled down on the house. The washing machine paused in mid-spin. The dryer ceased its energetic tumbling. No water rushed into the dishwasher. The Beatles stopped strumming their guitars. Wind no longer rushed from the hair dryer upon the synthetic curls of the occupant. The furnace sighed and purred no more.

Mrs. Appleyard showed great presence of mind. Though it would have been possible to make her chowder with melted snow, she prefers water and she promptly ran enough into a pitcher while there was some left in the tank.

"I'll make it over the fire," she told her daughter Cicely.

There were already flames licking around the white birch logs, for Cicely had called about the power failure and had been told it might take two hours to restore service. By the time Mrs. Appleyard had sliced the potatoes, there was a fine bed of coals in the fireplace and water was beginning to simmer in one of the kettles on the crane.

Here is the rule she followed. She is glad to say it works equally well over electricity except that a certain subtle flavor is missing. It's called smoke — in case you'd like to include it — and it's quite easy to duplicate. Just hold a piece of burning shingle over the kettle and let a few charred bits and a spark or two drop into the contents. When Mrs. Appleyard gets around to it, she plans to invent some genuine bottled smoke flavoring. Watch for it in your supermarket but in the meantime make your chowder this way.

NEW ENGLAND FISH CHOWDER (S.W.E.)

FOR EIGHT

6 medium potatoes
¼ pound salt pork, diced
3 large onions, sliced thin
a 4-pound haddock cut for chowder head and all
4 cups hot water
1 teaspoon salt
½ teaspoon black pepper (freshly ground)
¼ teaspoon thyme
¼ teaspoon marjoram

½ teaspoon paprika
2 tablespoons Instant Flour (Pillsbury's)
3 cups rich milk
1 cup heavy cream
2 tablespoons minced parsley
1 tablespoon minced chives
1 lemon, sliced thin
8 Montpelier crackers
butter for crackers

Slice potatoes as thin as fourpence. That's what Mrs. Appleyard's grandmother told her. Never having seen a fourpence, Mrs. Appleyard slices them as thin as a nickel. The point is not to have any chunks of half-raw potatoes in your chowder. Furthermore, salt pork dice means the kind of dice you use for backgammon, not unwieldy chunks. Fry the dice in your kettle till they are a delicate tan, skim them out and put them on a plate. Fry the onions in the pork fat until a delicate straw color. Skim out.

Lay in the fish cut in 4 pieces, head, tail, bones and all. Add the sliced potatoes, onions, and pork dice. Sprinkle in the seasonings. Pour over enough water to cover the fish and potatoes and cook until fish falls from the bones, about half an hour. Now swing out the crane and fish out the head and all the bones you can find. You won't get them all so say, "Beware of bones," to your guests. Thicken the juice with woman's best friend, Instant Flour: just stir it in. Cook 3 minutes.

Serving time has now come. Your milk and cream have been heating in your second kettle. Pour them over the fish. Brisk up the fire with some shingles thus providing a little extra smoke for flavoring and for the cook's eyes. Cook the chowder about 5 minutes. It should not boil or the fish will curdle the milk. Add the parsley and chives, freshly clipped from the plants in the window. Add the lemon slices.

Break 2 of the Montpelier crackers, which have been split and buttered and heated in a skillet over the coals, into a blue Canton soup tureen. Pour the chowder over them. Pass the others with the chowder, eat it by candlelight, and be thankful that the electricity came on in time to wash the dishes.

This fish chowder, made on an electric or gas stove — in case your favorite tune is not "Smoke Gets in Your Eyes," not to say a word about ashes and how your knees feel and the crick in your neck — is the basis for several different kinds of chowder.

Minced clams may be added to it, though Mrs. Appleyard prefers chowder made just with clams instead of fish. Oysters may be added the last minute after being cooked in butter until their edges curl. Shrimp, cleaned, cooked and fresh frozen, are a good last-minute addition and if you want something really deluxe, shrimp, lobster, and crabmeat can all be included. The original chowder rule was planned for six. With an extra cup of milk and half a cup of cream, the extra shellfish and extra crackers, you can serve eight or ten.

And if you have a beach near you and a fire built between some rocks, you can cook it there and get almost as smoky as Mrs. Appleyard did. She hopes you'll try it!

NEW ENGLAND BOUILLABAISSE APPLEYARD

FOR EIGHT

Bouillabaisse is really just a chowder with a French accent. It's a mixture of fish and shellfish seasoned with herbs and saffron. It's supposed to have mussels, shells and all, in it and thick slices of eels sometimes turn up in it. Mrs. Appleyard makes hers out of things easily found in your supermarket.

3 pounds haddock fillets (frozen)	2 bay leaves
1 pound flounder fillets	1 teaspoon thyme
1-pound slice of halibut	½ teaspoon pepper
1 cup oil (olive, safflower, or Wesson)	1 teaspoon paprika
2 large onions chopped fine	4-ounce can of pimentos
1 bunch of leeks, chopped	1 pint oysters
1 green pepper, sliced thin	1 pint Cape scallops (frozen)
1 tablespoon minced garlic	12 ounces shrimp (frozen)
1 tablespoon minced celery	1 teaspoon saffron
1 pound crabmeat	2 tablespoons lemon juice
1 pound lobster (frozen)	1 cup white wine
3 tomatoes, chopped	1 tablespoon minced parsley

half a long loaf of French bread

Cut up the fish in neat pieces, not too small. Mrs. Appleyard hopes you have some court bouillon (see p. 30) on hand but if you have none you can make it by simmering scraps of fish with herbs and seasonings. Put the oil into your biggest frying pan. Toss onions, leeks, green pepper, garlic, and celery in it until the onions are straw colored. Use the green tops of the leeks, chopped with the white part. Add the cut-up fish, the crab and lobster meat. Cook 5 minutes. Add tomatoes, bay leaves, and dry seasonings, except the saffron. (You may have to get saffron from the drugstore.) Add court bouillon and the pimentos cut in strips. Simmer 25 minutes, covered. Add oysters, scallops, shrimp. Cook until edges of the oysters curl, about 5 minutes. Stir saffron and lemon juice into the wine and add the mixture. Sprinkle in the parsley. Your French bread should be cut in slices 1½ inches thick and toasted. Lay 8 slices in a large hot tureen or casserole. Pour the bouillabaisse over it. (The correct French way is to serve broth and fish separately, but Mrs. Appleyard likes them in one dish and serves the mixture in soup plates.) With it serve the rest of the bread, sweet butter, radishes, olives — ripe and green — and raw celery. Have white wine to drink with it. Fruit and cheese will be all you'll want for dessert.

Some cold evening you might like

TOASTED CRAB SANDWICHES
FOR SIX

1 pound crabmeat	1 tablespoon lemon juice
½ cup mayonnaise	extra mayonnaise
3 drops Tabasco sauce	6 slices homemade bread
½ teaspoon Worcestershire sauce	6 slices Vermont cheese
1 teaspoon dry mustard	paprika

Use fresh or frozen crabmeat if possible, but canned will do. Flake crabmeat. Mix mayonnaise with Tabasco, Worcestershire, mustard, and lemon juice. Add crabmeat. Toast bread on one side. Spread the untoasted side first thinly with more mayonnaise, then with the crab mixture. Leave a narrow margin around the edge as the mixture tends to spread out. Top each slice with cheese. Sprinkle with paprika. Put slices on a cooky sheet. Slide them under broiler at least 2 inches away. Cook till cheese starts to melt and brown, about 5 minutes. Watch them.

HALIBUT IN FOIL
FOR FOUR

1½-pound slice of halibut   1 tablespoon lemon juice

Sprinkle halibut with lemon juice and wrap it in a sheet of heavy foil. Heat oven to 400°. Put ½ inch of hot water in a heatproof dish. Put in the fish. Start it over a top burner. When the water boils, set the dish in the oven. Use a meat thermometer inserted in the fish. Bake until it registers 145°, about 40 minutes. In the meantime make

EGG AND BUTTER SAUCE

¼ pound butter	2 hard-boiled eggs
1 tablespoon lemon juice	1 teaspoon grated lemon rind

Melt butter over low heat, add lemon juice and rind and the whites of the eggs cut up in ¼ inch pieces, the yolks flaked with a fork. Serve hot.

Any juice in the foil should be poured over the fish.

CLAM OR CORN CHOWDER
FOR TWO

Mrs. Appleyard's son Hugh invented this chowder. Mrs. Appleyard has made it using some of her own chowder (p. 21) as a basis, adding a 4-ounce can of minced clams and the corn. Hugh's rule is even simpler.

1 8-ounce can frozen clam chowder   1 tablespoon butter
1 cup rich milk, part cream   1 small can whole kernel Golden Bantam corn
3 Montpelier crackers, split, buttered, toasted

Heat chowder with milk and cream in the top of a double boiler. Melt butter, toss corn in it until very little liquid is left. Combine mixtures just before serving. Serve in hot chowder bowls. Crumble crackers in them or spread them with Mrs. Appleyard's Mint Chutney (*Winter Kitchen*, p. 191).

Challenge to the Frozen Chefs!

MRS. APPLEYARD sometimes disciplines herself by looking over a case full of frozen dinners, thus making herself happy about the humble meal she will have later — the carrot juice, the toasted sandwich of real cheese and real bread, the freshly cut grapefruit. She feels no yearning for the sea scallops (née skate), the seven crinkles of fried potato, the little hollow full of very green peas. How, she wonders, do they measure the peas? By the teaspoonful? Or do they count them?

These dinners do not all *look* the same: you can easily tell the turkey from the roast beef at a glance. Of course they all taste alike, so it does not matter which you buy. However, there is one *plat du jour* the frozen-computer chefs have not mastered — the New England boiled dinner. You may not like boiled dinner — lots of people don't — but you are never going to confuse it with fried chicken or Salisbury steak. Would you like something not synthetic for a change? Then try

BOILED DINNER
FOR TWELVE

6 pounds corned beef (brisket)   12 small beets, not peeled, cooked separately
2 pounds lean salt pork   6 medium onions, peeled and halved
12 whole carrots, scraped   3 small white cabbages, quartered
6 small turnips, quartered   12 potatoes, peeled

No seasonings are needed except a little black pepper from the grinder if you like.

The corned beef is the kind that looks brown, not red, when it is cooked. The pork should have plenty of pinkish streaks of lean in it. Put both into a kettle large enough to hold them and the vegetables, which will be added later. Cover the meat with cold water. It must simmer, not boil. When it starts to bubble, reduce the heat. Skim the broth carefully for the first 10 minutes, then cover the kettle and let it simmer until the meat is tender — about 3 hours. During the last hour add the carrots and turnips. Cook the beets separately.

Remove meat from the broth and set it aside in a warm place. Bring broth to the boil and add onions, quarters of cabbage and potatoes. Cook until potatoes are done — about 40 minutes. Return meat to the broth and simmer until it is well heated. Slip beets out of their skins. Have your biggest platter hot. Mrs. Appleyard likes a blue and white one but any cheerful color will do. Place the brisket in the middle. Slice the salt pork and arrange it around the meat. Make small heaps of vegetables, each heap containing cabbage, carrot, onion, turnip, potato and a beet, and circle the platter with them.

Of course if the vegetables all come from your own garden you feel unbearably complacent as you carry in the platter. However, an excellent result can be obtained from vegetables you buy. If no young beets are available canned ones will do. Mrs. Appleyard has heard it rumored that in New Hampshire the beets are sometimes cooked right in with the other vegetables and that in Massachusetts, her native state, parsnips are sometimes included. She does not say what she thinks about these practices.

RED FLANNEL HASH

This follows a boiled dinner as a rainbow follows a thunder shower. You may have to cook extra potatoes and beets for it. You need twice as much potato as meat and enough beets to give the hash a good red color. Let's assume you have 2 cups of corned beef left.

2 cups corned beef	4 cups cooked potatoes
2 cups vegetables from boiled dinner	4 small cooked beets
¼ pound beef suet	broth from boiled dinner

Do not grind meat or vegetables. Chop them in a large wooden bowl. Chop beef first, rather fine. Chop in vegetables, including beets. Chop potatoes in last, not too fine.

Cut suet in small cubes. Try it out in a large iron frying pan until you have about ¼ inch of fat and the suet cubes are golden brown. Skim them out, drain them on brown paper. Put in the hash, toss it in the fat for a minute. Moisten with the broth. Half a cup should be enough. Don't make it too wet. Smooth the hash gently. Cook it over very low heat until it starts to brown around the edge of the pan. It will then be brown on the bottom. This may take half an hour or a little more. Fold it like an omelet and slide it onto a hot platter. Serve it garnished with the beef cracklings and fresh parsley.

Mrs. Appleyard promises you that, like the boiled dinner, this is never synthetic.

Corned Beef

SOMEONE recently called Mrs. Appleyard's attention to the fact that she has told how to cook corned beef but not how to corn it. Beginning at once to study the problem, she was baffled by this statement: "Make a brine strong enough to bear an egg."

She tried another book. It said "float an egg." None of the old books came right out and told her just how large a piece of meat she was supposed to be working on, what sort of container to use, how long the meat should stay in the brine or whether the liquid should be hot or cold. Apparently the writers assumed that every daughter had seen her mother, grandmother and great-grandmother corn beef so she would automatically know these things. Only in this case, Mrs. Appleyard wondered, why did the bride need a cookbook anyway?

She herself certainly needed one. It must be old enough to assume that people still corned their own beef and modern enough to describe the process accurately. She did not wish to be told to take a crock big enough to hold a piece of beef of unspecified size and be advised to leave it in a brine strong enough to bear an egg until it was ready for use. Luckily she has a copy of *Miss Parloa's New Cook Book*, 1881.

Miss Parloa was regarded with reverence by Mrs. Appleyard's grandmother, who used the book until it almost fell to pieces. She added receipts of her own on extra pages carefully sewn in at the back. She went to lectures at Miss Parloa's cooking school, a forerunner of Fannie Farmer's school. If Mrs. Appleyard's memory is not at fault, Miss Parloa's graduates inspired superb cooking in their kitchens.

Christopher Columbus, some think, discovered America. Miss Parloa discovered France. She broke the news to New Englanders that they could make Béchamel sauce and still be respectable. She wrote for the *Ladies' Home Journal*. She was the first writer on cooking to suggest accurate measurements. Her endeavor — she says in her preface — "is to have directions, clear, complete and concise."

Mrs. Appleyard thoroughly approves but of course we all have moments of weakness.

In one of hers, Miss Parloa tells us to make Golden Frosting "by stirring into two egg yolks, enough powdered sugar to thicken and flavor strongly with lemon." Perhaps not feeling that she was quite living up to her ideals, she adds honestly: "This does not have so good a flavor as other kinds of frosting but it makes a change."

Luckily her directions for corning beef are more precise.

TO CORN BEEF

"For fifty pounds of beef, make a pickle of two gallons of water, four pounds of salt, one and a half pounds of brown sugar, one and a half ounces of saltpetre, half an ounce of saleratus [soda]. Put these ingredients on to boil and when they boil, skim and put away to cool. When cold, put the beef in it. Put weights on the meat to keep it under the brine."

From other old books Mrs. Appleyard learned that beef used for corning was usually the brisket, which is part of the forequarter. The meat should be turned often in the pickle. It is easier to keep weights on it if a large plate is put on top of the beef and if the weights are placed on that. Clean, heavy stones are recommended as weights, rather than flatirons, because metal must not touch the pickle. The best container is a large well-glazed crock with a cover. One writer warns you lugubriously that some crocks have arsenic in the glaze. There certainly were perils in home cooking. If all went well, the beef would be properly corned in about six weeks.

While she was studying this question, Mrs. Appleyard began to feel that she had been mixed up in some such project at some time. Turning beef in a large crock, for instance — hadn't she done that? Of course she had, only not in Vermont, in Virginia; only it was not called corned beef, but spiced beef and the piece used was the round instead of the brisket.

She remembers the result. It was delicious.

If anyone is in a mood to pickle beef, this is a method worth trying.

SPICED BEEF

Figure the time needed by the weight of the beef and the day you plan to serve it. The beef must stay in the brine one day for each pound of beef and you should allow three days extra for cooking it and for thorough cooling. It is served cold and should be sliced paper thin. This is impossible if it is not thoroughly cooled.

For a 12-pound round of beef allow fifteen days for pickling, cooking and cooling.

Make the pickle of

2 ounces saltpeter (from the drugstore)	2 ounces ground cloves
2 cups salt	2 ounces ground nutmeg
1 ounce ground allspice	1 ounce ground cinnamon

1 quart dark molasses

Put the beef into a stoneware crock big enough to hold it and which allows space to turn it. Mix the dry ingredients thoroughly with the molasses and pour this marinade over the beef. It will not cover it completely. That is why the meat must be turned every day. Juice will run out of the beef so you will have more marinade after a day or two than you had at first. Set the crock in a cool place on a bench or table of convenient height so that it will be easy to reach the meat for its daily turning. Cover the crock. Mrs. Appleyard has tried various implements to use in the turning, found out that the easiest way is to overcome any residue of fastidiousness that life may have left you and just plunge in with both hands and grasp the slippery mass firmly. If you keep a bunch of paper towels beside the crock, you will not regret it.

On the thirteenth day, remove the meat from the marinade, tie it in cheesecloth and set it on a rack in a large kettle. Add the marinade, two onions and two carrots, sliced. Add enough water so that the meat is covered. Put a lid on the kettle, simmer the beef till it is tender — 4 to 6 hours.

Never use a piece of meat with bones in it. You may use chuck — though round is better — but if you do, have the bones removed and the chuck tied in a round shape.

When the marinade has cooled, remove the beef and drain it, remove the cheesecloth, set the meat on a rack in a covered roaster or on a rack on a platter in a cool place. At the end of the day, put it in the refrigerator.

Now all you need is a skilled carver who can slice it so thin that you can read the Declaration of Independence through it. Your favorite carver will be delighted to accept your invitation.

Serve the spiced beef with chicken or turkey salad or with scalloped oysters. Hot rolls or toasted crumpets go well with it. So does horseradish with sour cream or mustard sauce (*Winter Kitchen* p. 100).

HORSERADISH SAUCE

½ cup heavy cream
2 tablespoons grated horseradish (fresh from the bottle.
    Add no salt; it's salted already and so is the beef)

½ teaspoon pepper
½ cup sour cream
1 tablespoon minced parsley

Whip the cream till it just starts to thicken. Stir in the horseradish and pepper. Stir in the sour cream. Put in a bowl and sprinkle it with minced parsley.

When the boiled dinner had finally disappeared in the form of hash, Vermonters often turned to the

SALT PORK DINNER

FOR SIX

6 small onions
3 turnips, cubed
3 carrots, sliced
3 beets, medium size
2 pounds salt pork
6 potatoes, for baking
½ teaspoon pepper
¼ teaspoon cinnamon

½ teaspoon paprika
1 cup flour
1 cup milk
4 tart apples, sliced
2 tablespoons brown sugar
2 tablespoons flour (extra)
1 cup sweet cream (thin)
1 cup thick sour cream

Start vegetables (except potatoes) cooking in separate kettles, in as little water as possible. Simmer salt pork for one hour, drain, dry on paper towels. Cool it and cut into quarter-inch slices. Start potatoes baking at 450°. Add dry seasonings to a cup of flour. Spread it on a plate and dip the pork slices first in milk, then in flour. Some people dip the pork in batter, but Grandmother Appleyard regarded that practice with suspicion, said it often resulted in greasy batter and half raw pork. Allow two slices for each person to be served. Lay them in a large cold iron frying pan and cook them slowly until they are a light cracker-brown on both sides. Some pork fat will be tried out of them. Put some of this into another frying pan and in it put the slices of tart apples, skins, seeds and all. Sprinkle them with brown sugar and when they are cooked, transfer them and the pork slices to a large hot platter. In the meantime you have turned the baking potatoes and reduced the heat of the oven to 350°. You have also checked the different vegetables to see if they are cooking properly. When the beets slip from their skins, skin them, dice them, keep them warm in a little of their own juice. Save any liquid left from vegetables and add it to your soup kettle or chill it and keep it in the refrigerator until you need it.

Take 2 tablespoons of pork fat and blend into it the extra 2 tablespoons of flour. Do this over very low heat and then stir into it first the sweet cream and then the sour cream. Increase heat and bring it to the boil but do not let it boil. Serving time has now arrived. Pierce the potatoes with a fork to let the steam out. Serve them in a separate dish, the other vegetables in little heaps around the platter of pork and apple slices. There should be some of all the vegetables in each heap. Put the sour cream gravy in one sauceboat; pour any pork fat in the frying pan into another sauceboat.

Mr. Appleyard liked this whole dinner served on old blue willow pattern dishes. His mother always had parsley growing in a sunny window and she used to put sprigs of it between the heaps of vegetables. Each guest took a baked potato, opened and mashed it, added pork, cutting it fine, then cut in what vegetables he liked. The sliced apples and some sort of relish, piccalilli or small green tomatoes pickled with dill, went alongside. The sour cream gravy went on top and some hungry characters added some of the pork fat. Probably all they had for dessert was a choice of three kinds of pie — what a hard winter!

Mrs. Appleyard thinks that these platters with the different foods heaped on them and the sauceboats of gravy were in a way ancestors of the casserole. The main difference was that you could avoid anything peculiarly abhorrent to your palate. For instance, when snow melted and people began to dig parsnips, there might be parsnips with a salt fish dinner but you could either ignore them or eat them. Let freedom ring!

Incidentally to many Vermonters who had been living all winter on the vegetables in the root cellar — the rather woody beets and carrots and turnips — parsnips seemed delicious and exciting and springlike. One of Mrs. Appleyard's neighbors told her the other day that one of the great moments in the year was when her mother served parsnip chowder.

PARSNIP CHOWDER (M.P.F.)

FOR SIX

¼ pound salt pork, diced
3 onions, sliced thin
3 potatoes, sliced as thin as a nickel
2 cups parsnips, peeled and cubed
2 cups boiling water

pepper to taste
3 cups milk
1 cup cream (thick)
6 Montpelier crackers, split, buttered, and toasted

Try out salt pork dice until they are amber brown. Skim them out. Drain them on brown paper. Cook onions in the pork fat until they are straw colored. Skim them out. Put in a kettle a layer of potato, onion, and parsnips. Repeat until kettle is well filled. Pour boiling water over the vegetables and cook them until they are soft, 20 to 30 minutes. Add pepper. (Since the pork is salt, no extra salt is needed.) Use pepper from the grinder. Scald the milk and cream and add them to the kettle. Bring the mixture just to the boil, take kettle off the fire. Scatter in the salt pork cracklings. Serve the crackers separately, to be broken into the chowder or eaten as they come.

Who Counts Calories?

WELL, certainly not Vermonters in winter, Mrs. Appleyard says. One thing good housewives always had on hand, long before electric freezers were invented, was frozen pies. It was not difficult to freeze pies; all you did was to put them on the pantry shelf where they soon became as hard as rocks. Heat, not cold, was the rarity in Vermont houses.

One of the oldest and most attractive houses Mrs. Appleyard knows has a peculiar feature. It still has much of its original woodwork, wainscots of single boards cut from primeval pines, great hand-hewn beams, wide ceiling boards, the enormous chimney with three fireplaces opening into it, the beehive oven, hand-made bricks of many colors. In the old kitchen there was something its new owners could not understand. The wide unpainted boards of the floor were one shade of golden tan in a half circle around the big fireplace. Outside the half circle they were several shades darker, almost as if they had been stained.

The mystery was solved when a grandson of the original owner came to call. He was eighty years old but he still remembered the winter nights — and days too — when frost lay thickly on the floor of the room, except in the half circle where the heat of the fire penetrated. The frost is what had darkened the outside boards.

He pointed out wooden pegs on the outer walls, told how his grandfather hung carcasses of beef critters on them and how the beef remained frozen right in the kitchen, ready when you needed it. Mrs. Appleyard, who occasionally goes into her own house in the winter and emerges with her teeth chattering, can well believe that every Vermont pantry used to be an automatic deep freeze.

One compliment paid a good housekeeper was to mention that "she's got more'n forty pies in her pantry, I wouldn't wonder."

This meant that her husband was reasonably sure of pie for breakfast. Mrs. Appleyard read somewhere recently a statement that this story about Vermont breakfast habits was not true. The writer seemed to think it was an ill-natured myth that made Vermonters ridiculous.

Mrs. Appleyard happens to know from personal observation that it was true fifty years ago and that there was nothing ridiculous about it. The man who was enjoying a good slab of apple pie at seven-thirty had been up milking cows since four o'clock. He had already done what most men would consider a day's work, and he would still be working twelve hours later. He very likely had pie twice a day and he needed it.

Apple pie and mince pie were the ones most commonly frozen for winter use but squash, pumpkin and cranberry were sometimes on the pantry shelf too. Frozen baked beans and brown bread, a kettle of boiled dinner, a chicken pie made in a big milk pan, were there too, ready to be thawed when needed.

Sometimes a woman went away for a day or two and when she was asked how her men-folks were getting on, she would reply, "Guess they're eating off the pantry shelf." No doubt they were and it was no hardship.

However, even with forty pies on hand Vermont cooks made other desserts, some of them even more nourishing. Grandmother Appleyard, for instance, specialized in a dish known as

FRIED PIES

FOR EIGHT

4 cups flour	6 tablespoons butter
¾ teaspoon salt	2 eggs, well beaten
2 teaspoons baking powder	1 cup milk

Sift flour, salt, and baking powder together three times. Cut in the butter with a pastry blending fork. Beat the eggs, add the milk, beat them together, and beat them into the dry mixture. Roll the dough out thin and cut it into 5-inch circles. Fry them in deep hot fat until the cakes are golden brown.

You are supposed to have dried applesauce on hand, a big crock of it in the cellarway. However, applesauce made with cider instead of water, well sweetened and spiced, will do. The fried cakes are arranged in heaps of four with the warm applesauce spread thickly between. These heaps are the pies. Wedge-shaped pieces cut from them are served with plenty of thick cream and a bowl of granulated maple sugar. This is perhaps the most filling dessert ever invented. Mrs. Appleyard has seen strong men eat second helpings of it but there is no record of anyone ever having a third. She herself once ate one helping. It was delicious and has lasted her nicely during the last forty-seven years.

Since the cellar had barrels of apples in it, apple desserts were favorites with the cooks. Luckily men liked them too. A great treat was

APPLE CHARLOTTE

This calls for some sort of jelly or jam besides the applesauce. The original rule suggested apricot jam but cupboard shelves were more likely to contain raspberry or strawberry jam or currant jelly, so these were often used.

Butter	spiced applesauce
three days old homemade bread	grated lemon rind
jam or jelly	sugar

Quantities will depend on the size of the mold used. Butter it well. Cut the bread the long way of the loaf to give you strips as long as the mold is high. They should be ¼ inch thick and 1½ inches wide. Butter them and spread half of them also with the jam or jelly. Line the mold with them. Fill it half full of applesauce. Cover it with bread strips. Sprinkle with lemon rind. Repeat. Cover top with bread strips. Dot with butter and sprinkle with sugar. Bake at 350° until delicately browned. Serve hot or cold with whipped cream or with Hard Sauce (*Winter Kitchen* p. 130).

CHARLOTTE RUSSE

If you are in a mood for controversy, bring up the subject of Charlotte Russe. There are several theories about the correct way to make it, each with staunch defenders. Mrs. Appleyard gives two versions and advises you not to get on the scales until several days after you have eaten either.

Charlotte Russe — 1st method:

Quantities depend on size of the mold used. Line it with ladyfingers. Fill it with whipped cream, sweetened and flavored with vanilla, allowing ⅓ cup of sugar and a teaspoon of vanilla to 2 cups of cream. Don't whip Vermont cream too long or you'll have butter. Set the mold into the refrigerator for 2 hours. At serving time carefully loosen ladyfingers with a silver knife. Put triangles of wax paper over the top of the mold, turn it out on your best flowered cake plate. Put whipped cream in a pastry bag. Decorate the molded cake with ropes and scallops of cream. Put bits of candied cherries and angelica at strategic places. Pull out the paper triangles. Serve quickly, saying in return to compliments: "Oh, it's really nothing — anyone could do it."

Charlotte Russe — 2nd method: For a 2-quart mold:

2 tablespoons gelatin	4 tablespoons sherry
1½ cups milk	1 tablespoon vanilla
10 eggs	2 cups cream
1 cup sugar	sponge cake

Soak gelatin in ½ cup milk. Separate egg yolks and whites. Beat yolks and sugar together. Add the rest of the milk, beat well, put mixture into top of a double boiler and cook over hot water until the mixture begins to thicken. Add the gelatin, stirring it in well. Pour into a large pan and set it in one containing cold water and ice cubes. Chill thoroughly. Beat the egg whites until they make stiff peaks, fold them into the mixture. Stir in the sherry and vanilla. Whip the cream. Fold it in. Have large mold ready, lined with thin strips of sponge cake. Pour mixture into it. Chill it in the refrigerator for 2 hours.

Miss Parloa thinks you have done enough at this point. Miss Beecher wants you to turn it out on an oval glass dish and "syringe candy sugar on it in fanciful forms." Mrs. Appleyard thinks this means boiled icing, definitely plans not to do it; might possibly decorate it like the first kind with whipped cream and candied cherries.

Miss Beecher uses Russian isinglass for gelatin and suggests taking a whole big sponge cake, baked in a round pan, not a tube pan, and slicing off the top, then hollowing out the sponge cake, filling it with the custard and cream mixture, using the top for a lid. Whichever method you followed, you had a dessert of significance and distinction. Probably after this adventure you were glad to go back to your barrel of apples. You might decide to make

APPLE DUMPLINGS
FOR SIX

These may be made with pastry, homemade (see Deep Dish Apple Pie, p. 173) or from a package. The old-fashioned way was to use a rich biscuit dough.

6 tart apples, medium size	2 teaspoons baking powder (Royal)
2 cups flour	1 teaspoon salt
1 tablespoon sugar	4 tablespoons butter
¾ cup rich milk, part cream	

First prepare your apples. Peel and core them. Mix together 1 cup light brown sugar, 4 tablespoons soft butter, 1 teaspoon cinnamon, ½ teaspoon nutmeg, pinch of cloves, grated rind of 1 lemon, 2 tablespoons fine dry bread crumbs. Fill the centers of the apples with this mixture, packing it in rather firmly.

Now make your biscuit dough. Sift flour, sugar, baking powder and salt. Cut in butter with pastry blending fork until butter is in very small lumps all through the flour. Make a well, pour in milk, mix thoroughly. Toss dough on floured board. Knead one minute. Roll out in an oblong shape about ¼ inch thick.

Cut the dough into 6 squares. Place an apple in the center of each one. Bring corners of dough up over the top. Moisten the edges of the dough with a little cream and press them together so the apple is well covered. It is farther around an apple than you think, Mrs. Appleyard says. Be sure your squares of dough are big enough. She makes a pattern for hers out of a paper napkin before she peels the apples.

Bake the dumplings at 350°, in a pan large enough so that they do not touch each other, until they are well browned, about 30 minutes. Do not feel abashed if they open up and let a little sticky, spicy juice run down the sides: it's delicious.

Serve hot with

LEMON BUTTER SAUCE

1 cup powdered sugar	½ cup hot water
4 tablespoons soft butter (½ stick)	2 tablespoons lemon juice
3 egg yolks	1 tablespoon rum (optional)

Mix the sugar and butter well together. Beat the egg yolks into them with a wire whisk. Beat in the hot water slowly. Cook over hot water till the sauce thickens. Remove from heat and stir in the lemon juice and the rum. Extra lemon juice may be added if you omit the rum.

This same sauce goes well with

CRACKER PUDDING (M.M.M.)

If you are going to serve this for supper, start in the morning.

6 Montpelier crackers	3 cups milk
¼ cup butter	1 cup cream
6 eggs	½ teaspoon nutmeg
6 tablespoons sugar	¼ teaspoon cinnamon
½ teaspoon almond extract	

Split and butter the crackers. Pile them in a buttered casserole. Beat the eggs with the sugar, add the milk, cream, and seasonings. Pour this mixture over the crackers. Set the dish in the refrigerator for at least 3 hours. Before supper preheat oven at 425°. Set in the dish of pudding and bake it 15 minutes. Reduce heat to 350° and bake until it is well puffed and brown, about 30 minutes longer.

Serve hot with Lemon Butter Sauce or with vanilla ice cream, sprinkled with small pieces of candied peel.

Perhaps you like homemade candied peel. In that case a cold day in February is the time to make it, for then Temple oranges and Indian River grapefruit are both at their best.

CANDIED PEEL

peel of 6 Temple oranges, cut into ¼ inch strips
peel of 2 Indian River grapefruit, cut into ¼ inch strips
1 quart water
syrup of 2 cups sugar and 1 cup water
½ can frozen orange juice diluted with ½ cup water
½ can frozen lemonade
extra sugar —about 1 cup

Wash peel and cut it into ¼ inch strips. Put it in a pan and pour a quart of water over it. Let it stand one hour. Drain off the water. Cover it with fresh water and cook it covered over medium heat for 1 hour. Turn off heat and let it soak, covered, 2 hours longer. Make a syrup of the sugar, water, diluted orange juice and lemonade. Add the strips of peel — there will be about 3 cups — and cook them until there is very little syrup left. Remove heat, stir peel thoroughly so that syrup is all through it. Cover a big space on your counter with paper towels and wax paper. Lay the strips of peel on the wax paper. Do not let them touch each other. Handle them with two small forks or a fork and a dessert spoon, whichever you find easiest. Leave them to cool for about an hour. When they are thoroughly cool, spread sugar on a platter and roll them in it. Line a tin box with wax paper. Put in the sugared peel. Cover the box tightly. It will keep well for at least a month.

RICE PUDDING (S.W.E. AND C.V.S.)

This pudding is not for those who like it made with eggs, raisins, and vanilla. It has its own subtle flavor, which comes because the slightly caramelized top layer is stirred into it. Its creamy consistency comes from long, slow cooking at a low temperature. Don't use instant rice.

¾ cup sugar   1 quart rich milk
2 tablespoons soft butter   3 level tablespoons real rice

Butter a straight-sided quart casserole. Mix sugar and butter. Stir in the milk, stir in the rice. Put mixture into the casserole and bake it at 300° for 3 hours. At least 3 times, oftener if you feel like it, stir pudding thoroughly so that the top "skin" is well distributed through the mixture. Leave it alone the last hour. When it is ready, the top will be a rich golden light brown in color. Chill the pudding. Serve it cold with cream. It is the consistency of thick cream itself.

One thing has not changed in a changing world: grandchildren still count on grandmothers to have cookies available. Mrs. Appleyard tries to keep Oatmeal Lace Cookies (*Winter Kitchen*, p. 110) on hand. Another grandmother of her acquaintance specializes in the best sugar cookies in the world. (This is Mrs. Appleyard's opinion, not the maker's, a rather modest type. Her grandchildren agree with Mrs. A.)

SUGAR COOKIES (C.V.S.)

¼ pound butter	1 egg
1 cup sugar	1¾ cups flour
1 tablespoon lemon extract	2 teaspoons baking powder
2 tablespoons cream	⅛ teaspoon salt

sugar (extra) mixed with cinnamon

Materials should be at room temperature. In a bowl large enough to hold the whole mixture, cream the butter and beat in the sugar. Stir in the lemon extract, then the cream and the egg. Sift three times the flour with the baking powder and salt. Your flour may then measure a scant 2 cups. It must not be more. Sift this in, beating well, until it is all used. Scoop dough out on a large piece of waxed paper. Wrap it up. Chill it in the refrigerator overnight.

The next day take about a third of the dough, roll it out thin, using a pastry cloth and covered rolling pin. Heat the oven to 375°. Cut cookies with various shaped cutters — rabbits, scotties, butterflies, crimped circles are all popular shapes. Don't roll out the pieces left in between again but use them just the way they are. They will be more tender and crisp than if you roll them again. If anyone asks what they are, C.V.S. says it's her contribution to abstract sculpture.

Put all the shapes on cookie sheets. Sprinkle them with sugar and cinnamon. Bake at 375° about 7 minutes.

These may be made either by hand or in an electric mixer. If you use the mixer, stir the butter and sugar and egg mixture and some of the flour well together before you start the machine. After all you'd rather have the mixture land ultimately in the cooky jar than on the ceiling, wouldn't you?

Make the whole batch of dough into cookies in one day or rewrap some of it again carefully and use it another day. If it has dried at all, work a few drops of cream into it on the dry part and it will soften up as you roll it out.

Warning: if you once start making these cookies, your grandchildren are not likely to let you stop.

SPRING
IN VERMONT

Spring in Vermont

VERMONT'S most confusing season can begin with a blizzard and end with a wreath of fireflies flashing signal lights in the forget-me-nots around a misty pond. Spring can produce any kind of day it chooses. One kind is a sort of cousin of Indian summer. It is called Squaw winter and is mentioned unfavorably during the nipping frosts of June.

Mrs. Appleyard once showed some old photographs of Appleyard Center to a well-seasoned Vermonter. She said she didn't know exactly when they were taken.

"Well, I can tell you one thing," said her guest. "It wasn't in July." He paused — Vermonters are masters of the anecdotal pause — and added: "No snow on the ground."

Mrs. Appleyard usually sets out her tomato plants on May 30th. After all she wants tomatoes before the August frosts. If frost comes in June, she buys new plants and starts over. Except for peas, which stand cold quite well, she does not plant anything before Memorial Day. The ground has not warmed up; nothing will sprout anyway. When days of sunshine come, the long hours of daylight make the garden grow faster than you expect. Before you know it, you have six kinds of lettuce, each so good that it spoils you for lettuce for the rest of the year. The first radish appears. Mrs. Appleyard can never really believe that those scarlet globes came from the uninteresting seeds she scattered among the carrots. She thinks even one radish makes it worthwhile to have a garden.

"And of course," said one of her city friends, "it must be a great economy."

This remark had an unusual result. It made Mrs. Appleyard speechless.

They were eating her whole asparagus crop — sixteen stalks. Having been brought up never to mention the cost of food at the table, Mrs. Appleyard did not tell her guest that she figured that the asparagus cost a dollar a stalk. This is inexpensive — two years ago it was five dollars.

Naturally the first real sign of spring is reading seed catalogues. This is a good occupation for a spring day that begins with a thick cold fog. The temperature is above freezing but the day feels colder than a crisp blue and silver one at zero. The fog is the sign of the snow's decision to go away.

Evergreens, white outlined in green yesterday, are suddenly dumping their white loads with the soft thud of snow on snow. Now they loom black through the fog. Snow slithers and slides off gabled roofs with a crash. It begins to melt and trickle into gutters. Icicles drip musically. Yesterday the waterfall at the old sawmill was carved pillars of ice. Today you can hear it dash, gurgle and splatter.

Ice is breaking up in the ponds. The river spreads over a field and carries the frozen flotsam and jetsam with it, leaving it in tumbled heaps. Streams that once purred and rippled are roaring. A tree, which has long bent low from the bank, falls across the hurrying water. Suddenly there is a dam with ice cakes piled against it and the stream behind is an icy log jam. Then the pressure tears out the last roots of the tree and the whole mass goes down the valley in grinding, cracking thunder.

Mrs. Appleyard realizes that it is time that she too started south. This is not the first time it has thawed this year. There have been other warnings that mud time is at hand. Slush scatters noisily from under the wheels of cars. Blue jays say "Ka-deedle" to their mates in sentimental tones instead of screaming at them. The bear that lives near the sugar place has stopped hibernating.

It's time I did too, thinks Mrs. Appleyard.

She reaches Virginia while it is still camellia time. The inhabitants have the pleasant custom of bringing visitors their most beautiful specimens — crimson, shining white, rose pink or a kind like scarlet and white marble. Orchards are foaming with peach blossoms. In bright green fields are black pigs as clean as freshly polished iron stoves. In a flowering crab redbirds are sitting, cocking their purple crests.

Mrs. Appleyard moves north with the spring. In Washington the cherry trees are in bloom. She has a favorite, one that leans with special grace toward the Potomac and has the pinkest of blossoms. It has a number. She shares this secret with the tree. No computer shall learn it from her.

Maryland gardens are scented with box. The new green leaves shine. Both Maryland and Virginia have Paulownia trees, big ones, as tall as a maple. The leaves, when they come, are like the ears of rather small elephants but the flowers come first and each tree is an enormous corsage of violet orchids. The ground is covered with them. A single blossom is a joy to hold in your hand and there are thousands and thousands of them.

Philadelphia has cherries in bloom too. Around Valley Forge dogwood is greenish white snow. Daffodils are sunshine against old houses of creamy tan and gray stone. Pennsylvania stonework, Mrs. Appleyard decides, is as beautiful as Virginia brickwork. Ivy looks well with both.

All the gardens in New Jersey are on fire with Red Emperor tulips. There are still red flowers on the swamp maples and lilac flowers on the Judas trees. The woods begin to

look wintry through Connecticut but in Boston the magnolias along Commonwealth Avenue are in full bloom. Swan boats are out in the Public Garden. The State House dome shines. Willows are drifting green-gold rain in the soft wind. Weeping cherries weep pink tears. Forsythia falls over old stone walls in fountains of green gold and Norway maples scatter flowers of gold green.

Mrs. Appleyard likes to remember that America is a melting pot for flowers as well as for people. Forsythia came from southern Europe and met the maple from Norway here. Japan sent the pink clouds of double cherries. From China came the most beautiful of the flowering crabs. Daffodils were asphodels in Greece. Hawthorns bordered Roman roads in England. The Greeks had a word for a yellow rock garden plant — alyssum. It meant madness. The English, however, call it gold dust. So does Mrs. Appleyard.

For a time, as she drove north to Vermont, she saw the same colors, the same patterns of shape and texture repeated. Then, almost as if a line had been ruled across the country, there was no more forsythia. She has often seen what a change this makes in the spring landscape. What was lush is suddenly bleak. You feel that everything that grows has to fight for its life — as indeed it has.

Yet, as she crossed the Connecticut and wound up into the Vermont hills, she began to feel that what she missed was only prettiness. Here the beauty was in the bones of the land, in its enduring compelling power. It showed in the determined green of new grass, in the thrust of pointed firs, in the rush and roar of foaming brooks, in the petals of cowslips in marshy places, shining like butter fresh from the churn.

There were flower buds of red or henna or green and gold on the maples, so Mrs. Appleyard knew that sugaring was over. Syrup made too late in the season is said, disapprovingly to have a "buddy" taste. Because the spring peepers are singing, it is also called frog-run — pronounced frawg-run.

One of Mrs. Appleyard's neighbors, hearing a radio advertisement of a substitute for maple syrup, said contemptuously: "Pure frawg-run."

Mrs. Appleyard had thought of trying it, for was it not luscious, generous, indescribably delicious? Not caring much for frog-run, she continues to eat syrup from maple trees without benefit of corn or cane. She felt sorry that in avoiding mud time she had also missed sugaring. One year she stayed through the winter and experienced sugar on snow, sugar that had been sap only the day before.

That same year she saw daphne in bloom along gray stone walls. This is the kind called mezereon or poor man's daphne. The lilac-colored sweet-smelling flowers come out before the leaves. There may be snow still on the ground near the roots of this valiant shrub, this lilac hedge in miniature, this assurance that spring has really come. This year when Mrs. Appleyard arrived, the shining laurel-like leaves of the daphne had already come out on the bushes near her stone wall. What would later be lacquered scarlet berries were already tiny green knobs.

Mrs. Appleyard's lawn, as she optimistically calls it, was starred with dandelions. If she picked them all and made dandelion wine, she could, she thought, intoxicate her entire acquaintance. She gave up this hospitable idea and went out to see her goldfish. Three years ago she had ten for a birthday present. That was the time she fell into the pond trying to teach one of them to swim. The goldfish recovered from this experience and so did Mrs. Appleyard but her new Paisley print dress was never the same. When she washed it, it shrank in many directions.

"I could wear it if I lost ten pounds," she said to her daughter Cicely, who replied: "Yes, but then everything else you have will be too big."

Struck by the good sense of this remark, Mrs. Appleyard gave up the idea of making herself fit the dress.

"I'll keep it till Roger Willard needs it for the scarecrow," she said, and happily poured herself another cup of Cream of Spring Soup.

She never saw the goldfish again that year. She assumed that kingfishers and blue herons had eaten them for hors d'oeuvres. Goldfish look so tropical and exotic that no one, including Mrs. Appleyard, supposed that they could survive a Vermont winter but they did. The next year there were hundreds. This spring there are thousands. Their ancestors, the original settlers — including the one she taught to swim — were red gold in color. Now there are many colors, gold with strange patterns of silver, gold, and black, plain silver, silver with dots of scarlet. There are fish with sharply cut plain fins and tails and dressy relatives who trail clouds of chiffon behind them as they move. Some are so big they are called carp. Others are no larger than anchovies. Mrs. Appleyard likes them all. She feeds them whatever she has including crumbs of oatmeal cookies. They are crazy about her cooking and fight with each other over every crumb.

When not lunching with her, they make a moving coppery-gold wreath around the pond. This is the pond's inner wreath. Outside it is one of green frogs waiting to have their heads tickled. Some of them — don't believe this if you don't want to — have blue heads. This helps the frog wreath to harmonize with the next one, which is the forget-me-not wreath. Outside that is the yellow wreath, which has, at different seasons, a sort of yellow sweet pea, dandelions, St.-John's-wort, goldenrod and, just before frost, wild sunflowers. Beyond that is the wreath of lupines, as many lupines as goldfish, more perhaps.

The pond was made several years ago by hollowing out a marshy place. Mrs. Appleyard wanted fresh water running through it, so she asked Roger Willard to go out on the hill with his dowsing rod and see if he could find a spring. Pretty soon he came back with his forked cherry stick in his hand.

"Did you find one?" asked Mrs. Appleyard.

"No." (Vermont pause) "Found three though."

The water from two of these springs now gurgles into the pond.

The muddy clay scooped out of it was apparently just what lupines like. When the dirt was still bare, Mrs. Appleyard raked it a little, collected seeds from the lupines in her garden and scattered them around, remarking, "I might get two or three clumps out of these."

The result is lupines of all the colors she had ever seen and more besides. They range from pure clear white through ivory white to pale yellows and shell pinks. The pink deepens to rose, grows still deeper. Suddenly it is bluish lavender and then all shades of violet from lilac to magenta. White mingles with all these colors. Sometimes it seems as if no two of the thousands of plants were the same. The lupines lead their own life. Any plant they don't want for a neighbor they quietly asphyxiate. They allow mint to grow near them, but they have no patience with goldenrod. This trait makes the lupines and Mrs. Appleyard rather congenial. A little goldenrod goes a long way. Only it's like garlic, there is no such thing as a little goldenrod.

The lupines were still only jade-green buds when she came home this spring and the scarlet knobs on the apple trees were just starting to unfold pink and white petals. Mrs. Appleyard stayed for a while in her apartment at Cicely's but worked every day — she claimed — at opening her house. Part of the opening process naturally meant a good many trips between her house and Cicely's. After all, she needed her vegetable juicer and that pink tweed suit — the one of which she has worn the right cuff through writing books. She's thinking of binding it with leather in case of another book coming on.

The trips to fetch such treasures can easily be extended in apple blossom time to drives of ten or fifteen miles. Luckily for Mrs. Appleyard she has the ability to forget how beautiful it was last year: it's always a surprise. An old orchard is a bank of pink snow. A turn in the road shows a bright green field with white trees shining along the edge. Down the next valley, trees are like clouds and clouds are like trees. Here is an orchard of young trees, Degas dancing girls in tulle and pearls with arms reaching to the sky. Beyond an old crab apple is a pink tower above a small gray house. Down below in the village every house has a red roof and an apple tree. The whole place looks like a big strawberry meringue pie.

Back in Appleyard Center, trees a hundred and fifty years old are full of blossoms and of bees among the gold stamens. In September deer will stand on their hind legs and knock down the apples. A deer silhouetted against a sky with a new moon in it makes an interesting design as it knocks down Golden Transparents, Dutchess and Wealthys. Any kind is acceptable to a deer. Mrs. Appleyard prefers the Dutchess, named for their original home — Dutchess County, New York. She planted that Dutchess tree near her corn barn herself, feels splendidly venerable as she looks at its gnarled trunk.

She planted the lilac hedge too, forty years ago. She planned to keep it eight feet high but of course the hedge has made its own decisions. If you want some of the purple plumes, you have to pull them down with a rake.

Mrs. Appleyard gets a suitable rake and begins work. While she is cutting lilacs, an oriole flies in and out of the apple tree. Bobolinks skim over the iris near the pond, singing as they fly. She fills a big copper jug with lilacs and apple blossoms and yellow tulips and sets it on the cherry chest under the Queen Anne mirror.

Now she has officially opened her house. Now it is spring.

Thanks to the Indians

ONE OF Mrs. Appleyard's favorite passages in literature is in a story by an Englishman. Broadmindedly he chose an American scene and with genial realism splashed in the background, thus: "It was autumn, the season called Indian summer, and under the red and yellow maples the Indians in their feather headdresses were gathering the maple syrup."

What an improvement this is over going out, with no feather headdress, on some raw, bone-chilling morning in early March to tap trees and hang sap buckets! You might, Mrs. Appleyard supposes, just as well catch the juice of the maple on its way down in the fall as on its way up in the spring, especially as, in Indian summer, there would be none of this nonsense about cooking down thirty or forty gallons of sap to make one of syrup. In that happy season, it seems, syrup comes right out of the tree. The fortunate Indians could serve it at once on waffles or — perhaps a little more handy — sagamite, that cornmeal mush to which Indian gourmets often added grasshoppers or crickets according to the season. Only how about sugar on snow? If it had not been for the Indian habit of collecting the spring run of sap, we would never have known that hot syrup poured over fresh snow makes a sort of crisp golden lace and tastes the way maple syrup smells. Ambrosia and nectar is a menu that has been favorably mentioned for quite a while: sugar on snow is like both only more nourishing because with it are served eggs that have been boiled in the sap, plain doughnuts of a substance splendidly absorbent and dill pickles with which you stimulate your palate for another round.

It used to be necessary to go right to the sugarhouse for such a treat but, thanks to the deep freeze, you can now have sugar on snow in lilac time, wild rose time, under a hot August moon or even in Indian summer. Until just the other day, Mrs. Appleyard's freezer contained a number of neat pasteboard dishes full of snow. In case you have some snow, either in the freezer or on the front lawn, this is how you cook syrup to use with it.

Into a kettle that will hold a gallon or more, put a quart of syrup and quickly bring it to the boiling point. Watch it! If you turn your back, it will boil over, leaving you with a cleaning job that will make you wish you could just pick up your wigwam and go somewhere else. Use a candy thermometer. If you like your sugar on snow waxy, cook the syrup to 230°. For the crisp and lacy kind, the right temperature is 232°. Call in the customers. Dribble the hot syrup over the snow. Ah-h-h!

Perhaps you prefer maple flavor in a more permanent form. Then butter a plate lightly. Cover it with nutmeats — butternuts, walnuts or pecans. Pour syrup at 232° into a big tortoiseshell Bennington bowl. Stir vigorously until the syrup turns from dark to pale amber and just begins to thicken. Pour it over the nutmeats. Mark in squares while it is still warm.

You may like granulated maple sugar. Cook the syrup to 238°. Pour it into a bowl. Stir it through various shades of amber to a pale golden beige. Use first a spoon with holes in it, then a strong pastry-blending fork. After a while it will begin to grain. Sift it through a large-meshed strainer. Break up any lumps that are left. It will look rather like brown sugar but it will taste of bare maples, like fans of black coral against a blue silk sky, of crunching crusty snow, of woodsmoke, of sap tinkling into buckets, of sun hot on your cheek — of, in fact, maple.

Serve it on ice cream or on freshly cooked homeground wheat, or Scotch oatmeal, with cream. Mr. Appleyard's favorite dessert was a slice of homemade whole-wheat bread generously sprinkled with this sugar and with cream spooned over it. He spooned it since, being Vermont cream, it was too thick to pour.

On a day when she was going to have some luscious unsalted rice and five steamed apricots for lunch, Mrs. Appleyard was heard to wish she were an Indian. However she soon realized she would be a squaw, busily gathering sap and boiling it, probably with a papoose grandchild on her back, while the braves smoked. Occasionally one would come around and say "How?" To this remark Squaw Appleyard would respond by swishing some syrup over the snow. If it was lacy enough, he would eat it and then she would be allowed to set the kettle in the snow and stir the syrup until it sugared.

She certainly thanks the Indians for this discovery and even more the white men who put the syrup in cans decorated with red and yellow leaves. Never mind if they wear imitation fur hats instead of war bonnets — she thanks them specially.

Mrs. Appleyard, during sugaring time, is often asked for rules for doughnuts. She usually explains that she would just as soon fry and eat a porcupine, quills and all, as make doughnuts. However, she does have her grandmother's receipt and last spring she sent it to an especially friendly sounding correspondent who says they turned out all right, so she repeats it here. It is adjusted for modern equipment.

TWO DOZEN DOUGHNUTS (S.W.E.)

2½ cups flour	1 tablespoon butter, melted
2 teaspoons baking powder	½ cup sugar
⅛ teaspoon (pinch) nutmeg	1 egg
1½ teaspoons salt	1 cup rich milk
¼ teaspoon cinnamon	2 pounds Crisco for frying

Sift flour and dry ingredients three times. Mix butter, sugar, and unbeaten egg in a bowl. Stir well. Add alternately the flour mixture and the milk. Use a pastry frame and a rolling pin cover for rolling dough. With your hands very lightly floured, shape mixture into a mound, then lightly roll it out ⅜ inch thick.

Heat the Crisco in a straight-sided pan, 8 inches across and 5 to 6 inches deep, or use a deep-fat fryer if you have one. Use a fat-frying thermometer to check temperature of the fat. It should be 370°. A 1-inch cube of bread will brown in it in 1 minute. A frying basket to fit your kettle is a great help, but you can manage with two long-handled slotted spoons or with a spoon and a fork if you prefer. It is important not to pierce the doughnuts with the fork.

Cut out your doughnuts with a lightly floured doughnut cutter. Cut out 4. Cook only 4 at a time. Slip the doughnuts gently into the fat. When they rise and are brown underneath, turn them carefully. Sweet-milk doughnuts should be turned only once. When they are just the right shade of rich golden brown, remove them from the pan, letting surface fat drip back into the kettle. Have two big pans full of crumpled paper towels. Drain the doughnuts in the first pan on one side, then move them to the second pan and drain the other side.

Check the heat of the fat. When it reaches 370° again, put in 4 more doughnuts. When you have cooked them all, cook the doughnut balls. It is better to make the scraps between the doughnuts into balls, patting them gently into shape, rather than rolling the dough out again as that tends to toughen it. If you like your doughnuts sugared, shake them in a bag with sugar when they are well drained and just barely warm. Either powdered or granulated sugar may be used. Add ½ teaspoon mixed spices — cinnamon, nutmeg, allspice — to a cup of sugar.

Doughnuts to be eaten with maple syrup or with sugar on snow of course should not be sugared.

Grandmother Appleyard made doughnuts using either sour milk and butter or sour cream. She used lard rather than Crisco for frying and she liked to be alone when she did it so she used to get up around five o'clock. At this time Mrs. Appleyard, a systematic sleeper, who seldom reads after midnight, was not likely to interrupt her. The results of this dawn cooking were excellent.

SOUR CREAM DOUGHNUTS (B.H.K.)

ABOUT THREE DOZEN

Crisco for frying	¼ teaspoon cinnamon
4 cups flour	½ teaspoon nutmeg
2 teaspoons baking powder	pinch of ginger
1 teaspoon soda	3 eggs, medium size
½ teaspoon salt	1¼ cups sugar
¼ teaspoon cloves	1 cup sour cream

Fat should be hot enough to brown a cube of bread in one minute (365° to 370°). Sift flour once. Measure. Sift again twice with dry ingredients. Spices may be varied according to taste. Beat eggs well, beat in sugar, stir in the cream, sift and stir in the flour mixture. Chill mixture while fat is heating. Roll it out and fry the doughnuts as in rule given above, but turn them several times. Toss in a bag with spiced sugar or serve them plain. Be careful not to get in too much soda. Modern soured cream may be used but it is not nearly so acid as cream skimmed off a big pan of clabbered milk. If you use it, Mrs. Appleyard thinks you had better reduce the soda to ½ teaspoon and add 1 teaspoon baking powder. The old rule called for real sour cream which was likely to have a little of the sour milk mixed in it. Doughnuts tasting of soda are a painful experience. Still, sour milk and cream make a very light tender dough both for doughnuts and also for biscuits, shortcake and pancakes. The art is worth mastering, even at the cost of one or two failures. Some chilly spring morning you might like to try

SOUR MILK GRIDDLE CAKES

FOUR 4-INCH CAKES EACH FOR FOUR PEOPLE

⅞ cup flour	1 tablespoon sugar
¾ teaspoon baking powder	1 egg (large)
½ teaspoon salt	1 cup sour milk
½ teaspoon baking soda	2 tablespoons butter (melted)

Taste the milk. If it is not very sour, reduce soda to ¼ teaspoon and increase baking powder to 1 teaspoon, or use 1 cup sour cream and omit the butter.

Sift flour once. Measure it. Sift twice more with dry ingredients. Beat egg light with a wire whisk. Quickly whisk in first the milk and melted butter, then the flour mixture. Do not overbeat. Heat an iron griddle or a well-seasoned iron frying pan. Do not grease but wipe with raw potato. Cut the end off the potato. Wipe it over the surface of the griddle while it is warm. Heat the griddle until drops of cold water dashed on it sputter and steam. Pour on the batter in 4-inch circles. After 2 or 3 minutes the cakes will begin to bubble and the bubbles will burst. Lift cakes with a pancake turner. Check to see if they are well browned, turn them and bake until they are well browned on the other side. Remove them to a warm platter set in an open warm oven. Cut a thin slice off the potato, discard it and wipe the griddle with the freshly cut surface. Do this between baking each batch of cakes. Butter the warm cakes. Stack them in heaps of 4. Serve them with maple syrup or with thick cream and granulated maple sugar.

BLUEBERRY PANCAKES

If you would like to make blueberry pancakes for a change, use this same batter and a cup of frozen blueberries right from the package. Do not mix them with the batter. Pour some batter on the griddle, spoon on some blueberries, cover them with a little more batter. Brown the cakes on both sides. Serve them with Vermont sausage and with butter. Some people add maple syrup too.

SAUSAGE MEAT

If you read the labels on modern sausages you will find that they contain water. This is a very expensive way to buy water which is in the sausage for a special purpose — to make it heavier. Your butcher, even in a supermarket if you go at a time when it is not crowded, will grind pork for you. Take with you, for 6 pounds of sausage meat, a plastic bag containing 6 teaspoons salt, 4 teaspoons powdered sage, ¼ teaspoon summer savory, ¼ teaspoon thyme, 3 teaspoons pepper from the grinder. (Some people omit thyme and savory.) Tell the butcher that there should be 6 pounds of lean pork, at least 4 pounds of lean meat. Ask him to sprinkle your seasonings over it and put it twice through the grinder.

At home you can mold this into rolls and wrap them in several thicknesses of wax paper or you can put the meat in tins lined with wax paper. You may freeze the sausage meat in either form. It will also keep all right in the refrigerator for at least a week. The frozen meat must be thoroughly thawed before being used. Shape it into patties or slice it and cook it with sliced apples. Use it in Turkey Stuffing (see p. 148) or make it into Meat Loaf with Veal (*Winter Kitchen*, p. 307) or make

SAUSAGE AND PINEAPPLE
FOR FOUR

8 sausage patties	8 slices pineapple
½ cup flour	½ cup brown sugar
⅛ teaspoon cinnamon	

Use two frying pans. Make the sausage meat into patties slightly smaller than the pineapple slices. Dip them in the flour. Start them cooking over low heat. When fat runs out of the sausage, put about 2 tablespoons in the other pan. Add the pineapple slices, sprinkle them with the brown sugar mixed with the cinnamon. Let them brown slightly. Be sure they do not scorch. Turn them. When the sausage slices have browned on the first side, turn them and brown them carefully on the other side. Put the browned pineapple in an electric skillet, put the sausage slices on top of the pineapple, simmer at 200° until the sausage shows no trace of pink color, at least an hour. Serve with Thin Scalded Johnny Cake (see *Summer Kitchen*, p. 158). If you have no electric skillet, have the pineapple slices in one frying pan, cover them with the sausage slices. Pour pineapple juice around them. Bake in a 250° oven until sausage is thoroughly cooked; at least an hour. Baste occasionally with the pineapple juice.

VERMONT SCRAPPLE MRS. APPLEYARD

You can use some of your sausage meat to make scrapple. This is a short-cut method, an imitation of Philadelphia Scrapple. Mrs. Appleyard has also made it by the method that starts with a pig's head and takes three days. She is no longer so energetic.

5 cups boiling water	2 cups yellow cornmeal
1 cup sausage meat	

Bring the water to a rapid boil in the top of a large double boiler. Sprinkle in the corn-meal a little at a time, only a few grains at first. Stir constantly to keep the meal from lumping. Reduce the heat and stir in the sausage meat, which you have broken up fine with a fork. Cook 5 minutes, stirring the meat thoroughly into the meal. Set the pan over hot water and cook one hour. Put the scrapple into pans lined with wax paper; cool. Keep in the refrigerator. When you serve it, cut it in slices about ¾ of an inch thick. Grease a frying pan with sausage fat or butter, cook over medium heat until one side is golden brown, then turn and brown the other sides of the slices.

Onions Simmered in Cream, Green Beans with Garlic Crumbs, tart jelly such as choke-cherry or elderberry, or Mrs. Appleyard's Tomato Conserve (*Winter Kitchen*, p. 142) all go well with scrapple on a snowy spring evening.

Golden slices of scrapple are also good with Chicken Breasts in Cream sauce (p. 26) or with Creamed Turkey made the same way.

Another way to use your sausage meat is to make it into small cakes and put them into the roasting pan around a turkey during its last hour of cooking. Turn them after half an hour, baste the turkey with the fat in the pan.

Sausage cakes also go well with Yorkshire Pudding, (*Summer Kitchen*, p. 221). The pudding can be cooked using sausage fat instead of beef fat. They are also delicious served with

VERMONT JOHNNY CAKE (B.H.K.)

This is halfway between johnny cake and spoon bread. Like all things made with sour milk, it takes judgment but it's worth learning to do, Mrs. Appleyard thinks.

1½ cups cornmeal	½ cup sour cream
½ cup flour	1 cup sour milk
3 teaspoons baking powder	1¼ cups sweet milk
1 teaspoon soda	2 eggs
1 teaspoon salt	1 tablespoon sugar
¼ cup sweet cream	2 tablespoons melted butter

Sift together the cornmeal, flour, baking powder, salt, and soda three times. Mix the sour milk and sour cream, the sweet milk, the eggs well beaten and the sugar. Make a well in the dry mixture and add the wet mixture, beating it in well. Melt the butter in a large (12-inch) iron frying pan. Pour in the mixture. Pour the sweet cream over the top. Bake at 400° for ten minutes. Reduce heat to 350° and bake until it is well browned, about 30 minutes longer. Do not overbake. The inside should be quite soft, almost like a soufflé. Serve maple syrup with it.

Also good with maple syrup (what isn't?) is Cream of Wheat spoon bread.

CREAM OF WHEAT SPOON BREAD
FOR SIX

⅔ cup Cream of Wheat	3 eggs, separated
2½ cups boiling water	3 tablespoons flour
4 tablespoons butter	1 teaspoon salt
1½ cups milk	3 teaspoons baking powder

Add the Cream of Wheat to the boiling water so slowly that it never stops boiling. Cook over hot water for 5 minutes. Add butter. Let mixture cool slightly, add the milk and the egg yolks well beaten. Sprinkle in the flour sifted with the salt and baking powder. Stir well. Fold in egg whites, beaten to stiff peaks. Put mixture into a well-buttered baking dish. Dot more butter over the top. Bake at 400° for 10 minutes. Reduce temperature to 350° and bake until well browned, about 35 minutes longer.

Vermonters keep their freezers filled with pans of spring snow so that if they feel in the mood they can have sugar on snow in August. There are, however, other desserts where maple is the theme. A simple one to prepare is

MAPLE TOAST

Allow one slice of bread for each person to be served. Toast them on one side. Butter the other sides. Sprinkle them generously with maple sugar but don't put it too near the edge as it tends to spread. Put under the broiler, 3 inches away, and broil until the sugar melts. Sprinkle slices with coarsely chopped pecans. Serve with thick sweet yellow cream or sour cream. Use either white or whole-wheat bread, whichever you prefer. You need firm homemade bread. Ordinary baker's bread will not do.

MAPLE SHORTCAKE
FOR SIX

Butternuts really belong with maple dishes but they are not often available. Shelling them is a special skill that is almost forgotten now. Mrs. Appleyard substitutes walnuts, black walnuts, or pecans, usually the latter.

pinch of salt	¾ cup maple syrup
4 teaspoons baking powder	1 tablespoon butter (extra)
2 cups sifted flour	2 egg whites
⅓ cup butter	1 cup cream, whipped
¾ cup milk	1 cup pecans, broken

Mix salt and baking powder with the sifted flour and put it through a triple sifter. Work in butter with the fingertips until mixture feels like coarse meal. Cut milk in with a pastry-blending fork. Toss dough on a lightly floured board and quickly make it into two mounds and roll each out ½ inch thick to fit two greased layer cake pans. Bake at 450° for 12 to 15 minutes.

In the meantime cook maple syrup and 1 tablespoon butter until mixture threads from the spoon. Beat egg whites stiff, and pour syrup on them, beating all the time with a wire whisk. Cool slightly. Whip the cream and whisk it into the maple mixture. Spread between layers and on top of the shortcake. Sprinkle pecans between layers and on top of the cream.

MAPLE MARRON MOUSSE
FOR SIX

1¼ cups maple syrup	24 chestnuts
yolks of 4 eggs	1 cup light cream
2 cups heavy cream	

This is easier to make than it used to be because chestnuts can now be bought already shelled in cans. Drain off the liquid.

Heat the syrup until it will spin a thread from the spoon. Beat the egg yolks until they are thick and lemon colored. Pour the syrup over them, beating all the time. Break the chestnuts into medium-sized pieces, add them to the mixture. Put the mixture into the top of a double boiler and cook it over hot water until it coats the back of the spoon. Stir in the light cream and cook a minute longer. Cool slightly. Whip the heavy cream and fold it into the mixture. Put it into a deep tray or a melon mold, rinsed in cold water. Set in your freezer or the freezing compartment of your refrigerator for at least 2 hours. Stir contents thoroughly to break up crystals three times during the first hour. Level it neatly after stirring it. When unmolding it, set the mold for half a minute into tray of lukewarm water, 100°. Watch it — the contents are not what you need for floor polish.

MAPLE TRIFLE

1 tablespoon gelatin	a little rum (optional)
½ cup almonds	2½ cups cream
¼ cup cold water	½ cup Candied Peel (p. 48)
1 cup maple syrup	¼ cup crystallized ginger
2 dozen lady fingers	½ cup cream (extra)

Blanch and skin the almonds. Brown them in butter. Soak gelatin in the water. Heat maple syrup, pour it on the gelatin, and stir well until it is dissolved. Cool slightly. Line a mold with lady fingers: sprinkle them with rum. Whip 2 cups cream. Fold it into the syrup mixture. Fill mold half full, lay on a few lady fingers, sprinkle with rum, scatter on some almonds, repeat. Top should be covered with lady fingers, no nuts.

At serving time remove from mold. Whip ½ cup cream. Decorate the trifle with it and also with the candied peel, ginger and a few whole almonds. Pecans may be used if you prefer. Mrs. Appleyard has relaxed sufficiently so that she no longer unmolds the trifle but makes it in a big Sandwich glass dish, decorates the top at serving time and serves it right from the dish. No complaints so far.

Spring Fever

EARLY explorers in North America usually had scurvy during the voyage across the ocean and in the winter after they arrived. Their provisions — salt fish, salt meat and ship's biscuit — supplied them with enough food so that they did not die from actual starvation but they were short on vitamins, especially vitamin C, so the weaker men sometimes died of the resulting scurvy.

Champlain, who was friendly with the Indians near Quebec, was generous to them even when his own supplies of food ran low. The result had a strange nutritional effect. Indians regarded salt as poison and felt that the white men were crazy in their use of it. Indians sometimes starved to death when the supply of fresh moose meat and venison failed but they did not have scurvy — at least not until they began to eat the white men's salt meat and fish. Then they did not die of starvation but they had scurvy, just like anyone else. However, they had a remedy and they told Champlain about it. A certain evergreen, probably some sort of spruce though it has never been identified, put forth green tips in early spring. The Indians ate these and advised the Frenchmen to do so. Apparently results were good.

Vermonters, even only fifty years ago, had a craving for green things after their winter diet of salt meats and root vegetables. Milkweed shoots, the fiddleheads of the ostrich fern, dandelion greens, sorrel, the first stalks of asparagus were all, quite literally, lifesavers. Parsnips and Jerusalem artichokes too were a welcome change from the winter diet. Mrs. Appleyard can remember when children in spring were dosed with sulphur and molasses and also cod liver oil to ward off spring fever. She is not sure which was most repulsive but her family were cod liver oil specialists so she votes for that fishy substance as the one least likely to win friends.

She was not very fond of parsnips either but she remembers that they could be tolerated in the form of parsnip fritters or — as Miss Parloa recommended —

PARSNIP BALLS
FOR SIX

1 pint boiled parsnips	2 tablespoons cream
2 tablespoons butter	1 egg, beaten
⅛ teaspoon pepper	beaten egg (extra)
1 teaspoon salt	fine dry bread crumbs

Mash the parsnips, removing any dry fibers. Add the butter, pepper, salt, and cream. Stir mixture over the fire until it bubbles and stir in the beaten egg. Cool. When it is well cooled, make the mixture into balls ⅓ the size of an egg. Dip them in beaten egg, then in crumbs. Put in frying basket, lower it into hot fat (370°) and cook until the parsnip balls are a rich brown.

JERUSALEM ARTICHOKES
FOR SIX

These have the flavor of the French globe artichoke and have the advantage of being without thistle fluff to choke the unwary eater.

1 pound Jerusalem artichokes	2 tablespoons minced parsley
¼ cup butter	¼ teaspoon salt
juice and grated rind of 1 lemon	½ teaspoon paprika
⅛ teaspoon pepper	

Wash and peel the artichokes. Drop them as you peel them into a quart of cold water with half a cup of vinegar in it to keep them from darkening. Drain. Cook in boiling water until soft, about 25 minutes. Check them often during cooking and remove from heat as soon as they are soft. They may get hard again if cooked too long. Melt butter, add lemon juice and rind, parsley and seasonings. Drain artichokes. Put them in a hot dish and pour the sauce over them.

MARINATED ARTICHOKES

1 pound Jerusalem artichokes	6 tablespoons olive oil
2 tablespoons tarragon vinegar	½ teaspoon salt
1 teaspoon garlic powder	1 teaspoon mustard (powdered)
½ teaspoon paprika	½ teaspoon pepper
½ teaspoon sugar	⅛ teaspoon curry powder

Wash, peel, and cook the artichokes as in the rule above. Put all the other ingredients in a jar and shake them well together. Pour this marinade over the artichokes while they are still hot. Chill thoroughly. Use for hors d'oeuvres or in salad. Use cider vinegar and Wesson or safflower oil if you prefer.

Artichokes and many other vegetables are good garnished with buttered garlic crumbs made like this —

GARLIC CRUMBS

3 slices dry homemade bread   3 tablespoons butter
1 teaspoon garlic powder

Roll the bread into rather coarse crumbs. Melt the butter over medium heat. Toss the crumbs in it until they are a delicate brown. Sprinkle garlic powder over the crumbs and stir it in well. Serve.

Mrs. Appleyard used to do this with real garlic mashed through a garlic press, but several reasons have made her change to the powder. The chief one, everyone will no doubt be glad to know, is a certain amount of inertia. It's a lot easier to sprinkle in powder than it is to peel garlic and mash it. Another reason is that people who won't tolerate the garlic at full strength often like the powdered form. Also real garlic is hard to keep. If you need some only occasionally — to rub a salad bowl or to crush for salad dressing or garlic butter — you often find that all you have is a dried, papery substance faintly flavored with garlic.

Of course there is no law that bread crumbs ever have to encounter garlic at all. They are good just browned in butter and sprinkled over the vegetable.

MILKWEED SHOOTS
FOR SIX

One of Mrs. Appleyard's Vermont neighbors was always on the lookout for the first milkweed shoots. This is how she served them, picking them when they were only a few inches high.

24 milkweed shoots	2 tablespoons flour
6 slices buttered toast	pepper and salt to taste
1 hard-boiled egg	½ cup milk
2 tablespoons butter	½ cup light cream

Rub the shoots between your hands to loosen the woolly covering and wash the shoots in several changes of water. Have a large pan of boiling water ready and have more hot water in your teakettle. Boil the shoots until they are tender, about half an hour. Change the water twice during the cooking period. This is to wash away the milkweed juice.

Make the toast and butter it. Chop up the hard-boiled egg, not too fine. Melt the butter and make a roux with the flour and seasonings. When the roux is well blended and smooth, remove pan from the heat and work in first the milk, then the cream. Return to the fire. Cook over low heat, stirring constantly for at least five minutes. Add the chopped egg. Turn off the heat. At serving time, drain the milkweed shoots, put them on toast, bring the sauce to the boiling point. Pour it over the milkweed.

DANDELION GREENS

Picking dandelion greens is a fine nutritious project, splendid exercise if you don't mind standing on your head, and wonderful for the lawn. Greens should be dug before the blossoms come. Cut off the roots, buds, and coarse outside leaves. Wash greens thoroughly. Even when young and tender, dandelions are quite bitter. Put them into a vegetable cooking basket and lower it into rapidly boiling water. Cook the greens 15 minutes, change the water, cook until tender, about 10 minutes longer. Drain, chop, reheat. Serve sprinkled with crisp bacon or tried-out cubes of salt pork or of beef suet and sliced hard-boiled eggs. If it's all the same to you Mrs. Appleyard would rather have spinach.

FIDDLEHEADS

When people tell you about fiddleheads, the coiled tops of the ostrich fern, they always say, "They are like asparagus." They are the same people who tell you that frogs' legs and rabbit are like chicken. It is true that a frog's leg resembles chicken more than it does a nice porterhouse steak and it is also true that fiddleheads are more like asparagus than they are like parsnips or beets, but they have their own texture and flavor and if you are looking forward to chicken and asparagus, Mrs. Appleyard thinks perhaps that is what you had better eat. She could not possibly encourage anyone to eat her favorite blue-headed frogs although she has cooked and eaten frogs' legs and rather likes them. There's something less personal about fiddleheads than about frogs. Here is how you deal with them:

Fiddleheads must be picked before they unroll, and the shortest possible time before they are cooked. They are rather furry and this fur — or perhaps it should be called hair — must be carefully rubbed off. You also have to get rid of the tough ends of the stalks and also the dry scales. Some of the scales are in the coiled tips of the ferns.

A folding steamer, the aluminum kind that adjusts itself to the kettle used, is a good thing to use in cooking fiddleheads. Pull out the legs of the steamer to their greatest length. Set it in rapidly boiling water. Heap in the fiddleheads — allow 6 to a serving — cover the kettle, steam them half an hour.

Serve in the same way you do milkweed shoots, on buttered toast with cream sauce, or with Egg, Butter and Lemon Sauce (p. 47).

BEET GREENS

Mrs. Appleyard, who has been confronted with her quota of tough bitter beet greens, came across an entry in her cooking diary which says, "Beet greens properly cooked — for once." This happy event took place in 1959 and has been a secret until this moment. She began by thinning out her row of beets until she had half a peck of young greens. She says they were so fresh that the crinkled leaves rustled. She began by cutting off the roots, which were just starting to form into young beets, and putting them into a bowl of water. She scrubbed them well and removed all the strings and washed them in several changes of water. She cut all the thick red stems into ¼-inch pieces with scissors and put them on to steam with the young beets. She steamed them 25 minutes. During this time she washed the leaves, cut them up with scissors and then put them on to cook just with the water that clung to them and 2 tablespoons of butter. She cooked them 5 minutes, chopping them all the time, added another lump (about 2 tablespoons) of butter and left them until serving time. She then added the cooked beets and stems and cooked them about 3 minutes. Most of the liquid had then been absorbed. Both the beets and the greens were tender and well colored. They were served with sour cream.

"Even I liked them," records the diary.

Soup in Spring

THERE are many spring evenings in Vermont when a bowl of hot soup is a cheering item on the menu. There are also occasional hot days when the same soup, chilled in pottery jars, makes a refreshing luncheon dish. The soups given below may be served either hot or cold. They are lighter than winter soups and are variations on two themes — on chicken stock, cream sauce and vegetables or on clear soups made with beef stock. Stock is not hard to make. The last time Mrs. Appleyard was simmering a batch of it she was also waxing floors, mending stockings, doing laundry and revising proofs of *He Went with Hannibal*. She also visited the compost heap and put out sunflower seeds for the chickadees. The soup stock was then ready.

CHICKEN STOCK

1 pound wing tips and necks of chicken   3 pounds veal bones
carcass of roast chicken with scraps of meat   4 carrots, washed and sliced
  and stuffing   2 onions, peeled and sliced
2 stalks of celery, cut fine   celery tops, cut fine
1 tablespoon minced parsley   pinches of basil, rosemary, oregano
1 bay leaf   ¼ teaspoon thyme

Put all the ingredients in a large kettle. Add 2 gallons of cold water. Bring to the boiling point and simmer for 4 hours. It will cook down so that you have about 2½ quarts of liquid. Strain it, chill it, skim it when chilled. Pour it into pint jars. It will jelly and it keeps well in the refrigerator.

BEEF STOCK

Mrs. Appleyard — perhaps you have noticed — mentions stock pretty often. This is not much of a task if you have a burner over which you can keep a kettle of stock simmering. Stock is not made by hard-and-fast rules. You need some beef bones with some meat on them, a knuckle of veal, a carrot, an onion, a turnip or some small radishes, and some herbs and spices: thyme, rosemary, basil, pinches of cinnamon, cloves, and nutmeg. Add the carcass of a chicken if you like.

Put the meat and bones to cook in cold water. As it starts to boil, skim the broth, simmer it either all day or all night. If you have a real simmering source of heat, less than 200°, there is no danger of the kettle's cooking dry. Strain the stock into sterilized Mason jars, cool, put it in the refrigerator. A cake of fat will rise to the surface. Remove this when you use the stock. If the stock has not jellied it will do so if more of the water is cooked out.

Once Mrs. Appleyard absentmindedly cooked some down so long that she pretty nearly made

PORTABLE SOUP

A friend of hers lent her one of the most fascinating of books: Mrs. Sylvester Gardiner's *Receipts for 1763*. Mrs. Gardiner was the wife of Dr. Gardiner of Gardiner, Maine. He was one of the few physicians anywhere in the region and he often rode on horseback many miles to visit a patient. Inns were few and far between but Dr. Gardiner had something nourishing in his saddle bags: he always carried a few squares of Mrs. Gardiner's Portable Soup.

The rule calls for "two legs of beef, about fifty pounds weight." After you had taken off the skin and fat, you put the bones into a large pot with about nine gallons of salt water. (Sea water perhaps?) Onions and anchovies and spices went in too. The whole mixture was simmered for eight or nine hours. Then it was strained, and cooled, the fat was removed and the broth was cooked down until it was like a thick jelly. This was spread out in shallow pans and allowed to cool. Then it was scored in squares of uniform size and set where it would dry. When finally cut in pieces, the squares were the consistency of horn.

When Dr. Gardiner was tired, hungry and thirsty after a fifty-mile ride, all he needed was some hot water into which he dropped a piece of Portable Soup and he soon had a delicious and refreshing drink.

Unfortunately the twentieth century has improved on this idea by substituting monosodium glutamate for the meat essences. This substance, so cleverly devised for the hardening of the arteries, is an expensive way of buying salt. An ounce of m.s.g. and 5 pounds of salt cost about the same. Why not make some Portable Soup? A shinbone of beef with some meat on it, weighing about 5 pounds, would be the basis for a good batch and as you probably are not going to ride out into the wilderness to set anyone's leg very often, you could have it on hand for quite a while, in case of emergencies. You might, for instance, make

ONION SOUP WITH CUSTARD
FOR FOUR

Mr. and Mrs. Appleyard had this once in a (Bostonian) French restaurant and he liked it so much that she went swiftly home, snatched up the Portable Soup squares with which she had been experimenting and made something upon which he kindly beamed approval.

4 large onions	¼ cup red wine
4 tablespoons butter	1 teaspoon Worcestershire sauce
4 Portable Soup squares	1 cup grated dry Vermont cheese
4 cups water (hot)	4 slices French bread, toasted

Slice the onions. Fry them in butter to a delicate straw color. They should be tender but not mushy. Melt up the Portable Soup squares in the hot water and pour over the onions. Add the wine and Worcestershire and let the soup just simmer a while. You can do this all in the morning and reheat it at supper time.

In the morning, if you are going to serve it for supper, make the custard. Make another cup of Portable Soup and use some of it in the custard. Drink the rest to strengthen you for your day's toil, such as reading the *Notebooks of Henry James*.

SAVORY CUSTARD

1 egg	4 tablespoons cream
yolk of another egg	½ teaspoon salt
2 tablespoons Portable Soup	¼ teaspoon pepper
pinch of nutmeg	

Beat all the ingredients together. Have a small buttered mold ready. Mrs. Appleyard has an ancestral baking powder can with a lid that fits over the edge of the can, which she uses for this purpose: it's about 2½ inches in diameter. Fill the mold two-thirds full of the custard, put it on a rack in a rather deep pan and surround it with boiling water. Cook it in a 350° oven until it is set and a silver knife comes out clean: 10 to 12 minutes. Chill thoroughly.

When serving the soup, unmold the custard, put a slice of toasted French bread in a blue Canton soup plate. Cover the bread with a slice of custard. Slicing it is a slippery business. Be firm but not rash. Mrs. Appleyard has done it. So can you. Pour the steaming hot soup over this. Be sure each plate gets its share of onions. Sprinkle the grated cheese over the onions. Pass some more cheese and some more of the toasted bread with the soup.

And thank Mrs. Gardiner for her invention.

CREAM OF SPRING SOUP
FOR FOUR

3 tablespoons butter	2 cups chicken stock
1 medium onion, sliced	2 cups fresh watercress
3 tablespoons flour	1 package frozen peas, cooked
salt to taste	6 stalks of asparagus, cooked
pinch of nutmeg	½ cup cream
1 cup milk	2 egg yolks

1 tablespoon minced parsley

Melt the butter. Cook the onion in it until onion is translucent, rub in the flour and dry seasonings. Remove pan from heat. Slowly stir in the milk. Add the chicken stock. Cook mixture until it melts and starts to thicken, about 5 minutes. Put a cup of the mixture, the watercress, half the peas, and the asparagus into your blender and run it half a minute. Pour the purée mixture into the top of a large double boiler and blend in the rest of the stock and the vegetables. Add the cream and cook over hot water for at least half an hour.

At serving time, beat the egg yolks in a pint bowl. Add the soup mixture to them a tablespoon at a time, stirring well, until you have about a cup of the egg mixture. Stir this back into the soup and cook it over hot water until it thickens slightly, about 5 minutes. Stir it carefully. Add a little more milk if it seems too thick.

Serve hot, sprinkled with parsley, with Souffléd Montpelier Crackers (*Winter Kitchen*, p. 221) or pour it into pottery jars to be chilled and served cold with hot French bread with garlic butter.

CREAM OF ARTICHOKE AND CRESS SOUP

Make this like the Spring Soup above but substitute 2 cups of cooked Jerusalem artichokes for the peas and asparagus. Just before serving it, stir in 1 tablespoon lemon juice and 1 tablespoon butter. Serve either hot or cold with Thin Scalded Johnny Cake (*Summer Kitchen*, p. 158).

CREAM OF ASPARAGUS SOUP

Make this like the Spring Soup (p. 73) but substitute 3 cups of cooked asparagus for the other vegetables. You may use well-washed spinach leaves in place of the watercress, if the cress is not available, or fresh young lettuce leaves from the garden.

CRÈME SENEGALESE

FOR FOUR

Mrs. Appleyard heard that you could buy this in New York for eight dollars a quart. She immediately planned to make her fortune. Making the soup was not difficult. Distribution was no problem at all: the consumers came and got it. Collections, however, proved slow; in fact Mrs. Appleyard forgot all about them. Perhaps you will have better luck.

2 cups chicken stock	¼ teaspoon nutmeg
pinches of marjoram, thyme, oregano	½ teaspoon curry powder
1 teaspoon dried onion flakes	½ teaspoon paprika
3 tablespoons fat (skimmed from chilled chicken stock)	2 cups heavy cream
	2 tablespoons minced chives
3 tablespoons flour	Garlic Croutons (p. 120)

Heat chicken stock with marjoram, thyme, oregano, and dried onion flakes. Melt chicken fat and make a roux with the flour seasoned with nutmeg, curry powder, and paprika. (Add a little salt if you like.) Strain the chicken stock through a fine sieve. Remove roux from the fire and work in the stock. Cook until it thickens — about 5 minutes. Chill. Set it in the refrigerator. At serving time stir in the heavy Vermont cream. Pour the soup into bright orange bowls. Set them for 5 minutes in the freezer. Serve sprinkled with the chives and garlic croutons.

Mrs. Appleyard has also served this hot. She added a cup of cubed white meat of chicken to the mixture and served hot Parker House rolls with it.

"Not bad," one of her Vermont relatives remarked.

Blushing at this blatant praise, Mrs. Appleyard turned her attention to the rest of the meal.

First Catch Your Trout

"WHAT DO I need to cook my trout?" Mrs. Appleyard's son Hugh asked.

His mother, who was busy inventing a way to make an ashtray from a plaster cast of a catamount's foot, promptly turned her attention to trout. No one can say she has a single-track mind.

"Trout?" she said. "Why you just take some woodsmoke, a waterfall — not very large, it's just for background music — curls of bacon, cornmeal, bacon fat and a frying pan. What more could anyone need?"

Hugh said he knew how to cook trout that way.

"This is for indoors," he said. "Something elegant, sophisticated and gourmetical. We have company. City folks."

"Have you caught them?" his mother asked.

She meant the trout. City folks are no problem to catch. They are, Mrs. Appleyard knows, because she belongs in this class herself, as plentiful as black flies. They are mentioned by Vermonters in much the same tone of weary acceptance. Both are inevitable and keep the inhabitants mentally alert.

Hugh said the trout had been out of the water fifteen minutes and it was time to begin. Mrs. Appleyard had been turning over the pages of a large and ancient French cookbook.

"I think this is what you are looking for," she said. "Write it down as I translate. Here's a pencil."

" 'Remove the fins. Draw by the gills and neatly wipe six very fresh brook trout. Make a spiral incision from head to tail on both sides of each fish. Place in a sautoire, make a maître d'hôtel butter. Use two ounces (good) table butter. One teaspoon finely minced parsley, one half teaspoon chervil and one eighth teaspoon white pepper. Mix well with a fork and spread over fish. Next lay over a dozen fillets of anchovies. Pour over a teaspoon anchovy essence mixed with two ounces white wine. Cover with buttered paper. Set in the oven for thirty minutes, basting often. Meanwhile prepare a Hollandaise sauce as follows.' "

Hugh groaned slightly but wrote bravely on.

" 'Place in a small enameled pan one light teaspoon freshly crushed whole white pepper, four tablespoons good tarragon vinegar, one good teaspoon fresh lemon juice, four leaves well mashed and strained parsley and the same of chervil. Set the pan on the corner of the range and let slowly reduce to one half the quantity, gently mixing once in a while. Then press through a cheesecloth.' "

"The pan?" Hugh asked.

"The contents. Don't be frivolous or the sauce will curdle," his mother said and went on translating. " 'Crack one (fresh) egg yolk. Sharply mix with a whisk for one minute, then carefully drop, drop by drop, one gill melted (good) butter, briskly and continually mixing with a whisk. Season with salt and pepper. Briskly whisk for one minute. Press through a cloth and serve.' "

"What are the fish doing all this time?"

"There is juice in the sautoire. You put a tablespoon of it into the Hollandaise and mix well. Pour the sauce over the trout. Sprinkle with chopped truffles and serve."

"Is that all?" asked Hugh.

"Yes," said his mother, shutting the book firmly, "and it's precisely my idea of how *not* to cook brook trout."

She took pity on her son and handed him a card from her own catalogue. It read:

BROOK TROUT

Clean 6 trout. Dip lightly in milk, then roll in flour seasoned to taste with salt and pepper. Melt 4 tablespoons butter in a large iron frying pan. Just as the butter starts to brown, lay in the fish and cook briskly 5 minutes on each side. Have a hot platter ready. Squeeze lemon juice over the fish. Sprinkle them with finely chopped fresh parsley. Add a tablespoon of butter and one of lemon juice to the juice in the pan. Stir well, heat slightly, pour it over the fish. Wreath them in sprays of parsley. Serve them forth.

"This was how your grandmother taught me to cook trout," Mrs. Appleyard added. "After about thirty years I read a cookbook and found it was trout meunière I'd been making. I felt like the character in Molière, who had been speaking prose all his life and didn't know it."

"Come down to supper in half an hour and have some trout that are pure poetry," Hugh said.

Mrs. Appleyard is now in a position to say that the diagnosis was correct.

The evening was warm, lilacs were coming out. There were yellow butterflies on the lilacs. Redstarts darted in and out of the cedars. Hermit thrushes sang in the sugar place. Of course there were also blackflies but Mrs. Appleyard always serves 6-12 as a sort of cocktail before an outdoor meal in spring so the flies did not have her and her friends for supper as they had doubtless planned.

What else did the Appleyards have for supper? Well, besides the trout there was also Asparagus, Country Style (*Winter Kitchen*, p. 191) and Popovers (*W.K.*, p. 13) made by Mrs. Appleyard while her son and grandsons cooked the fish at the stone fireplace according to directions already given.

Probably most fishermen like trout best cooked over an outdoor fire but sometimes it has been raining while they have been fishing and they have no objection to having their trout broiled on an electric grill.

BROILED TROUT

FOR SIX

6 fair-sized trout, cleaned   lemon juice
butter   parsley

Preheat the broiler. Grease the rack with a paper napkin dipped in a little butter. Lay on the trout, skin side up. Brush with melted butter and sprinkle with lemon juice. Have rack not more than 3 inches from the heat. Broil 5 minutes. Turn fish. Brush with melted butter. Sprinkle with lemon juice. Broil until delicately browned, 4 to 5 minutes longer. Lay fish on a very hot platter. In the broiler pan put ½ cup of water. Set it over a burner and mix all the juice and fat in the pan with the water. Let it boil up. Add a tablespoon of lemon juice and a tablespoon of minced parsley. Pour it over the fish and serve them at once.

Trout don't come to the bait every day. Perch are a little more reckless. One of Mrs. Appleyard's neighbors brings them around all cleaned and skinned and ready for the pan. She dips them first in milk, then in seasoned flour and cooks them in butter, about 4 minutes on each side, serves them with sprays of parsley and sections of lemon.

One of Mrs. Appleyard's favorite ways of cooking fish is to plank it. She is lucky enough to have an oak plank cut with the well-and-tree pattern. These are hard to find now but a cast aluminum one can be used instead with good results. She likes a properly boned shad best but has substituted haddock, halibut, mackerel and swordfish at different times.

PLANKED SHAD

FOR FOUR

Begin by greasing your broiler and broiling the skinside of the fish 3 inches from the flame for 7 minutes. Have ready mashed potato, Glazed Carrots (*Summer Kitchen*, p. 152), cooked peas, sliced green pepper sautéed in butter, tomato slices baked with garlic crumbs. Oil the plank, lay the fish flesh side up on it, build a wall of mashed potato around the edge, mark it with a fork in a crossbar pattern and brush it with melted butter. Put on small heaps of carrots, alternating with the peas and tomatoes and green pepper slices. Brush the fish with melted butter and lemon juice. Broil until the fish is delicately browned, about 4 minutes. Watch it. Tuck in some sprays of parsley. Set the plank on a large platter. The well in the plank will contain some delicious juice which should be spooned over the fish as you serve it.

A thick slice of halibut or swordfish will take longer to broil than shad but the principle is the same. The fish should be almost cooked before you put it on the plank and so should the vegetables. The final moments under the broiler are to be sure that the whole combination looks attractive and is hot when you serve it.

BLACK BASS, BAKED

If someone in the family catches a good-sized black bass perhaps he would like it baked as a change from broiled fish. Cut it along the sides almost to the backbone and put thin strips of beef suet into the cuts. Make the following stuffing:

½ teaspoon onion flakes	salt and pepper to taste
¼ cup cream	½ teaspoon paprika
2 cups bread cubes	½ teaspoon thyme
1 egg, beaten	¼ cup butter, melted

Soak the onion flakes in the cream while you make the bread cubes. Do this by cutting crusts off slices of homemade bread and cutting the bread into very small cubes. Beat the egg, add the cream and onion, sprinkle in seasonings. Add the melted butter. Stir all together and pour the mixture over the bread crumbs. Stuff the fish. Lay it on a rack in a pan. Bake at 425° for 10 minutes and for about half an hour longer at 350°. Baste it with the juice in the pan three times during the cooking.

More energetic cooks than Mrs. Appleyard advise you to sew up baked fish. If she does any sewing it will be crewelwork or perhaps some smocking. She gets the fish out of the pan successfully with two pancake turners, puts it on a hot platter, garnishes it with lemon sections and parsley.

Black bass is a rare visitor. Haddock is easier to come by and can be stuffed and baked in the same way. Mrs. Appleyard sometimes adds a few shrimp to the stuffing or, in the right months, oysters.

Spring Desserts

WHEN the maples begin to flower, the time for keeping forty frozen pies on hand is definitely over. Desserts must be made. This is hard on housekeepers who like to get out and find bloodroot shining white by the road and wild violets in the grass, who like to watch the shadows of great sailing clouds and pick sprays of shadbush and wild plum. Mrs. Appleyard, who has all these tastes, suggests some desserts that do not need to be watched while you are outdoors.

APRICOTS IN JELLY

FOR SIX

Mrs. Appleyard makes this with her own conserved apricots. She always keeps some on hand, made this way.

2 packages dried apricots	2 cups boiling water
1¼ cups sugar	½ teaspoon almond extract

Put the apricots in a folding steamer over the boiling water, which should not touch the fruit. Cover. Steam 12 to 15 minutes, until fruit is tender. Pack the apricots into a sterilized quart jar. Add sugar to water remaining in the saucepan. Cook until syrup just starts to color — 5 to 7 minutes. Cool slightly, add almond extract, pour the syrup over the apricots.

For the Apricots in Jelly use

1½ tablespoons plain gelatin	2 cups cold water
½ cup apricot syrup	juice of 1 lemon
½ cup cold water (extra)	thin lemon peel
2 cans frozen orange juice	1½ cups Conserved Apricots
½ cup blanched almonds, slivered (optional)	

Soak gelatin in the extra ½ cup cold water. Heat the apricot syrup and pour it over the gelatin. Stir until gelatin is dissolved. Dilute frozen orange juice with 2 cups of cold water. Add the lemon juice and thin yellow peel of the lemon cut in small pieces, the apricots and almonds. Add the dissolved gelatin. Rinse out custard cups with cold water. Pour a little of the mixture into each cup. Chill. When it starts to stiffen, spoon apricots and almonds into each cup, pour the rest of the juice over them and set them into the refrigerator. Do this early in the morning. At suppertime set the cups in lukewarm water — 100° — and leave them one minute. Unmold them into dessert glasses. Serve thick cream with them.

Prunes in jelly may be made in much the same way. (Details are in *The Summer Kitchen*, p. 222.)

APRICOT WHIP

FOR FOUR

This may also be made in the morning and served at night.

1 tablespoon gelatin	¾ cup conserved apricots, cut fine
¼ cup cold water	pound cake or sponge cake or lady fingers
½ cup apricot syrup	1 cup thick cream
1 cup milk, scalded	candied cherries and peel

Soak gelatin in cold water. Mix apricot syrup with scalded milk. Pour mixture over the gelatin. Stir well. Add the apricots. Let mixture cool. Line a glass dish with cake sliced thin or with ladyfingers. Whip the cream and fold it into the fruit mixture. Pour about half the mixture into the dish. Cover with ladyfingers or cake, repeat. Save some of the mixture to cover the top layer of cake. Decorate with cherries and candied peel. Serve from the dish.

AVOCADO WITH WATER ICE

Allow half a well-ripened avocado for each person to be served. At serving time fill each half with lemon or orange water ice. Sprinkle it with crystallized ginger.

BARLEY CREAM (S.H.L.)
FOR EIGHT

½ pound barley	2 tablespoons flour
1 gallon water	½ cup sugar
2 quarts milk	2 tablespoons sherry
2 eggs	½ cup cream, whipped

Drop the barley gradually into a gallon of boiling water. Cook until the mixture is thick and the barley is tender like boiled rice. Drain. In the top of a large double boiler put the milk. Scald it. Beat the eggs, beat in the flour. Add a little of the milk and beat it in. Keep adding milk and beating it until you have about a cup of the mixture. Add this to the hot milk. Set the pan over hot water. Stir. Add the hot barley. Add the sugar. Cook until mixture thickens, about half an hour. Taste. Add more sugar if you like. Stir in the sherry or use vanilla or lemon or almond flavoring if you prefer. Chill thoroughly. Serve in glasses with whipped cream on top.

MARLBOROUGH PUDDING
FOR SIX

1 cup Montpelier cracker crumbs	¾ cup sugar, extra
½ cup sugar	juice of 1 lemon
¼ teaspoon nutmeg	grated lemon rind
6 tart apples	6 eggs
½ cup butter	½ cup thick cream

Butter a baking dish thoroughly. Roll cracker crumbs very fine. Mix them with half a cup of sugar and the nutmeg. Coat the inside of the baking dish and the bottom with the crumb mixture.

Pare and core the apples and grate them or chop them fine. Cream the butter and extra sugar together, stir in the lemon juice and rind, add the eggs well beaten and the cream. Stir in the grated apple. Old rules for this suggest adding rosewater (made by pouring brandy over rose petals) extra nutmeg and cinnamon. Add a tablespoon of brandy if you like. Mrs. Appleyard prefers it with only the apple and lemon flavors. Pour the mixture into the baking dish. Bake at 350° for one hour. This is really a custard mixture. It is done when a silver knife blade pressed into the middle comes out clean. Chill and serve cold.

Mrs. Appleyard does not know any season when her friends and relations won't eat chocolate. With this fact in mind and some paper cups and instant potato flakes on hand she invented

CHOCOLATE CREAM
FOR EIGHT

1 cup boiling water	1½ cups sugar
2 teaspoons instant coffee	¾ cup butter
5 squares Baker's chocolate	2 tablespoons rum (optional)
1⅛ cups instant potato flakes	3 egg whites (beaten stiff)
3 egg yolks	1 cup heavy cream

Into the top of a double boiler put half a cup of boiling water. Add instant coffee. Stir well. When it is dissolved add the chocolate and cook over low heat or over hot water until chocolate is melted. Into the blender put the other half cup of boiling water and the potato flakes. Press them down well and run the blender half a minute. Then add egg yolks, sugar, butter, rum, and the melted coffee-chocolate mixture. Blend until the mixture is smooth, about half a minute. Remove from blender. Fold in the beaten egg whites and all but 4 tablespoons of the whipped cream. Pour the mixture into the paper cups. It filled 16 of the size Mrs. Appleyard had. She can't remember the exact size; realizes it isn't much help to say they had butterflies on them. She decorated the tops with the remainder of the whipped cream.

Sign of Spring

WHEN rhubarb pushes up bright pink stalks with big crumpled green fans at the tops, Mrs. Appleyard really believes spring has come. Of course there are also blue-eyed ponds looking up out of green fields. Spring peepers sound like chimes of sleigh bells. Lacquered gold cowslip stars catch and reflect every ray of sunshine. Small scarlet knobs show where apple blossoms will soon make gnarled gray trees into hills of rose and snow. All these things she enjoys peacefully but when she sees rhubarb leaves, she knows the time for lethargy is over. Rhubarb is at its best when the stalks first come. By the time the ivory flower plumes appear, it is tough and stringy. Young "strawberry" rhubarb makes the best pie.

When Mrs. Appleyard's friends, the Dobsons moved to Vermont from Texas, they were prepared for sleet, hail and snow but the perils of spring — mud, slush, dandelion greens and rhubarb — were unknown to them. When Alice made her first rhubarb pie, Simon did his best to eat it but after a while asked gently, "Do we have much of this in the garden?"

Alice at once telephoned to Mrs. Appleyard who came to the rescue. Later she received a candid camera shot of Simon happily eating pie with the caption: "Appleyard Recipe for Rhubarb Pie Saves Vermont Marriage."

To be sure your marriage is happy, make rhubarb pie like this:

RHUBARB PIE

3 cups rhubarb	⅛ teaspoon each of cinnamon and nutmeg
2 tablespoons flour	1 egg well beaten
1½ cups plus 2 tablespoons sugar	2 tablespoons butter cut into 12 bits

Use only "strawberry" rhubarb so young and tender that it needs no peeling. Discard leaves and lower ends and cut the stalks in ½-inch pieces. Sift flour, sugar and spice together. Line a 9-inch pie tin with pastry. Mrs. Appleyard prefers her own but she says some of the packaged brands make very satisfactory crust. Leave a good margin of pastry around the edge of the tin. This is to be turned up over the upper crust and pressed with the back of a fork so no juice will run out. Mrs. Appleyard mistrusts her own skill in this matter so she sets a fruit pie on a square of chef's foil and turns the edges up to make a box, says it's less work than cleaning the oven.

Scatter ¼ cup of the flour, sugar and spice mixture over the lower crust. Add half the rhubarb cubes. Add half the remaining mixture, then the rest of the rhubarb and the rest of the mixture. The rhubarb should be heaped slightly toward the center of the dish: it will sink while baking. Pour the beaten egg over the pie, dot with bits of butter. Put on the upper crust. Gash it well so that steam can escape. Bake at 450° for 15 minutes. Reduce heat to 350° and bake until fruit is tender and the crust brown and puffed — about 40 minutes longer. If it browns too quickly, cover it with a sheet of buttered brown paper. A snapshot of your husband eating it will be gratefully added to Mrs. Appleyard's collection.

Strawberries come while rhubarb is still good. They combine well in

RHUBARB STRAWBERRY CONSERVE

2 cups pink rhubarb cut in ½-inch pieces	thin peel, cut fine, and juice of 2 oranges
3 cups small whole strawberries	4 cups sugar
1 cup diced pineapple (no juice)	¼ teaspoon ginger
1 cup golden seedless raisins	

If you cannot get golden raisins, use extra strawberries or pineapple. Ordinary raisins darken the conserve too much.

Mix fruit, orange juice, sugar, and ginger in a large shallow enamel pan and let them stand several hours. Set the pan into the oven at 375° and cook for one hour. Now cook the conserve on top of the stove till juice thickens on a cold saucer. This amount fills six 6-ounce glasses, plus what was wheedled away from you to spread on corn muffins to see if it was just right.

RHUBARB SAUCE

Never add water to rhubarb. You will only have to cook it out again.

4 cups of strawberry rhubarb cut in ½-inch pieces   3 cups sugar

Mix fruit and sugar in a large shallow enamel pan. The pan should not be more than half full. Set it into a 350° oven and cook till fruit is tender but not mushy — about one hour. Taste for sweetness. Add more sugar if necessary. This sauce can be sealed in sterilized jars. It keeps well in the refrigerator. Mrs. Appleyard sometimes adds some of the juice to her fruit punch.

She always plans to make more next year. She also thinks she might make rhubarb Brown Betty or wine or ice cream but after all she has other duties. She has to listen for hermit thrushes and sit on a hill top where, at sunset, eagles sometimes fly over screaming. This is the year when she thinks she's old enough to take up painting: not the front porch — pictures. Besides there's that miniature kneehole desk she never finished . . .

Relax, rhubarb. Wave your plumes. You are safe now until next spring arrives.

Spring came and went all too fast — as usual. The next time it came around Mrs. Appleyard made

RHUBARB FIZZ
FOR SIX

4 pounds rhubarb   1 cup sugar
6 cups water   1 quart pale dry ginger ale
       ice cubes

Wash pink rhubarb. Do not peel it. Cut it up into small pieces. Cover with water and simmer until tender, about 25 minutes. Strain, discard pulp, add sugar to the liquid. Stir until sugar is dissolved over medium heat. Chill. At serving time combine with ginger ale and pour over ice cubes in tall glasses.

One of Mrs. Appleyard's pleasant childhood memories is of being served glasses of fruit punch by a landscape painter who always slipped a spray of flowers into children's glasses.

She remembers meeting larkspur blossoms and bluebells and forget-me-nots in these congenial surroundings; thinks a small spray of lilac blossoms might go well in rhubarb fizz. It's distinctly optional.

RHUBARB RASPBERRY WINE

8 pounds strawberry rhubarb	1 yeast cake
2 packages frozen raspberries	1 tablespoon gelatine
8 quarts boiling water	1 cup lukewarm water
8 pounds sugar	

Wash rhubarb. Slice in ¼-inch pieces. Add the raspberries. Put the fruit in a large enamelware kettle. Pour boiling water over the fruit. Cover. Let stand three days. Then dissolve yeast and gelatin in lukewarm water. Strain liquid off the fruit into a stoneware crock. Add yeast, gelatin and sugar. Stir until sugar is dissolved. Cover crock and let mixture stand three days longer. Pour into sterilized cider jugs. Put into a cool place — the cellarway has an even temperature — and leave it for three months. Then strain through sterilized cheesecloth, put wine into clean ginger ale bottles, press sterilized caps down firmly. Label and date.

She also experimented with

RHUBARB ICE CREAM
ONE QUART

3 cups rhubarb, cut fine	1 teaspoon lemon juice
2 cups sugar	1 cup heavy cream

Choose young tender stalks of very pink rhubarb. Slice thin. Put into a baking dish in layers with sugar scattered between them. Top layer should be sugar. Add no water. Bake one hour at 350°. (You may cook it in the top of the double boiler if you prefer. It will take a little longer.) Cool slightly. Put half the cooked rhubarb into the blender and run it 10 seconds. Add the rest of the rhubarb and blend until you have a thick purée — about 15 seconds longer. Put into a bowl and chill 20 minutes. Stir in the lemon juice. Whip the cream until it will stand in soft peaks. Fold in the rhubarb purée. Put the whole thing into a plastic container holding one quart. Do not cover. Set it in the freezer or freezing compartment of your refrigerator. After 15 minutes, stir the ice cream well with a rubber scraper to break up the crystals that have formed. Do this twice more the first hour. Cover it. Freeze it 2 hours longer.

RHUBARB STRAWBERRY ICE CREAM
ONE QUART

Make and freeze this like the plain rhubarb ice cream but use 2 cups of rhubarb and 1½ cups of sugar. When you blend the cooked rhubarb add a cup of cut strawberries and ½ cup sugar and blend them with the rhubarb, or use a package of frozen strawberries. This makes a pinker ice cream than you have when rhubarb alone is used.

By raising strawberries, Mrs. Appleyard discovered that it is a lot less work to have one of her good neighbors appear at the door of the summer kitchen and say: "Don't suppose anyone wants any berries today?"

He is wrong as usual and the next step is

STRAWBERRY SHORTCAKE
FOR SIX

1 quart strawberries, crushed	⅛ cup butter
1 cup sugar	milk
2 cups flour	1 cup heavy cream
4 teaspoons baking powder	extra butter
½ teaspoon salt	extra whole berries

Crush the strawberries with the sugar. Set the bowl over hot, not boiling, water. They should be warm but not hot. Heat spoils their delicate flavor. Light oven: 450°. Mix and sift flour, salt, and baking powder three times. Work in butter with your fingertips until the mixture feels like rather coarse meal. Cut milk in with a pastry-blending fork. Toss the dough on a lightly floured board and roll it out gently. Handle it as little as possible. Divide it in halves. Pat half of it into an 8-inch buttered circular pan. Brush the dough lightly with melted butter, put the other half on top. Bake at 450° until shortcake is delicately brown, about 12 minutes. In the meantime whip the cream. When shortcake is baked, split it, using a fork. Butter the cut sides with soft, not melted, butter. Put the bottom half, cut side up, on a round platter. Cover the cake with half the crushed fruit. Lay the second piece, also cut side up, on top of the first half. Cover it with the rest of the cut fruit, spoon on the whipped cream. Decorate with the whole berries. Serve at once.

You can make good shortcake with a biscuit mix, only before wetting the dough you should work in about 2 tablespoons of butter with your fingertips. You may also, of course, make individual shortcakes and serve them with cream so thick it has to be spooned out of a bowl or with whipped cream and an enormous whole berry on top of each shortcake. You may double the rule and bake the dough in a large oblong pan in a form called, by the young Appleyards and their friends, Hayberry Long Cake. The one thing you may not do with Mrs. Appleyard's blessing is to split a dry sponge cake snatched from some handy shelf, add a few half-thawed berries and some synthetic whipped cream and call the result by the honorable name of strawberry shortcake.

Mrs. Appleyard has not finished making that miniature kneehole desk yet but she has at least made

RHUBARB PANDOWDY

She made a batch of Rhubarb Sauce (p. 83), baking it in an iron enamel casserole. When the rhubarb was tender, she moved the heat up to 400°, made some biscuits of the same kind she uses for Apple Pandowdy (p. 172), dropped pieces of the dough on top of the hot sauce, baked it until they were well browned and served Hard Sauce (*Winter Kitchen* p. 130) with it.

She says that if you do not use rhubarb when it is first picked, you can keep it crisp by standing it in a pitcher of cold water and setting the pitcher in a cool place for a day or two.

SUMMER
IN VERMONT

Summer in Vermont

WINTER, Mrs. Appleyard thinks, is Vermont's most beautiful season. Spring is a rainbow of unpredictable excitement. Autumn has moments of unequaled splendor.

Her favorite season is summer.

Yes, she knows it's monotonous with all those green hills and valleys. Landscape painters who come to Vermont complain because they have to use so much green on their palettes. There is certainly plenty of green and Mrs. Appleyard loves every leaf, every blade of grass, every spray of ground pine, of myrtle, of maidenhair fern.

Winter has the distinction of a Dürer etching, of Whistler's portrait of Thomas Carlyle, of white-ruffed, black-coated Dutch burghers by Rembrandt. Spring has the charm of little girls painted by Renoir. Autumn outblazes any painting. So why does Mrs. Appleyard choose summer?

Perhaps because it's familiar: she feels a certain kinship with a Colorado visitor to Vermont.

He said: "I believe if you could scrape all this mess of grass and trees off this state, you'd have some mighty pretty country."

He was homesick for his rocks — so colorful or so gravely monotone, so rough hewn or worked with such exquisite care, so clean; always changing, always the same. There are so many reasons why a thing seems beautiful. Especially, Mrs. Appleyard thinks, because it changes. Human beings, like their cousins the apes, are restless: they want something going on.

Naturally she is as inconsistent as anyone else. She approves of simplicity, of economy of effort and emotion, of peace and restraint. Yet the rooms in which she is happiest seem to have a good many different colors and textures, not to mention a good many objects,

89

in them. Is it really restful to have a hundred and nineteen pieces of Delft pottery in your bedroom?

Oddly enough, it is. They are part of the familiar background; in spite of their fragility, always a link with the past. The little flowered cup from a doll's tea set came to Appleyard Center in 1797. That big blue and white charger has survived more than two hundred years of adventure. So has the highboy on which it stands. It was already an antique when the Appleyards loaded it on an ox sledge and started for Vermont.

Mrs. Appleyard knows it so well that she can walk right past it and never notice it until — fortunately — it occurs to her that, now that mud time is over, there is enough dust to make dusting worthwhile. She likes to dust.

Summer has other pleasures for her. Every year she signs her personal Declaration of Independence. To be free to drive her car without thinking of snow, sleet, slush or mud is to her a sort of Liberty Meringue Pie. She does not have to pursue happiness. It comes to her every time she walks out into her yard and breathes in the Elixir of the Day — apple blossom, lilac, spice-pink, syringa, mown hay, each in its season. Freedom of speech, she enjoys even in winter. After all she has a telephone. Summer brings different freedoms. It is a series of festivities.

Another thing Mrs. Appleyard likes about summer is that she can sit out on the porch and whittle. This may be the summer when she will finish the miniature kneehole desk she started two years ago. Perhaps not, though.

In summer she usually makes something by the Lost Wax process. Her method is different from Benvenuto Cellini's. She invented it herself. A friend, who was doing over an old room, picked up a carved eagle from her table and said, "I wish I had one like this for my mantelpiece."

A look that has often terrified Mrs. Appleyard's children came over her face as she said gently, "I think I could do that."

She began next day by melting up ancestral candle ends. (The Appleyards never threw anything away: it might come in handy.) She put them in an ancient Britannia metal coffeepot, melted them, poured the hot wax into the pan she makes a triple rule of brownies in. She let it cool and when she thought it was just right, she pressed the carved eagle face down into it. The impression of every feather was clear and precise.

Mrs. Appleyard set the wax mold in her freezer. While it hardened she mixed up plaster of Paris and Elmer's Glue All and a certain amount of water. It turned out to be the right amount. She poured the plaster into the wax mold. It stiffened. All was going well — so far. She lighted the oven of her gas stove and set the pan into it. The small hole in the pan passed unobserved by her. Though little more than a pinprick, it was plenty big enough to let wax drip on the gas flame. Soon oily smoke seeped out into the kitchen. The rest of the details are not completely clear. In the resulting explosion, she was blown through the screen door onto the porch, that peaceful place for whittling. Picking herself up and finding, rather to her surprise, that she had the usual number of arms and legs, Mrs. Appleyard returned to her craft shop-inferno (or **Summer Kitchen**.) This time she turned the gas off.

She also managed to remove the brownie pan from the oven. After a while the wax ceased to burn. The eagle, you will be glad to know, was done to a turn. Only a little of its maker's hair was scorched. On the whole the experiment, since the house is still standing, is considered one of her successes.

All the eagles in the neighborhood of Appleyard Center are not plaster ones. Last summer Mrs. Appleyard was invited to supper at a house on a lonely hilltop. Just as she stepped out to see the sunset, purple and gold in the west, a great bank of pink cloud in the east, her host said, "What's screaming?"

Mrs. Appleyard said, "It sounds like eagles," and there they were, right overhead, beating through the air with that fierce thrust of wing that she has never seen except in an eagle's flight. It carried them forward with such speed that, in less time than it has taken to write this, they were only dim shadows in the pink haze. Then, still screaming, they vanished and in a moment were no longer heard.

It has become the fashion lately to speak disparagingly of eagles, to describe them as lazy and incompetent gangsters of the bird world. Yet during those moments of swift flight, Mrs. Appleyard knew why the eagle is called the Bird of Freedom. Any time they come screaming by, they will be welcome.

One reason why Mrs. Appleyard is on the roads so much in summer is that it is so much warmer outdoors than in. After all, her car has a heater. Visitors to other states send postcards home saying: "We sleep under blankets." Visitors to Vermont write: "We sleep under *electric* blankets" — as if that were unusual.

Sometimes it is warm enough, if you have a camel's-hair robe, to lie out on the front porch and read the complete works of Jane Austen. Mrs. Appleyard knows them so well that she often sandwiches in a look at the landscape between sentences. She can look across her covered bridge, the smallest in Vermont, and see the wind making green and silver waves and ripples in the uncut hay. In the pasture Jersey cows are conscientiously nibbling down the grass to green velvet. Hummingbirds are emeralds and rubies among the larkspur spires. Sky roses of cloud drift by. She can hear the brook dashing down the valley.

This, she realizes suddenly, is the day to hunt for The Waterfall. She has waterfalls nearby — one eight feet high, one twelve feet, one more than twenty. Each is all a waterfall should be. They rush, they roar, they breathe coolness from ferny banks, they make rainbows in white foam. Under the biggest one, forty years ago, Mrs. Appleyard once gave herself a shampoo. Not even her hairdresser, whom she hastily visited, knew why her hair looked such an interesting color.

The waterfall she wants to find is on the other side of the county and is known simply as The Waterfall. Simon and Alice Dobson, whose marriage Mrs. Appleyard saved by timely instructions about making rhubarb pie, wrote: "Come and see us. We live near the waterfall."

Mrs. Appleyard visualized a nice standard waterfall, perhaps a little bigger than the one where she received her shampoo combined with mudpack facial. She was not prepared for one as high as Niagara. The waterfall is not so wide as Niagara, in fact it is narrow.

It falls almost straight down for more than half a mile, a high slender spire of foam. Big boulders jut into it here and there, making white fountains as the water hurries down from Turtle Head Lake three thousand feet above. Great spruces and firs lean over it, forming dark arches above the ferns. The stream falls so steadily, so swiftly that in the distance it is a pillar of carved marble. Under the bridge it boils up green and white and goes thundering on down to the river. No doubt it is The Waterfall.

On her way home Mrs. Appleyard went to see the Hands and Feet. They were cut in a dark slab of slate stone by Indians hundreds of years ago. The hands are more exposed to the weather than the feet so they have suffered more from erosion but the feet show clearly. They are placed just as Indian feet should be, exactly parallel with each other, each toe separate and clearly indented in the rock. They are as sharply engraved as old Italian intaglios cut in black onyx. You half expect, if you look farther, to see the dying Gaul or the profile of Marcus Aurelius.

Beavers have raised the level of the pond near the cliff. The slap of their tails is like the crack of a giant whip as they dive among the water lilies. At night, when you see flares of light along the road, they may be the eyes of porcupines or raccoons or baby foxes. A young fawn stands for a moment looking into the headlights of the car, then capers off across the muddy isthmus to the almost-island. Mrs. Appleyard always looks with affection on this dumpy collection of rocks and white birches. Somewhere on it is a gold seal ring of her father's with his crest cut on it. One of his grandsons lost it there about 1935. Gold mining followed on various occasions but the ring was never found. Is that gold the moon is shining on tonight?

Yes — on water lily stamens and on ripples in the moon's path. It is time to go home but it is summer and Mrs. Appleyard can exercise her four freedoms. They are: Freedom to stay at home and have company, Freedom to build (with Roger Willard's assistance), Freedom to go and — her favorite — Freedom to stay out.

Is it any wonder that summer is her favorite season?

A Sound of Summer

THE MOST summery sound, Mrs. Appleyard says, is the music of new peas shelled into an ancient tin pan. The symphony orchestra that first gets this instrument correctly played will really have something. Perhaps, indeed, it will have Mrs. Appleyard, for who else has a tin pan of proper size and resonance, the skill to open pods with such a sharp staccato pop and to run them, *allegro ma non troppo*, into the pan so musically? She plans to wear black velvet with a large white apron and look rather like a benevolent penguin.

In the meantime she will, as usual, be cooking peas within half an hour of the time they are picked. If you drop in some day, you may find her fixing peas and new potatoes in cream.

PEAS AND NEW POTATOES IN CREAM

To serve eight you will need:

half a peck of peas
2 quarts tiny, freshly dug potatoes
½ pound salt pork or beef suet, diced

small onion, finely minced
1 cup thick cream
no seasonings

Shell the peas. Do this outdoors where you can watch the hummingbirds flashing in and out of the larkspur spires. Scrub the potatoes well but do not peel them. Have water boiling in a fire proof casserole big enough to hold both peas and potatoes. Drop potatoes into just enough boiling water to cover them. Cook them about 20 minutes while you are trying out the pork or suet cubes (Mrs. Appleyard prefers suet) until they are a delicate straw color. Skim them out and cook the chopped onion in the fat until straw colored. The potatoes should now be done. Don't cook them too long or they'll be mushy. Most of the water should have cooked away. Add the suet and the onion to the potatoes. In a separate pan have half a cup of water boiling. Add the peas and cook them 3 minutes after the water boils again. Add them with their juice to the casserole. Simmer a few minutes over a low flame so that everything will blend well. Add the cream. When it just begins to bubble around the edges, bring the bowl to the table.

Boston Brown Bread goes well with this dish, which may also be made on a cold winter evening with your own

FROZEN PEAS

Pick only enough peas to make 2 pints when they are shelled. Have everything ready, the right saucepan, freezer set well below zero, your favorite containers — Mrs. Appleyard prefers glass freezer jars. Never blanch or salt vegetables you are freezing. Blanching is a process often recommended but not by Mrs. Appleyard. She says the salt used only makes the vegetables tough and rubbery, and that when you pour off the blanching liquid, you pour vitamins, minerals and flavor right down the sink. Add salt next winter just before serving.

Shell the peas, drop them into half a cup of boiling water. Cover. Cook 4 minutes after water boils again. Put them in the jars with the liquid evenly divided. Set the jars in cold water for 3 minutes. Put on covers, wipe jars dry, freeze. When you cook the peas next winter, you will need to add very little water. They will taste almost as if they just came out of the garden.

Do this as often as you have time, strength and peas hanging among the leaves. You will not regret it.

If you make several plantings of peas, you can still be eating them when corn is tasseled out but the time arrives — alas! — when you come in with the last picking and a sparse one at that. This is a good moment for fresh pea soup.

FRESH PEA SOUP

1 cup shelled peas	¼ teaspoon nutmeg
2 cups jellied chicken stock	⅛ teaspoon curry powder (optional)
1 tablespoon onion, finely minced	salt to taste
2 tablespoons butter	1 cup heavy cream
2 tablespoons flour	2 tablespoons minced parsley
½ teaspoon paprika	2 tablespoons minced chives

Put the peas and the chicken stock into the blender and blend to a velvety green purée. Toss the onion in the butter until the onion is soft and transparent. Do not brown. Work in the flour and seasonings over very low heat. Blend it with the purée. Simmer the mixture five minutes. Stir in the cream. If soup seems too thick, add a little milk. Heat until it just starts to bubble around the edges. Sprinkle with minced parsley and chives. Serve with toasted Montpelier crackers. In hot weather try serving it well chilled.

When peas are over, Vermont pessimists (what other kind of Vermonter is there?) begin to shiver and say grimly, "It won't be long now." Actually snow seldom falls in August but it is twinkling up there at night along with the Aurora Borealis in a rather sinister way. Still, Mrs. Appleyard thinks, there is something to be said for a climate that produces a vegetable so appealing to all five senses as peas — the shining green of the pods, their satiny texture under the fingers, their fragrance while they are cooking, their sweet and soothing flavor and that happy tintinnabulation as they strike the pan.

Any orchestra that needs this percussion instrument — and peas for supper after the concert — will please let Mrs. Appleyard know at once. She has to get that apron ready.

Summer's Come

THE OTHER day Mrs. Appleyard heard someone state that salmon and peas were never served on the Fourth of July by anyone in New England. The speaker, who she afterwards heard was born in Kansas, was so young and strong and opinionated that Mrs. Appleyard did not feel vigorous enough to contradict him. Perhaps he was talking about some different part of New England, one paved with concrete and ornamented with billboards showing those seductive New England mountains and lakes in full raw color and the rolling ocean, complete with gulls; the New England of the bulldozer, the used-car lot, the imitation brick siding, the western ranch house made of plastic stone so like Turkish nougat.

STEAMED SALMON
FOR SIX

In Mrs. Appleyard's New England, salmon and peas and egg sauce are as traditional on Fourth of July as turkey and pumpkin pie at Thanksgiving. She means eastern salmon from Maine or from the Gaspé, the kind that cooks to a delicate shell pink. In Mrs. Appleyard's youth a whole salmon used to be cooked in a fish boiler. She still has the fish boiler but she has not had a whole fish to put in it lately. She buys a 3- or 4-pound chunk of fish, and puts it either on the rack in the fish boiler or in a steamer. Water should not touch the fish. It should be tightly covered and cooked in steam as quickly as possible. Insert a meat (and fish) thermometer and cook salmon until the internal temperature registers 145°. The time of cooking will depend upon the amount of fish you cook and how thick it is cut. For fish cut one inch thick allow 20 minutes; for 2 inches thick, 30 minutes; for 3 inches thick, 35 minutes. Check the thermometer after 15 minutes. While it is cooking make the egg sauce. You can hard-boil the eggs in the water — or court bouillon if you prefer (p. 30) — under the fish. Cook them 15 minutes.

EGG AND CREAM SAUCE

2 tablespoons butter	½ teaspoon paprika
½ teaspoon onion, put through garlic press	¼ teaspoon pepper
2 tablespoons flour	1 cup milk
½ teaspoon salt	1 cup cream
2 hard-boiled eggs	

Melt the butter and put in onion crushed through a garlic press or very finely minced. Cook it until it is straw colored. Lower the heat and rub in flour mixed with seasonings. Cook very slowly for 3 minutes. Do not let it brown. Remove from heat. Stir in half the milk a little at a time, rubbing the mixture smooth with the back of the spoon. When you have a smooth paste, stir in the rest of the milk and the cream. Return to the fire and cook until the sauce just starts to bubble, then put it in the top of a double boiler and leave over hot water until serving time. Add the eggs, chopped, not too fine. If sauce seems too thick, add a little more milk.

Put the fish on a very hot platter and pour the hot sauce over it. Put sprigs of parsley around it or put the peas around it in little heaps.

GREEN PEAS

The peas should be picked and shelled as short a time as possible before they are cooked. Mrs. Appleyard has recently discovered that you can save much of the fresh sweetness of peas by putting them in the refrigerator as soon as they are picked and then shelling them just before they are cooked.

Use only just enough water to cover the bottom of the pan and have it boiling well when you put the shelled peas in. They are full of juice and will make their own liquid to some extent. Stir them during cooking. Taste them. Remove them from the fire as soon as they are soft, probably in about 5 minutes. Ladle them out with a spoon with holes in it and put lumps of butter on them. Cook liquid remaining in the pan so that you have only 2 table-spoons of it. Pour this over the peas. Never add soda to them: they will be a natural shade of green — pea green in fact — and meltingly sweet.

Boiled new potatoes with butter, chopped parsley and a few minced chives go well with the salmon and peas. Giant strawberries with the hulls on, arranged around mounds of powdered sugar follow. No one who is offered oatmeal cookies (*Winter Kitchen*, p. 110) or Baked Fudge Brownies (*Winter Kitchen* p. 117) at this time seems to refuse them.

There's a white wine from California, Almaden, that is fine for drinking the health of the Founding Fathers or to express sympathy for those with whom salmon and peas are not traditional on Fourth of July.

If you had a lot of salmon and only a few guests, it is possible that you have some salmon left over. Mrs. Appleyard suggests some ways of serving it, adds that there is no law that says that you can't cook it on purpose, chill it and serve it as suggested.

SALMON AND RED CAVIAR

1 teaspoon finely chopped onion	1 green pepper
4 ounces red caviar	oak leaf lettuce
1 cup sour cream	red caviar, extra, 4 ounces
2 cups cold salmon in inch cubes	½ teaspoon paprika

Mix onion, 4 ounces of caviar, and cream. Mix in the cubed salmon and put the mixture into a chilled bowl. Set it into the refrigerator. At serving time clean the seeds from a green pepper and slice it in very thin rings. Unmold the salmon. Surround it with oak leaf lettuce and with the pepper rings. Put a spoonful of the extra caviar in each ring. Sprinkle molded salmon with paprika.

SALMON IN A FISH MOLD

A copper fish mold looks handsome on the wall of the kitchen but it ought to be used to mold fish occasionally.

2 pounds steamed Gaspé salmon

4 tablespoons olive oil

2 tablespoons white wine vinegar

2 teaspoons minced chives

2 tablespoons minced parsley

½ teaspoon pepper

1 cup sour cream

1 small cucumber

6 large stuffed olives

garden lettuce

3 ripe tomatoes, medium size

3 hard-boiled eggs, sliced

1 red onion, sliced in rings

Cut the salmon into inch chunks. While it is still warm, pour over it a marinade made of the oil, vinegar, chives, parsley, and pepper. Chill. When thoroughly cold, add the sour cream with ¼ cup of finely sliced and diced cucumber. Oil a fish mold with a pastry brush dipped in oil and wipe it out with a paper towel. Put a large slice of a stuffed olive where the eye of the fish is and put in the mixture. Chill at least one hour. At serving time, unmold fish on a large platter. Surround it with Bibb or oak leaf lettuce. Arrange slices of tomato, paper-thin slices of cucumbers, olives, slices of eggs and onions around it. Sprinkle all the vegetables with French dressing.

Another way of using a fish mold is for Salmon in Tomato Aspic (*Summer Kitchen*, p. 71).

SALMON MOUSSE, HOT

FOR FOUR

1 pound raw Gaspé or Maine salmon

1 tablespoon lemon juice

2 eggs

¾ cup cream

1-inch thin lemon rind

7 grains of cayenne

salt and pepper to taste

Put everything through the blender or a Foley food mill. Rinse out glass custard cups with cold water. Fill them with the mixture, not quite full. Use a rubber scraper to fill them and press the mixture down smoothly. Set them on a rack over hot water and bake at 350° — until the blade of a silver knife comes out clean — about 20 minutes. Do not overcook or custard will separate. Serve with Hollandaise Sauce (*Winter Kitchen*, p. 127) or Fish Sauce, made as follows.

FISH SAUCE

2 tablespoons butter

2 tablespoons flour

1 cup court bouillon

½ cup heavy cream

1 cup light cream

2 egg yolks

2 tablespoons white wine

salt and pepper to taste

The bouillon should be jellied. If it is not, take a cup and a half of it and cook it down to one cup. Melt the butter. When it bubbles, rub in the flour smoothly. Cook gently 3 minutes. It must not brown. Remove from heat. Add bouillon, slowly at first, and then the cream. Return to low heat. Beat the egg yolks. Mix hot sauce into them a tablespoon at a time till you have half a cup of the mixture. Pour mixture back into the sauce. Stir it well until it thickens. Add the wine and seasoning. Do not let it boil.

Sprinkle it with minced chives or parsley. Unmold the fish mousse on separate plates. Add stalks of freshly picked and cooked asparagus. Pour the sauce around the mousse, put butter on the asparagus. Have a lemon section on each plate. Serve corn dodgers (*Summer Kitchen* p. 89).

FLYING FISH

Fish often arrives in Vermont on wings, at least lobster does. The wings, it is only fair to state, are not their own but belong to an invention Mrs. Appleyard has heard about but never tried: it's called an airplane. What won't they think of next? (She herself is busy inventing a way of telephoning with words instead of numbers. Her own call name is of course Vocabeloch.)

Lobsters come over from Maine, fresh though not aggressive; Maine clams, seaweed and all find themselves in clambakes on the shores of many a Vermont lake. Mrs. Appleyard is not sure whether swordfish arrives on wings but anyway it reaches her favorite market in excellent condition and there, wandering amid the artificial flowers, walking in time to the artificial music and hovering in fascinated horror over the synthetic cakes, she sometimes buys a slice of genuine swordfish. It is a great favorite of her daughter Sally's and this is the way Sally likes it cooked.

BROILED SWORDFISH

FOR FOUR

2-pound slice fresh swordfish, 1 inch thick	½ stick butter, softened
juice of one lemon	parsley

The fish was cold from the refrigerator. The time of cooking would be less if it were at room temperature but if you measure the internal temperature with a thermometer and check it carefully, all will be well. Brush one side of the fish generously first with lemon juice, then with soft butter. Insert the thermometer. Preheat the broiler. Mrs. Appleyard uses an electric one but gas is all right too. Cook until the fish is well browned, about 15 minutes. Turn it with two pancake turners. Spread the second side with lemon juice and butter. Cook until the thermometer registers 145°, about 12 minutes longer, and until it is beautifully browned. Serve with the juices from the pan poured over it. Wreathe it with parsley.

Fish cooked quickly to 145° is completely cooked but still holds its natural juices. Fish cooked slowly for a long time and allowed to reach a higher temperature breaks down. Its juices are carried off as a fishy smell and the fish is dry and tasteless. This principle applies to all the kinds of fish Mrs. Appleyard has cooked. If she finds some kind that responds to long slow cooking, she'll let you know.

With the swordfish she served some Broiled Tomatoes (p. 103) and Corn Pudding (*Winter Kitchen*, p. 101). Nothing much for dessert, just Strawberry Shortcake (p. 85) and whipped cream.

When the first small white onions and radishes and carrots come, either in your own garden or in the market, and you have peas is a good time to make

BEEF STEW
FOR SIX

½ cup flour	1 large onion, chopped
½ teaspoon oregano	12 radishes
¼ teaspoon cinnamon	6 new potatoes, cubed
½ teaspoon garlic powder	12 small white onions
½ teaspoon thyme	6 young carrots
½ teaspoon nutmeg	1 cup peas
⅛ teaspoon cloves	beef cracklings
5 pounds chuck	2 tablespoons minced parsley

Have your market man cut up the meat in inch cubes and have him give you the bones and the fat. Cover the bones with cold water and simmer them 2 hours. Do this the day before you make your stew. Pour off the stock and chill it. Cut the fat into small cubes and try it out. Drain the cracklings on brown paper. Save the fat. Remove the fat from the top of the chilled stock and save it also. Next morning begin making your stew by sifting together the flour and seasonings. Put the mixture in a paper bag, put in the cubes of beef and shake the bag until the meat is well coated.

Melt beef fat and cook the chopped onion in it until it starts to brown. Add the floured meat and brown it on all sides, removing it as it browns to an electric skillet or to a pan from which it can be served. Heat the stock, pour it over the browned meat and simmer (200° on the electric skillet) for 2 hours. When it has cooked an hour and a half put a cup of boiling water in a pan big enough to hold the vegetables. Add all but the peas and cook, covered, until they are tender but not mushy, about 35 minutes. The radishes will taste like very delicately flavored young turnips. Let most of the water cook away but if necessary add more boiling water to keep them from scorching. Add the peas (use a package of frozen ones if fresh ones are not available). Cover the pan and cook until peas are tender, 6 to 8 minutes longer. Stir all the vegetables and the water in which they were cooked into the stew and let it simmer a few minutes to blend all the flavors. If the gravy seems too thin, thicken it with a little Pillsbury's Instant Flour, that non-lumping miracle that prevents a lot of nervous breakdowns, Mrs. Appleyard thinks. If you add salt, this is the time to add it, never while the meat is cooking. Your own judgment about the amount will be better than Mrs. Appleyard's. Put the stew in a handsome dish, scatter it with the beef cracklings and the parsley.

Serve piping hot Popovers (*Winter Kitchen*, p. 13) with it.

BRAISED VEAL (C.B.)
FOR FOUR

One of Mrs. Appleyard's neighbors sent over some braised veal one day and was also good enough to send the instructions for making it.

At your market have a pound of veal cut thin, about ¼ inch thick. Lay the slices on a board and pound into them with the edge of a thick china plate all the flour they will take. Pound the meat in a crisscross pattern on both sides. Season the flour as you like with pinches of thyme, oregano, rosemary. Salt to taste may be added later but do not add salt during the pounding process or during cooking.

Into a heavy iron frying pan put a little butter and a few very thin slices of onion. Brown the meat over moderate heat — *keep looking at it* and turning it. When it is well browned add a small amount of water. Cover it and simmer until it is tender, about an hour. You may have to add small amounts of water from time to time. Serve with the gravy poured over it.

New potatoes, cooked with the skins on and sprinkled with parsley and chopped chives, served in a dish with melted butter in it and new peas go well with the veal. So do Blueberry Muffins (*Mrs. Appleyard's Kitchen*, p. 41) and a

VEGETABLE SALAD
FOR SIX

garden lettuce, several kinds	½ cup young beets, cooked, cubed
1 cup baby carrots, raw	1 cup new peas, cooked
¼ cup chopped cucumber	green onion tops, sliced
6 young onions, chopped	4 slices crisp bacon crumbled
1 cup green beans, cooked, cut fine	1 tablespoon chopped nasturtium stems

1 tablespoon chopped chives

Mix the vegetables and marinate them with French Dressing (p. 122). Use just enough dressing to moisten the vegetables slightly. At serving time mix in the crumbled bacon. Arrange the lettuce in a big wooden bowl, add the vegetables. Mask the vegetables with salad dressing made of ⅔ cup sour cream, ⅓ of chili sauce.

For dessert — fresh raspberries, thick cream, brownies. To drink: Pouilly Fuissé, chilled.

Thin slices of pounded veal may also be made into

VEAL BIRDS

FOR FOUR

Trim the pounded veal into pieces 2¼ x 4 inches. Allow 3 slices to each person to be served. You will need also

trimmings of veal, minced	1 cup jellied stock (beef, veal or chicken)
4 tablespoons tried-out beef suet	1 teaspoon garlic powder
1 cup Montpelier cracker crumbs	½ teaspoon freshly ground pepper
1 cup dry bread crumbs, rolled fine	4 tablespoons butter
1 beaten egg	4 ounces Underwood's Deviled Ham
1 teaspoon mixed herbs	½ pound mushrooms
1 tablespoon lemon juice	toast slices
1 tablespoon onion, put through press	½ cup sour cream
1 egg, beaten with 1 tablespoon water	parsley

Mince the trimmings of the veal and add the beef suet, 1 cup of finely rolled bread and cracker crumbs, herbs, lemon juice, onion pulp, beaten egg, and 2 tablespoons of the jellied stock. Spread this mixture on the slices of veal, keeping it toward the center of each slice, and roll meat around it. Fasten with toothpicks. Mix the garlic powder and pepper from the grinder with the remaining cup of finely rolled bread and cracker crumbs. Dip the "birds" in this, then in beaten egg and water, then in crumbs again. Melt the butter in a large iron frying pan or electric skillet and brown the birds in it. When they are golden brown, add stock. It should come up to about half the thickness of the birds. Cover pan and simmer till meat is tender, about one hour. While it is cooking make toast, trim it into long pieces slightly larger than the birds. Spread each with Deviled Ham. Cut mushrooms in parasol-shaped slices and sauté them in the extra butter.

At serving time there should be only a little gravy left in the pan with the birds. Lay the birds on toast slices on a hot platter. Add the sour cream to the gravy. Heat it well but do not let it boil. Garnish the platter with the mushrooms and sprigs of parsley. Pour the hot sauce over the birds.

The mushrooms Mrs. Appleyard used for this dish the last time she made it came out of her own field just beyond her covered bridge. Mushrooms are not quite so reliable as — for instance — beets so Mrs. Appleyard admits that she has been known to use Broiled-in-Butter mushrooms out of a can. At such times she adds a little sherry to the sauce, heats it well then adds the sour cream.

With the veal birds she likes to serve Corn Pudding (p. 105), tossed salad of garden lettuce, new peas or glazed beets cooked like this.

GLAZED BEETS (APPLEYARD)
FOR FOUR

Use young tender beets, none bigger than a ping-pong ball. Wash and scrub them well, cook them in plenty of boiling water until they are tender — 30 to 40 minutes. (Discard any that are not tender.) Slip them out of their skins, slice them and put them in a double boiler over hot water.

2 cups cooked beets	2 tablespoons lemon juice
1 cup beet juice	2 tablespoons Burgundy
1 tablespoon minute tapioca	1 teaspoon sugar
pepper and salt to taste	

(Just to indulge Mrs. Appleyard, *please* do not substitute cornstarch for the tapioca. Just give up the whole idea and cook some frozen French-cut beans or serve the beets with butter only.)

Strain beet juice through a fine sieve. In ¼ cup of it soak the tapioca at least 5 minutes. Cook the beet juice down until you have one cup. Add the lemon juice, wine, sugar, seasonings and the soaked tapioca. Stir this mixture into the hot beet juice. Cook till it starts to thicken. Pour it over the beets. Serve hot.

BEETS WITH BROCCOLI

Cook beets and glaze them or just add butter to them if you prefer, heap them in the middle of a round hot platter and surround them with a ring of cooked broccoli flowers. One advantage of using broccoli from your own garden is that you can cut the flower heads off with very short stems. Wash them, put them in a steamer, and cook them until tender. No peeling of stems is necessary. They should be cooked in 12 to 15 minutes. You don't want them mushy and you do want them to keep their green color so don't overcook them. Arrange them in a ring around the beets. Pass a sauce of lemon juice and melted butter with them — 2 tablespoons of lemon juice to half a stick of butter.

Mrs. Appleyard likes to serve different color combinations of vegetables. She likes the way they look and also the fact that she then has one dish to wash instead of two. Some of her favorite combinations are:

Beets and Broccoli reversed — broccoli in the center beets around the edge. Hollandaise sauce.

Carrots, Glazed (*Summer Kitchen*, p. 152), in the center. *Green beans* around the edge. Garlic crumbs scattered over the beans.

A small cauliflower (that's the only kind her garden ever produces) in a wreath of broccoli. Sprinkle the broccoli with hot lemon butter sauce and the cauliflower with buttered garlic

crumbs. Cauliflower takes longer to cook than broccoli. Have water boiling hard in a pan, put in cauliflower, cover it tightly. It should be cooked in 20 minutes.

Cauliflower surrounded by green beans.

Green Beans surrounded by slices of Broiled Tomatoes Appleyard.

For this choose medium-sized tomatoes that are showing color but are not completely ripe. Slice off and discard the stem ends. Slice tomatoes in halves. Place slices on a buttered fireproof pan. To 12 tomato slices allow 1 cup homemade bread crumbs, 4 tablespoons melted butter, 1 tablespoon garlic powder, pinch of mixed herbs, 1 teaspoon paprika, 2 tablespoons light brown sugar. Spread this mixture on tomatoes. Put the pan in the oven and bake 20 minutes. Then top each slice with a thin slice of Vermont cheese. Run the pan under the broiler until cheese melts.

Green Beans with Mushrooms (*Winter Kitchen*, p. 67) in the center, border of

Broiled Zucchini Slices.

Remember to pick your zucchini when they are not over 8 inches long. Mrs. Appleyard is really giving herself this advice. She has a habit of forgetting them until they would make nice hors d'oeuvres for elephants.

Slice the zucchini ⅜ inch thick. Dip them lightly in flour seasoned with mixed herbs. Put 3 tablespoons of olive oil in an iron frying pan and toss 2 beans of peeled and sliced garlic in it. Put in the zucchini slices. Brown them on both sides. Set pan in the oven for 10 to 15 minutes. Slice a seeded green pepper thin. Cook the slices in a little olive oil for 3 or 4 minutes. Add them to the pan of zucchini. Cover slices with thin slices of Vermont cheese. Run pan under the broiler until cheese melts.

Brussels Sprouts may be used as the center vegetable with either broiled tomato or zucchini slices for a border. Pour hot lemon butter over the sprouts.

Peas may be the center of a three color combination, surrounded first by a ring of *Glazed Carrots* then by one of match stick *Buttered Beets.*

Never throw the water vegetables have been cooked in down the sink. Either cook it down to a tablespoon, add butter and pour it over the vegetable or keep it to add to stock or iced vegetable cocktail. You can always cook the juice down to a cupful so that storing it is no problem. Use it in making V–12 Juice Appleyard which is the juice of whatever is in the garden — vegetables and herbs put through an energetic machine called a juicer. It makes you almost strong enough to cope with the machine.

All Tasseled Out

THE NEWS that corn tassels are green is always welcome at Appleyard Center but days of anxiety follow. Will the tassels turn golden and the ears push out from the stalk at the proper angle before frost comes? Will a masked bandit with stripes on his tail visit the garden some crisp moonlight night? He always knows which ears are ready. Mrs. Appleyard, not so smart as a raccoon, has to test a kernel of golden Bantam by running her thumbnail into it. If milk spurts out, corn appears in some form at every meal until frost.

The principle of cooking corn is the same however you serve it. Pick it just long enough ahead of the meal to husk it and cook it. Guests should wait for corn, never corn for guests. If you must pick it ahead of time, put it unhusked into your refrigerator till just before you cook it. This way you will keep most of its special sweetness.

Start the water to boil in a large kettle. Fill it about a quarter full. Pick the corn, husk it, pack it into the kettle, cover it tightly. It will stop boiling. Watch it and check the time when it steams hard again. This will vary with the size of the kettle and the amount of corn in it. Cook it for 5 minutes. Have ready a hot platter with a damask napkin in it. Heap on the corn, cover it with another napkin. Have plenty of Vermont butter on hand.

Someone is sure to say: "I never ate corn like this!"

No doubt a true statement but he might like it even better cooked outdoors over hot coals. Build a stone fireplace in some convenient pasture near the corn patch. Maple wood makes good coals and fragrant smoke. Mrs. Appleyard picks the corn while the flames are high. Her corn patch has a friendly scarecrow in it. She has lent him her coat for the summer but will get it back when winter comes.

Put a grate over the fire. Lay on the corn, still in the husk. As it cooks, keep turning it with a forked stick and move the ears from one end of the grate to the other, changing the left hand one often to the right hand end. The corn is done when the tassels have scorched away and the husks begin to brown. Test a kernel. The milk should now be thick and creamy. This happens in about 15 minutes. A large jar of melted butter is at hand. Everyone husks his steaming hot ear and dips it into the jar. The view from Mrs. Appleyard's fireplace is rather nice but no one looks at it. The corn is too good.

CORN CHOWDER

FOR SIX

You can make corn chowder either outdoors or in. While someone is picking and husking the corn, cook salt pork or suet cubes slowly until crisp in a big kettle. Remove them. Cook a thinly sliced onion till it is straw colored. Add 3 potatoes, sliced thin and cover them with hot water. Score — slit with a sharp knife — and scrape a cupful of corn from the ears. Add it to the chowder. Add also, if you like, a cup of minced clams. When the potatoes are tender, add a pint of milk, a cup of cream, salt, pepper and paprika. Do not let it boil except just around the edges. Sprinkle in diced pork or suet and plenty of minced parsley. Serve toasted Montpelier crackers with it.

BAKED CORN WITH CRACKLINGS

8 ears of freshly picked Golden Bantam
1 teaspoon sugar
¼ teaspoon pepper
½ teaspoon salt
¼ teaspoon garlic powder

4 tablespoons butter
½ cup light cream
½ cup beef suet cracklings, diced and lightly browned
1 tablespoon minced parsley

Score and scrape uncooked corn from the cob. Add seasonings. Melt 2 tablespoons of butter in a casserole. Put in the corn and the rest of the butter cut in small pieces. Pour cream over it. Bake at 350° to 375° till corn is crusty brown around the edge of the dish, 35 to 40 minutes. Scatter with cracklings and parsley and serve.

Toasted mushroom sandwiches and a tossed salad go well with this.

CORN PUDDING

FOR FOUR

Mrs. Appleyard invented this once when she had six unexpected visitors and not enough corn to go around.

6 tablespoons melted butter
2 teaspoons baking powder
½ teaspoon salt
¾ cup cornmeal

1 cup boiling water
2 cups milk
3 eggs
1½ cups corn cut from the cob

Melt 2 tablespoons of butter in a casserole. Mix baking powder and salt with cornmeal and add the rest of the butter. Scald mixture with boiling water. Beat. Add milk and beaten eggs. Beat well. Stir in the cut corn. Bake 35 to 40 minutes in a 375° oven until it is puffed and brown around the edges. There should be brown crust on the bottom of the dish. The Appleyards like this part best.

Country sausage and ham both go well with this dish. So do Broiled Tomatoes (p. 103) topped with buttered garlic crumbs. This rule serves four generously.

FROZEN CORN

If you grow your own corn, you had better freeze some. Pick it, husk it at once, score and scrape it from the cob. For a pint of cut corn, boil 3 tablespoons of water in a quart pan. Add the corn. Cook covered 3 minutes. Set pan in cool water. Put corn with all the liquid in the pan into a package and freeze. Next winter when you use it, the cooking water is right in the package so none of the flavor is wasted. This is next best to corn straight from the garden.

Use it in chowder, corn pudding, soup or in

CORN AND PEPPERS
FOR SIX

Do this in a chafing dish or a double boiler. Serve it on English muffins, split, buttered and browned under the broiler.

3 tablespoons butter	½ cup cream
1 tablespoon minced onion	½ teaspoon salt
1 green pepper, seeded and shredded	½ teaspoon paprika
1 cup corn	½ teaspoon mustard
2 pimentos, cut fine	1 cup grated Vermont cheddar cheese
1 cup milk	3 egg yolks beaten with a fork

Melt butter. Add onion and green pepper and sauté till onion is straw colored. Add frozen corn and pimentos. Cook till corn is tender — about 3 minutes after ice melts. Add milk and cream. From now on mixture must not boil or it will separate. Add seasonings and cheese. When it melts, add some of the mixture to the beaten egg yolks. Keep adding and stirring with a fork until you have about ¾ of a cup. Now stir it into the chafing dish. Cook one minute and pour the mixture over the toasted muffins which should be ready on hot plates.

With a salad — avocado, orange, grapefruit with paper thin onion rings, perhaps — this is all you need for supper on some frosty evening such as Vermont so generously provides in summer.

Mrs. Appleyard begins to shiver. She really must get her coat off that scarecrow. Luckily she has a suitable hat to go with it. And lots of corn in the freezer. Let winter come!

A one-dish meal, good to serve on a cold evening in corn season, is

CHICKEN AND CORN SOUP
FOR FOUR

4 tablespoons flour	1 large onion, minced
pinch of nutmeg	tops from a bunch of celery
1 teaspoon mixed herbs	½ cup minced parsley
½ teaspoon garlic powder	1 quart fresh tomatoes
3-pound frying chicken, cut up	1 cup white wine
4 tablespoons butter	2 cups corn, cut from the cob
2 tablespoons sherry	

Mix flour and seasonings in a paper bag. Shake the pieces of chicken in it until they are well coated. Melt butter in a large iron frying pan. Add the onion and the chicken pieces and cook over low heat until the chicken is lightly browned, turning often. Add the celery tops, the parsley, the tomatoes, peeled and cut up, the wine and enough hot water to come well up around the chicken. Simmer for about 2 hours, adding more hot water if necessary. Just before you serve it remove chicken from the bones, put it in a fireproof dish and keep it hot. Sprinkle the cut corn into the pan, add the sherry. Cover the pan and cook until corn is done, 10 to 12 minutes. Pour the soup over the chicken and serve with Souffléd Montpelier Crackers. (*Winter Kitchen*, p. 221)

HOT VEGETABLE "SALAD"
FOR FOUR

This is a mixture of garden vegetables. Mrs. Appleyard serves it with Roast Lamb (*Winter Kitchen*, p. 242) with new potatoes roasted around it and mint sauce.

1 red bell pepper, seeded, cut fine	1 cup green beans, cut diagonally
1 green pepper, seeded, cut fine	4 tablespoons butter
4 carrots, cut in matchstick pieces	4 tablespoons light brown sugar
4 stalks celery cut in ½-inch pieces	pinches of cinnamon, nutmeg and allspice
12 scallions, cut in inch pieces	4 tablespoons cream

Toss vegetables in butter. Do this in a fireproof dish in which they can be served. Sprinkle on the sugar and spice. Almost cover with hot water. Cook until carrots are tender but not mushy. Add water if necessary but it should all cook out. At the last minute add the cream. Salt to taste. Stir well and serve very hot with Garlic Croutons (p. 120).

CIDER MINT SAUCE
FOR FOUR

1 cup mint leaves, stripped from the stem	2 tablespoons cider vinegar
¼ cup sugar	¾ cup fizzy apple cider

Put all the ingredients in the blender. Blend until mint is finely cut. Simmer until liquid cooks down to about half a cup. Turn off heat. At serving time reheat, serve very hot.

MINT SAUCE
SHORTCUT

½ cup water	1 glass apple-mint jelly
½ cup cider vinegar	4 tablespoons finely chopped mint

Boil water and vinegar, add jelly. Stir until it melts. Add the mint. It is ready to serve when you are.

POTATOES

Most of us realize that corn and peas freshly picked from our own gardens are better than some weary travelers from Texas or California. Very few of us however know that even carrots and potatoes are especially good if they are cooked as soon as possible after they leave the soil.

Perhaps you are going to eat cold lamb some night. Try smothering a few potatoes to go with it.

SMOTHERED POTATOES
FOR FOUR

4 medium or 8 small potatoes	1 teaspoon onion, put through garlic press
¼ pound butter	salt to taste
	pepper from grinder

Peel the potatoes, slice them thin. Cut the butter into small bits. Mix it and the onion with the potato. Add the seasoning. Wrap in chef's foil. Put package in a heated iron frying pan. Set pan in the oven. Bake at 450° for 10 minutes. Reduce heat to 350° and bake until done, about half an hour longer. Serve in a very hot dish.

POTATOES APPLEYARD
FOR SIX

7 good-sized potatoes	½ teaspoon pepper
¼ pound butter	1 teaspoon paprika
¼ pound mild Vermont cheese	salt to taste
1 large onion, minced	½ cup milk
	½ cup cream

Peel potatoes. Slice them thin. Melt 2 tablespoons of the butter in a large iron frying pan. Put a layer of potatoes into the pan. Dot it with butter, sprinkle it with cheese, crumbled, the minced onion and some of the seasonings. Repeat this until you have 4 layers. Put extra butter on the top layer. Now pour the milk and cream into the pan. The liquid should come up to the top layer but not cover it. It is difficult to give the quantities of milk, cheese, cream, and butter accurately because potatoes vary in size and so do frying pans. When in doubt, be generous.

Bake the potatoes for 10 minutes at 450°. Reduce heat to 350° and bake 35 to 40 minutes longer. They should absorb all the liquid and be brown on top and a glazed brown underneath. Cut them into pie-shaped serving portions on a hot platter. If your pan is thoroughly buttered to begin with, you can get the pieces out rather easily with a spatula and a pancake turner.

Those who "never eat potatoes" eat these.

POTATOES HASHED IN CREAM
FOR SIX

6 baking size potatoes	1 tablespoon finely minced onion
6 tablespoons butter	pepper and salt to taste
1½ cups thin cream	parsley sprigs

Bake the potatoes for ½ hour at 450°. Peel them and chop them rather fine. Melt 2 tablespoons of butter in an iron frying pan. Warm the cream. Add the rest of the butter, onion, and seasonings. Stir in the chopped potatoes. Put the mixture in the pan and cook over very low heat until the cream is all absorbed and you see brown around the edges. This will probably be 20 minutes longer. Loosen the potato mixture around the edges. Treat it like an omelet: make a fairly deep cut across at right angles to the handle of the pan. Turn the top half over the other. Slide the folded "omelet" out, bottom side up on a hot platter. Put parsley around it and serve.

When potatoes are big and corn comes, summer is almost half over. Already occasional bright flags show on the maples, crickets look about for hearths to chirp on, goldfinches are getting thistledown for their nests. It's also cucumber time.

A cucumber is one of the most versatile as well as one of the most controversial of vegetables. It can be served hot or cold, in soup or in salads, green or ripe, fresh or pickled. Any time Vermont gourmets are gathered together the word "cucumber" stimulates such differences of opinion that Mrs. Appleyard sometimes thinks the United Nations ought to step in and pacify these dedicated eaters. One maintains that cucumbers should never be peeled ("the vitamins are in the skin and act as a digestive solvent"). Another says that even a quarter inch of skin is poisonous. She just wants them peeled, cut into chunks and soaked for hours in salt and water. A third chef claims that they should be peeled and all the seeds should be removed. Her friend across the table (they were playing bridge until the battle began) says, "It's the pulp that's poisonous — seeds are the nourishing part. One seed has all the energy in it to start a new cucumber."

Mrs. Appleyard, who occasionally eats a sunflower seed or enough of an apple pip to grow a wild new tree, is embarrassed by this thought.

"What have I been doing with all that energy I've absorbed?" she said guiltily to her daughter Cicely who replied, "Plenty!" and helped herself to another cucumber sandwich.

The cucumbers for the sandwiches were prepared according to Mrs. Appleyard's theory of how to treat this dangerous vegetable.

CUCUMBER SANDWICHES

Peel the cucumbers, young green ones freshly picked, not more than 7 inches long, with the kind of vegetable peeler that takes off a very thin peeling. With a sharp-tined fork, score the cucumber lengthwise all around its surface. This indents each slice around the edges. Now slice the cucumber so thin that you can read *Vermont Life* through it. Cut small rounds of bread just a little bigger than the cucumber slices, using a cooky cutter. If the bread is homemade, slice it very thin. Save crusts and extra corners for bread crumbs.

Mrs. Appleyard sometimes uses firm slices of Arnold bread, splitting each slice into two, horizontally. She learned how to do this from her daughter Sally. It takes very little more skill than that used in flute playing, deep sea diving, or translating Aristotle. Mrs. Appleyard has learned, so can you. Start at the lower right hand corner of a slice of bread and insert the blade of your bread knife (a Christy knife preferably) exactly in the middle of the slice. Keep the knife still but move the slice, always counterclockwise. When you have gone around the whole circumference of the bread in this way, you may move the knife gently through the central portion of the slice.

Now cut out your small rounds of bread, spread them lightly with softened, creamed butter. Add a very thin coating of mayonnaise. Lay the cucumber on one round of bread and cover it with the other. Mrs. Appleyard never finds she has any trouble in disposing of these even to the most extreme cucumber theorists. As she makes them she likes to remember Grandmother Appleyard's theory about cucumbers. It was very different from the others mentioned.

When she felt restless on a warm moonlight night, she used to walk out into the garden in her nightgown, pick a cucumber and eat it as if it were an unpeeled banana. She said it was a guarantee of a good night's sleep. Mrs. Appleyard has not tried this sedative.

She does, however, use cucumbers in other ways. With broiled fish — halibut, mackerel, haddock, flounder — she likes

MARINATED CUCUMBERS

1 small cucumber, peeled, scored, sliced thin	1 tablespoon minced parsley
¼ cup vinegar	1 bean of garlic, peeled
1 bay leaf	½ teaspoon fresh thyme
½ teaspoon salt	¼ teaspoon freshly ground pepper
2 small onions and tops, chopped fine	½ cup olive oil
½ tablespoon minced tarragon	

Mix all together. Pour over the cucumber and let stand in the marinade at least an hour. At serving time remove the bay leaf and the garlic.

CUCUMBER SALAD
FOR SIX

garden lettuce   1 thinly sliced cucumber
1 thinly sliced green pepper

YOGHURT DRESSING

¼ cup yoghurt   ½ cup soured cream
1 tablespoon minced chives   1 tablespoon cider vinegar or lemon juice
1 teaspoon sugar   1 teaspoon dry mustard
salt and pepper to taste

Mix all the ingredients well. Pour them over the sliced cucumber and pepper. Line a shallow bowl with different kinds of lettuce — bronze, curly, oak leaf, Bibb. Add the cucumber mixture and serve.

MOLDED CUCUMBER SALAD
FOR SIX

1 package cream cheese (8 ounces)   1 tablespoon chives, minced
¼ cup sour cream   lettuce
1 cucumber, peeled, seeds removed, chopped   6 large ripe tomato slices
mayonnaise

Moisten the cream cheese with the sour cream. Add the chopped cucumber and the chives. Stir well. Arrange lettuce on a platter. Lay the tomato slices on it. Pack the cream cheese and cucumber mixture into a custard cup and unmold it on a tomato slice. Repeat till all the slices are covered. Pass mayonnaise with the salad.

Cucumber slices go well in

ICED BEET SOUP
FOR FOUR

1 pint jellied beef stock   1 onion, sliced
½ cup red wine   thin cucumber slices
1 pint clear beet juice   sour cream

Heat the beef stock and the wine. Pour them and the beet juice over the onion. Chill. Strain the soup off the onion. Serve in cups with 3 cucumber slices to a cup. Pass sour cream.

SHELL BEANS

Shell beans are ripe when corn is ripe. This, Mrs. Appleyard supposes, is the reason why Indians invented succotash. Shell beans were ready when corn was and it was easier to cook them in one kettle than in two. Vermonters think of succotash as being made with shell beans rather than with limas because it is a rare season when limas ripen before frost comes.

There are rules in *The Summer Kitchen* for Shell Beans and Mushrooms (p. 212), also for succotash and succotash casserole using shell beans. Mrs. Appleyard's favorite variety is French's Horticultural bean. They are ready to shell and cook when the pods are splashed with crimson. The beans themselves have a delicate, almost chestnutlike flavor.

SHELL BEANS WITH TOMATOES

2 cups shell beans	beef cracklings
1 cup thick cream	Broiled Tomatoes

Start beans cooking in boiling water. Cover. Cook until tender, about 25 minutes. Ladle out the beans into the top of a double boiler. Cook liquid down to about 2 tablespoons. Add the cream, bring it just to the boiling point, pour mixture over the beans. Add salt and pepper to taste.

While the beans are cooking try out small cubes of beef suet to a golden brown, drain them on brown paper. At serving time heap the beans in the center of a hot circular dish. Sprinkle the cracklings over them and surround them with Broiled Tomatoes (p. 103).

BAKED SQUASH

Amiable members of the squash family are Acorn, Buttercup, and Butternut. All are good baked, like this. Allow half a medium-sized squash for each person to be served. Split, clean out seeds and strings, lay face down on a well-buttered baking sheet. Bake at 350° until tender, about 40 minutes. Cut small pieces off the curved sides of the squash so they will stand evenly. Turn them over in the pan. Prick upper sides all over with a fork. Dot with butter. Sprinkle each piece with a grating of orange and lemon rind. Mix 2 tablespoons lemon juice, 2 tablespoons orange juice, 2 tablespoons sherry. Pour some of the mixture over cut side of the squash and into the hole in the center. Cook 15 minutes longer. Baste once with liquid in the center.

SQUASH WITH SAUSAGE
FOR FOUR

Squash can also be used for the main dish. Hollow out the center well and bake it as described above. Cook 1 pound sausage meat over medium heat, breaking it up with a fork and tossing until it shows no pink color, about 10 minutes. Drain off the fat. Heap the meat in the centers of the squash. Return squash to the oven and bake 10 minutes longer. With it serve broccoli with lemon butter sauce and broiled tomatoes. For dessert, Fruit Cup (*Summer Kitchen*, p. 79) and Madeleines (*S.K.*, p. 160).

SUMMER SQUASH

This most uninteresting member of the squash family somehow always gets planted in Mrs. Appleyard's garden, though she tries to remember not to buy any seeds. She says that if you want to arrange a big wooden bowl of vegetables for the table on the back porch, summer squash gives a good note of color. If there were absolutely nothing else in the garden to eat she might consider slicing it and cooking it like Zucchini (p. 103). If you serve plenty of Tomato Sauce (p. 153) with it, you really won't know you are eating it. Mrs. Appleyard always hopes that when her friends come to pick things out of her garden they will take some of the summer squash but she has not had much luck so far. Apparently they don't like it either.

CREAMED CELERY
FOR FOUR

Creamed celery is often half-raw celery coated with flour paste. This need not be.

2 tablespoons butter	½ cup hot water
1 tablespoon minced onion	½ cup thick cream
best stalks of 2 heads of celery	pinch of nutmeg
cut in ½-inch pieces	1 tablespoon sherry
2 egg yolks	

Melt the butter, add the onion and the celery and toss them in the butter 5 minutes. Do not let butter brown. Add the water and cook until celery is tender and most of the water has cooked away, 10 to 15 minutes longer. Add cream and nutmeg. Heat. Beat sherry and egg yolks together with a fork. Dilute yolks with a tablespoon of the hot cream, repeat twice, stirring well. Then add mixture to cream in the pan. Cook over low heat until mixture thickens, stirring all the time. Serve from the pan in which it was cooked.

CABBAGE WITH CREAM CHEESE AND CREAM

It is not necessary to let the whole neighborhood know at 10 o'clock that you are planning to have cabbage for lunch.

2 tablespoons butter	¼ cup cream
2 cups shredded white cabbage	½ teaspoon paprika
½ cup boiling water	salt and pepper to taste
3 ounces cream cheese	1 tablespoon minced parsley

Melt the butter. Sauté the cabbage in it, stirring well until the cabbage is "al dente." Add the boiling water. Cover. Cook about 5 minutes longer. Most of the water should cook away. Mix cream cheese and cream. Stir it in, let it melt and come to the boil, but do not boil. Add seasonings and parsley.

Any Hot Evenings?

MRS. APPLEYARD always hopes there will be some hot evenings when her guests will like fruit punch. Last summer there were several such evenings and luckily they coincided with the presence of Company. Also luckily, Mrs. Appleyard regards Company (it is always capitalized in Vermont) with pleasure. She likes to get out her biggest punch bowls and fill them with some cooling mixture such as

CHERRY PUNCH
ABOUT TWO GALLONS

2 cans frozen lime juice	6 lemons
4 cans frozen lemonade	2 pounds sugar
2 quarts water	2 cups dark red cherries, stemmed
3 quarts pale dry ginger ale	and stoned
6 limes	2 quarts orange ice

Dilute the frozen lime juice and lemonade with the water and put it in the refrigerator. Chill the ginger ale. Remove very thin peel from limes and lemons. Squeeze the juice and add it to the frozen lime and lemon juice. Put the thin peel into a bowl and sprinkle sugar over it. Pound sugar and peel with a wooden pestle until the sugar is well mixed with the peel. Add the cherries and crush them gently. Add this to the lime and lemon mixture.

Rinse out the bowl with an extra cup of water and add this to the mixture. Chill thoroughly until serving time. Then put orange ice in the punch bowls. Put some ice cubes around it. Mix the fruit juice and the ginger ale and pour it over the orange ice. Theoretically a gallon of punch serves sixteen people but not on a very hot evening and not if they like it, Mrs. Appleyard says. She thinks about twenty-four people absorbed the two gallons.

FOURTH OF JULY PUNCH
FOR FORTY

First make your Basis. Do this the day before you serve it.

6 lemons	4 tablespoons tea
3 oranges	2 gallons water, cold
3 cups sugar	¼ teaspoon peppermint extract
2 quarts water (boiling)	2 cups strawberries

Slice the lemons and oranges very thin. Pound the sugar into the fruit for about 2 minutes. Bring 2 quarts of water to a bubbling boil. Throw in the tea. Boil exactly one minute, no more no less. Strain at once over the crushed fruit into a large kettle. Cool. Add the 2 gallons of cold water, the peppermint extract and the strawberries, slightly crushed. Stir well. Cover and let stand in a cool place.

At serving time put a gallon of the Basis into a punch bowl. To each gallon add

2 cans frozen orange juice	2 cans frozen lemonade
1 cup pineapple juice	12 ice cubes
1 cup ginger ale	½ cup brandy
1 cup white wine	sprigs of mint

Do not dilute the frozen orange juice and lemonade. They will chill the mixture as they melt.

Mrs. Appleyard usually makes a bowl for the children and for herself without the wine and brandy. Garnish the bowls with sprigs of mint.

RASPBERRY SHRUB

6 quarts red raspberries   6 cups cider vinegar
Sugar

Spread the fruit out in shallow dishes, press it slightly with a wooden pestle but do not crush it. Pour vinegar over it, cover and let stand for a whole day and night. Set a big strainer over a bowl. Line it with cheesecloth. Then pour in the fruit and let the juice drip through. Allow 1 cup of sugar for each quart of juice. Stir well, bring it to the boil, but do not boil. Pour into sterilized preserve jars. Keep it in a cool place. This is good poured over crushed ice with a little water added or it may be added to fruit punch.

SWITCHEL

In order to enjoy switchel you have to be a haymaker, not the kind that makes hay up into cakes like shredded wheat but a man who mows with a scythe. In the woods next to the hayfield, down among the ferns, he has a stoneware jug of switchel. It has been kept in the spring or in a cool well overnight and if there is a spring or a brook near the field he will stand the jug in the water. This is how his wife mixed it.

1 cup brown sugar	1 cup dark molasses
1 tablespoon powdered ginger	1 cup cider vinegar
1 gallon water	

In a big pitcher mix the sugar, ginger, and molasses. Pour the vinegar over mixture and stir all together. Add the cold spring water. Stir well. Pour the switchel into a stone jug. Rinse out the last of the molasses in the pitcher with a little extra vinegar and add it to the switchel. Cool the jug in the spring. When the ringing noise of scythes being sharpened ceases and no figures are seen in the hayfield, it is pretty sure that the mowers are passing the switchel jug from hand to hand and drinking out of it. Mrs. Appleyard is afraid it has to be drunk that way, not out of paper cups. That's one reason why she's never tried it. She would undoubtedly pour it down her neck, right over her pearls. She has heard it rumored — though never having done any hayfield drinking she has no firsthand evidence on this point — that good old New England rum occasionally found its way into the switchel jug. Presumably this happened between the well and the woods. Grandmother Appleyard's cookbook doesn't say a word about rum, just calls switchel "most refreshing."

SALADS

On hot evenings salad with cold cuts — chicken, ham, and tongue — makes a good center for the meal. Mrs. Appleyard mentions a few favorites here and adds some rules for salad dressing.

When she finds a small head of white cabbage in her garden she makes

COLESLAW
FOR SIX

4 hard-boiled eggs	1 teaspoon onion, put through garlic press
4 cups finely chopped cabbage	1 tablespoon Worcestershire sauce
1 tablespoon butter	2 teaspoons dry mustard
2 tablespoons sugar	salt and pepper to taste
1 teaspoon celery seed	1 cup cider vinegar

Chop the whites of the hard-boiled eggs. Add them to the cabbage. Cream the butter, work in the egg yolks with a fork. Add sugar, celery seed, onion, Worcestershire sauce, mustard, salt and pepper. Bring vinegar to a boil. Stir in the mixture and pour it slowly over the chopped cabbage, stirring it well. Chill for at least 2 hours. Serve cold.

Use part purple cabbage and add some finely grated carrot, if you like.

CRABMEAT AND SHRIMP SALAD
FOR FOUR

½ pound fresh crabmeat
½ pound fresh-frozen cooked shrimp
½ cup finely cut celery
½ cup French dressing
3 hard-boiled eggs, stuffed

1 teaspoon crushed onion
½ cup mayonnaise
lettuce
radish roses
tomato slices

Mix the crabmeat, shrimp, and celery and marinate in French dressing for at least ½ hour. Cut hard-boiled eggs in halves. Mash yolks with crushed onion and mayonnaise. Stuff the whites with the mixture. Arrange garden lettuce on a platter. Heap the crabmeat mixture in the center. Mask it with mayonnaise. Arrange stuffed eggs, radish roses, and tomato slices around the platter. Pass extra mayonnaise.

SHELL BEAN SALAD
FOR FOUR

garlic oil marinade
2 cups cooked shell beans
½ cup diced celery
lettuce
⅛ cup Mrs. Appleyard's Chutney (*Summer Kitchen* p. 103)

2 tablespoons minced chives
1 teaspoon chopped mint
2 tablespoons chopped parsley
mayonnaise
chili sauce

Make the marinade of ½ cup oil, 2 beans peeled and slivered garlic, ¼ cup vinegar, 1 teaspoon mustard, 1 teaspoon sugar, salt and pepper to taste, ½ teaspoon paprika. Pour this over the shell beans and celery and let them stand in a cool place at least ½ hour. Arrange lettuce in a shallow wooden bowl. Add the Chutney, chives, mint, and parsley to the beans. Mix well. Put in center of bowl, mask with ½ cup mayonnaise into which you have stirred 2 tablespoons of chili sauce.

Serve with cold ham and Corn Dodgers (*Summer Kitchen*, p. 89).

SARDINE AND ANCHOVY SALAD
FOR FOUR

crisp garden lettuce	sliced radishes
4-ounce can sardines	sliced stuffed olives
4-ounce can anchovies	whole ripe olives, stoned
12 shrimp (fresh-frozen, cooked)	2 hard-boiled eggs

French dressing (made with garlic and red wine vinegar)

Arrange this on individual plates. Use garden lettuce, oak leaf if possible. Lay it on the plates and lay over it a sort of log cabin of sardines and anchovies. In the center of each log cabin put 3 shrimp. Around the edge put the radish slices, the green and the ripe olives. Chop the hard-boiled egg whites and scatter them over the shrimp. Mash the yolks with a fork and sprinkle the powdered yolk over the plates. Pass French Dressing (p. 122) or Anchovy Dressing (p. 75) if you prefer.

This is an appetizer rather than a main-dish salad so it should be followed by something to use your appetite on — Red Flannel Hash, for instance (p. 38) and Thin Scalded Johnny Cake (*Summer Kitchen*, p. 158).

For a more substantial fish salad try

HALIBUT AND FLOUNDER SALAD
FOR FOUR

½ pound flounder fillets	green peas, cooked and cooled
½ pound slice of halibut	radish roses
2 hard-boiled eggs, chopped	egg water lilies
½ cup mustard pickle	celery stalks
garden lettuce	tomato flowers

Boiled Dressing (p. 123)

Steam the fish to internal temperature of 150°. Cool. Flake it and stir into it the chopped eggs and the mustard pickle. Pack it into a bowl rinsed out with cold water and chill in the refrigerator for at least 2 hours. At serving time turn the fish out on a round platter. Cover with boiled dressing or mayonnaise. Surround it with garden lettuce, heaps of green peas, the radish roses, egg water lilies, celery stalks, and tomato flowers.

RADISH ROSES

Wash radishes, cut off stems so radish will stand evenly on plate. Cut off tops. Score the radish in lines to make petal shapes and cut thin petals back about two thirds of the way to the base of the radish. Put in a bowl with ice cubes.

EGG WATER LILIES

Cut hard-boiled eggs in halves. Remove yolks and powder them fine with a fork. Cut white of each half into pointed petal shapes. Cut them only about two thirds of the way to the base of the egg. Cut a small slice from the base so that the egg will rest upright on the plate. Put powdered yolk back into the halves to represent the centers of the lilies.

TOMATO FLOWERS

Cut rather small peeled tomatoes into five sections each. Cut about three fourths of the way to the stem end. Spread out the petals and sprinkle powdered egg yolk in for the center.

Large tomatoes may be cut in the same way and filled with chicken salad or with a mixture of finely cut vegetables. In either case marinate the filling with French dressing and top it with mayonnaise.

MEAT AND VEGETABLE SALAD

FOR FOUR

This may be made of many combinations of meat and vegetables. For instance

1 cup tongue, chicken, ham, cut in neat cubes	mixture of salad greens, lettuce,
½ cup diced celery	romaine, watercress, endive
½ cup shredded white cabbage	2 tablespoons crisp bacon, crumbled
French Dressing (p. 122)	2 tablespoons chopped ripe olives

Marinate the meat, celery, and cabbage with the French Dressing. At serving time toss the mixture in a bowl with the greens, bacon and chopped olives.

With it serve

GARLIC FRENCH BREAD

Mrs. Appleyard has a friend who not only makes long loaves of French bread but generously hands it out to hungry gourmets. Sometimes you can buy real homemade French bread at a food sale and there are a few bakeries that make a long crusty loaf of firm bread. Mrs. Appleyard does not wish to sound too morose on this subject, but she feels it her duty to mention that just baking any old dough in a long loaf does not make French bread any more than Russian caviar can be made from cod roe and shoe polish.

If you really enjoy garlic bread you'll like it better made with real garlic than with garlic powder.

Cream ¼ pound butter. Peel 4 beans of garlic. Put them through the garlic press. Stir the crushed pulp into the butter. Add — if you like — 2 tablespoons minced parsley and 1 tablespoon minced chives. Slice the bread almost through to the undercrust. Make cuts about ¾ of an inch apart. Put the loaf into a 350° oven and leave it long enough to warm it through — 3 or 4 minutes. Remove it from the oven. Put it into a dripping pan and put some of the softened garlic butter between the slices. This is done most easily with a round-ended, flexible kitchen knife.

Set pan back in the oven and leave until you can smell it as you drive into the front yard — about 7 minutes longer.

Mrs. Appleyard occasionally advised you to sprinkle something with

GARLIC CRUMBS OR GARLIC CROUTONS

Use the same mixture as above. Melt it in an iron frying pan. Toss crumbs or croutons in it until they are lightly browned — about 5 minutes. If you feel conservative about garlic, use 1 teaspoon garlic powder to ¼ pound of butter.

Garlic is also good (or so Marco Polo says) to help your ponies breathe easily while crossing the Himalayas. Be sure to take some if you go.

SALMON SALAD PLATTER
FOR SIX

As summer slips by Mrs. Appleyard realizes that it will be almost a year before she can get real salmon again so when she sees salmon from the Gaspé in the market, she buys a two-pound chunk of it.

2 pounds Gaspé salmon	3 hard-boiled eggs, chopped
1 cup cooked young beets, cubed	1 cup sour cream
2 cups green beans, cooked	3 tablespoons chili sauce
2 cups green peas, cooked	¼ cup young onions, chopped fine
garden lettuce	1 tablespoon minced chives
12 perfect tomato slices, big ones	2 tablespoons peeled, seeded
1 cup tiny carrots, raw, sliced	cucumber, chopped fine
2 tablespoons minced parsley	

Steam the salmon to internal temperature of 150°. Cool. Chill at least 2 hours. Chill the cooked vegetables. On your handsomest big platter arrange different kinds, shapes and colors of crisp garden lettuce. Put the chunk of salmon (no bones) in the center of the platter and arrange vegetables around it in little heaps. Peas may be gone from your garden but perhaps you froze some for just such an emergency. S. S. Pierce carries tiny frozen peas which, if cooked in very little water for 5 or 6 minutes bear quite a resemblance to garden Green Peas (*Winter Kitchen*, p. 199). Beans should be cut on a long diagonal and cooked as soon as picked in the smallest possible amount of water.

Stir the chopped hard-boiled eggs into the sour cream. Add the chili sauce, chopped onion, chives and parsley and the chopped cucumber. Mix well. Mask the salmon with it. Sprinkle with minced parsley. Put spoonfuls of it among the heaps of vegetables.

Parker House Rolls (p. 8) go well with this combination.

Summer would not be legal in Vermont without an occasional jellied fruit salad. There are as many varieties as there are makers and they always disappear rapidly at community suppers, Mrs. Appleyard notices. Sometime you might feel in the mood to try

GINGER ALE ORANGE RING

2½ tablespoons gelatin	2 cups orange sections
2 cups ginger ale	3 ounces cream cheese
½ cup sugar	½ cup mayonnaise
2 tablespoons lemon juice	watercress
½ cup frozen lemonade diluted	sprigs of mint
with ½ cup water	¼ cup crystallized ginger, cut
1¼ cups orange juice (frozen)	rather fine

Soak the gelatin in ¼ cup cold water. Heat a little of the ginger ale with sugar. Pour it over the gelatin and stir until gelatin is dissolved. Add the lemon juice, frozen lemonade, orange juice and the rest of the ginger ale. Rinse out a 2-quart ring mold with cold water. Pour in a little of the mixture. Chill. When it hardens distribute fruit sections evenly around the ring and pour in the rest of the juice. Chill overnight. At serving time set the ring into lukewarm water, 98° F. for 30 seconds. Wipe it dry. Turn a large platter over it, center it carefully and reverse it.

Have ready the cream cheese mixed with mayonnaise. Put it in the middle of the mold. Wreathe the mold with watercress and sprigs of mint. Sprinkle crystallized ginger over the dressing.

SALAD DRESSINGS

For fruit salad you might like this dressing.

CURRANT CREAM

2 tablespoons currant jelly	½ cup sour cream
1 tablespoon juice from frozen raspberries	½ cup mayonnaise

Beat jelly and juice together with a wire whisk until you have a smooth mixture. Stir in the cream and the mayonnaise.

MAYONNAISE IN THE BLENDER

1 whole egg	1 tablespoon lemon juice or vinegar
1 teaspoon dry mustard	1 teaspoon sugar
½ teaspoon salt	pepper (optional)
½ teaspoon paprika	1 tablespoon olive oil
grated rind of 1 lemon	1 cup Wesson oil (or ½ Wesson and ½ olive oil)

Break the whole egg into the blender. Add the mustard, salt, paprika, pepper, grated lemon rind, lemon juice (or vinegar), and sugar. Blend for 5 seconds. Add 1 tablespoon olive oil. Blend again for 5 seconds. The mixture should now be fairly thick. Now add the salad oil, ¼ cup at a time, blending for 10 seconds after each addition.

Use lemon juice when you make mayonnaise for fruit salads and vinegar for meat and fish salads. If you like tarragon vinegar you can make it easily for yourself by putting a sprig of tarragon into a bottle and pouring cider vinegar over it. Add a little white wine if you like.

FRENCH DRESSING

Mrs. Appleyard has a bottle with a shaker top in which she keeps a mixture of dry ingredients for her brand of French Dressing. You might like a different combination but it is a convenience to have them all assembled and ready to use. Do not add salt to the bottle because it makes it hard to get seasonings out of the bottle. This is her winter combination: in summer she uses fresh herbs.

This is the basic mixture. Multiply it as many times as you need to fill your bottle.

1 teaspoon dry mustard	⅛ teaspoon curry powder
½ teaspoon pepper from the grinder	½ teaspoon sugar
¼ teaspoon thyme	½ teaspoon paprika
½ teaspoon mixed herbs	¼ teaspoon oregano
1 teaspoon garlic powder	

In mixing your salad allow 2 teaspoons of this mixture to ⅓ cup of olive oil, ⅓ cup Wesson oil, 3 tablespoons of red wine vinegar, 1 tablespoon chopped chives, 1 tablespoon of chopped parsley, ½ teaspoon salt. Put all these ingredients in a screw-top jar. Tighten the cover and shake all well together. Dip a crust of bread into the mixture and taste it. Add more vinegar if you like or more of any of the other ingredients if your palate so dictates.

At serving time pour some of the dressing into a wooden bowl. Lay a wooden fork and spoon over the dressing and put whatever combination of greens or vegetables you like to rest on the fork and spoon. Mrs. Appleyard always chooses some conscientious guest and says, "Please toss the salad *exactly* twenty-seven times. I'd like every leaf coated and no dressing left in the bowl."

Men are very efficient at this task. She checks up on their activities of course and pours in more dressing if necessary. She rather feels she has made this method sound complicated when it's really simple.

If the process sounds troublesome to you, you have her permission to assemble the dry ingredients you like in a large spoon, rub the bowl with peeled and cut garlic, fill the spoon, stirring well with the fork, once with vinegar and three times with oil. Then put in the salad greens and toss the mixture till every leaf is coated. This sounds simpler but really isn't because it has to be done at the last minute. Choose the method that suits your temperament and way of life.

However you make French dressing, you may vary it by adding grated Parmesan cheese or crumbled Roquefort or Danish Blue cheese or chutney or chopped green olives and ripe olives and pimento.

Another variation is *Russian Dressing:* ½ cup French dressing, 2 tablespoons finely minced green pepper, 1 tablespoon minced green onion, 2 tablespoons chili sauce.

Thousand Islands Dressing is ½ cup of French dressing, 1 tablespoon chopped stuffed olives, 1 teaspoon grated onion, 1 tablespoon minced green pepper, 1 hard-boiled egg, chopped, 1 tablespoon minced parsley.

BOILED DRESSING

When Mrs. Appleyard first came to Appleyard Center there were two kinds of salad served. One was lettuce with vinegar and sugar. The other was potato salad with Boiled Dressing. This is how Grandmother Appleyard made it.

2 tablespoons lemon juice (or vinegar)	½ teaspoon paprika
1 teaspoon dry mustard	1 teaspoon salt
½ teaspoon white pepper	4 egg yolks (large eggs)
1 teaspoon sugar	1 cup thick cream

Into a double boiler over hot but not boiling water put the lemon juice and the dry seasonings. Stir until the seasonings are mixed and dissolved. Then, with a Dover egg-beater, beat in the egg yolks. Beat well and then beat in the cream, a third of a cup at a time, beating well after each addition. Keep beating until the mixture coats the beater. Remove from fire. Chill.

Made with lemon juice, this is good with fruit salad. Make it with vinegar if you use it on potato salad. Mrs. Appleyard is sorry to have to say, not for the first time, that outside Vermont so-called "Heavy" cream is what in Vermont is called light cream and "Light" cream is what she would call milk. She refrains from comment on what city folks call milk, just says that if you can't get really thick cream for Boiled Dressing, you had better use sour cream.

In Case of Winter

ONE OF summer's most necessary tasks is to get ready for winter. It is not easy to forget this in Vermont. Even if you yourself are absentminded for five minutes, one of your neighbors will make some gloomy remark. Preserving and freezing naturally follow. You had just better be thankful that you don't also have to dry apples, corn beef, salt fish, can peas, smoke hams and pickle martinoes (whatever they are).

Mrs. Appleyard has tried to find out about martinoes without success. All she knows is what Miss Beecher told her — you must "gather them when you can run a pin head into them and, after wiping them, keep them ten days in weak brine, changing it every other day. Then wipe them and pour over boiling spiced vinegar. In four weeks they will be ready to use."

But how? Mrs. Appleyard wonders.

Miss Beecher also gives good advice about pickling mushrooms.

"Stew them in salted water. When tender pour off the water and pour on hot spiced vinegar. Then cork them tight, if you wish to keep them long. Poison ones will turn black if an onion is stewed with them and then all must be thrown away."

Mrs. Appleyard thinks perhaps it would be better to throw the poison mushrooms away before you pickle them rather than after but perhaps in the Beecher family this would have been considered extravagant. After all, there was always a chance the mushrooms might be all right and they would be nice in case of company.

Another piece of advice Mrs. Appleyard likes is when she is told to "throw cauliflower heads into spiced vinegar" — a satisfying gesture for a cook to make, she thinks. Her own career as a food preserver is less exciting.

FREEZING VEGETABLES

Mrs. Appleyard has told how she freezes peas (p. 93). She uses the same system in freezing other vegetables.

Before she goes to the garden for the vegetable she has everything ready. She turns the freezer to its lowest point, puts out plastic bags, gets out folding containers and a marking pencil, clears work spaces that will be needed, sharpens knives. She never brings in more than enough vegetables for two packages (pints) at a time and never cooks more than enough for one package at a time. This means that the vegetable is really fresh when you freeze it and that you do the freezing only as long as your endurance lasts. It is, of course, something where an extra pair of hands is a great help. Mrs. Appleyard often manages to do it alone but she would much rather have company.

She never blanches vegetables, a process which consists of cooking them in brine and throwing the flavor, vitamins and minerals down the sink and freezing the tasteless residue. She cooks the vegetable in a rather small amount of boiling water about half the time she would cook it if she were going to serve it immediately. Then she cools it by setting the pan in ice water and puts the vegetable and the water in which it was cooked, without seasonings, into a plastic bag. She then puts the bag into a box that folds into a square and labels it.

She says square boxes pack to the best advantage in the freezer. Always put them in for sharp freezing with plenty of space between them so the below zero air can circulate freely around them. Later they can be packed tightly together. Don't try to freeze too many packages at a time or they will not get the intense cold they need. Six is plenty for most freezers. Vegetables frozen in this way — not blanched, cooked enough to sterilize them, packed so they are airtight, frozen at a very low temperature — keep in perfect condition for — how long?

Mrs. Appleyard recently (1964) ate some peas dated 1960 and found only the same slight difference between them and peas from the garden that she would have noticed if she had opened them in a few weeks. The enemy of frozen food is dryness. The air in a freezer is extremely dry and will absorb moisture from the nearest possible source. If your vegetables are not put into airtight containers, plastic bags and properly sealed, they will lose some of their moisture. If a package feels very light in weight and the contents are dry and tasteless, it is because they were not properly packed before freezing.

It is important to have the liquid in which you cooked the vegetables in the package with them. It contains minerals, vitamins, and flavor and helps keep the vegetables from drying out. When they are cooked — say in two years! — you add only just enough water to the pan to keep them from burning and cook them very briefly. Putting a lump of butter on top of them speeds up the cooking time. If you add other seasoning, do so just before you serve them.

GREEN BEANS

Pick enough beans to fill 2 one-pint packages. Cut off tops and tails. Discard any that offer any resistance to the knife. Cut the beans in very thin pieces on a long diagonal or if you prefer, split them in halves lengthwise. Have ½ cup of water boiling hard. Put in the cut beans. Cover the pan. Boil them 10 minutes. Have some ice cubes in a pan of cold water. Set the pan of beans in the cold water for 5 minutes. Put beans and their liquid into a plastic bag, enclose it in a folding cardboard box, label and date it. Freeze at the coldest setting of your freezer.

When you serve these beans — say at Christmas time — put ¼ cup of water in a pan. When it boils add the beans. Cover. After 3 minutes uncover them and add a lump of butter. They should be done in about three minutes more. Watch them. The water will cook away and they might burn.

BROCCOLI

Broccoli may be cooked and frozen in much the same way. Cut off the flower heads. Do not include anything but the most tender stems which should be sliced fine. The young leaves next to the head have a good flavor so add a few of those. Cook and freeze as directed for beans.

SHELL BEANS

Shell the beans. Cook like green beans but increase the time of cooking to 15 minutes. Freeze like green beans.

SUCCOTASH

Mrs. Appleyard has frozen this but has decided that it is better to combine the beans and corn next winter and cook them when you wish to serve succotash. She has never had enough of her own lima beans to freeze any; thinks they are wasted on succotash, would certainly not freeze them as succotash, but freeze corn and beans separately and combine them at serving time if she felt like it.

CAULIFLOWER

Mrs. Appleyard says that her frozen cauliflower, like the professional kind, was always slightly rubbery. She has given up freezing it and buys fresh cauliflower as she needs it.

CARROTS

Use your own as long as they last and then buy them from Texas in plastic bags, Mrs. Appleyard advises. She has occasionally glazed a pint or two of carrots (*Summer Kitchen*, p. 152) and frozen them as she does the beans. At serving time they can be thawed out in the top of a double boiler.

ASPARAGUS

Mrs. Appleyard never has enough of her own to freeze. Once she bought some from a neighbor and froze it "country style." That is, she washed it, scraped it, cut it into inch pieces. She kept the tips separate. Cook the rest of the stalks, she says, in boiling water to cover about 6 minutes. Drop in the tips and cook 4 minutes longer. Freeze like green beans. At serving time cook the asparagus in a small amount of water. Serve it on rounds of buttered toast with Butter-and-Egg sauce (p. 36).

TOMATOES

Tomatoes are better canned than frozen. Mrs. Appleyard sometimes freezes them in the form of Tomato Sauce (p. 153) but is more likely to use them in Tomato Conserve (*Winter Kitchen*, p. 142) or Chutney (*Summer Kitchen*, p. 103).

PUMPKIN

Pumpkins and other members of the squash family keep so well that Mrs. Appleyard does not usually freeze them. However, she has occasionally made Pumpkin Pie Filling (as on p. 138) and has packaged and frozen it and thawed it out in the top of a double boiler when she needed it. She thinks that on the whole it is not much more trouble to make it at the time you make the pies.

MUSHROOMS

One year when mushrooms were very plentiful, she tried freezing them in various ways — raw, partly cooked, as a sandwich spread, as soup, as sauce. The most useful packages proved to be those containing sauce. The raw mushrooms and the partly cooked ones were rather rubbery. The sandwich spread being solidly packed took so long to thaw out that she found it was easier to make it fresh when she needed it. Soup can be made more easily in the blender with fresh mushrooms.

SOUP

She also used to freeze other kinds of soup but that was before her Blender Period. She finds it much quicker to make any kind of soup with the help of the blender than to thaw out the frozen soup. She has a generous amount of freezer space available but she feels it is important to use it for the things she needs most. Materials for soup are a good deal easier to come by than, for instance, fresh corn from the garden.

FREEZING FRUIT

Freezing fruit is a good deal more restful than doing vegetables.

BLUEBERRIES

These are the easiest. Pick them over, discard any bruised berries, leaves, and stems. Use no sugar. Pour the berries into plastic bags, package, label, freeze. They will be good next winter in muffins, pancakes, and pie.

STRAWBERRIES

Mrs. Appleyard thinks they are best hulled, sliced, and sugared. She allows ¾ of a cup of sugar to a pint of sliced fruit. Freezes them like blueberries.

RASPBERRIES

Pick them over carefully. Worms can be frozen right in them or even wasps, but somehow they look rather unattractive next winter. Sprinkle about half a cup of sugar into a pint of raspberries. Freeze like blueberries.

PEACHES

Mrs. Appleyard thinks professionals do a better job on these than she ever did. In spite of being carefully peeled and sprinkled with lemon juice, the peaches somehow always darkened slightly.

MIXED FRUITS

Mrs. Appleyard says that Kraft does a better job on sections of grapefruit and orange than she could ever possibly do. This does not prevent her from doing things to the frozen fruit so that Mr. Kraft would be surprised to meet it and think that he spent all that time arranging those sections so neatly in the jars. See *Summer Kitchen*, p. 142 for one of Mrs. Appleyard's variations on this theme. Sometimes she uses white wine instead of red and combines fresh fruit and whatever is at hand with the frozen mixture.

PRESERVES

When there are windless bright blue days and crystal-cold nights Mrs. Appleyard begins to worry about her tomato crop. She carries bushel baskets of them — green, half ripe, ripe — into the house. She arranges half-ripe ones in rows along window sashes and sills, or spreads them out on tables. The green ones she uses in mustard pickle or in piccalilli or in Lemon Mint Chutney (*Winter Kitchen*, p. 191). With the ripe ones she makes another kind of chutney which also contains Dutchess apples (*Summer Kitchen*, p. 103). She makes a gallon of tomato juice, bottles it and keeps it in the refrigerator. Last year the crop was especially big and she soon ran out of pint jars. She used any size from 2-ounce baby food jars up to 2-pound honey jars. There were so many jars that her shelves were so crowded that she took to giving them away to anyone who dropped in. Thus all problems were solved: the tomatoes were not frozen, there were no empty jars in the house, pretty soon there were almost no full ones either.

One of the favorite kinds she put into circulation was

RED PEPPER RELISH

12 sweet red peppers	2 lemons, sliced thin
6 green peppers	1 quart cider vinegar
3 large onions	2 cups sugar
6 large ripe tomatoes	1½ tablespoons salt

Split the peppers and take out all the seeds. Chop them, not too fine, in a big wooden bowl. Cover them with boiling water. Let them stand 5 minutes. Drain. Add the onions, finely chopped. Peel the tomatoes. Mrs. Appleyard does this by putting them on a wooden-handled fork and holding them over a gas flame until the skin pops. It then peels off easily. It makes the gas burner messy to clean and you may prefer to put them briefly into boiling water. Skim them out and peel them. Chop them with the peppers, not too fine. Add the thin lemon slices cut in 6 pieces with seeds removed. Heat the vinegar. When it is almost boiling add the sugar and salt. Boil 5 minutes. Add the pepper mixture. Boil 10 minutes. Cover. Let stand overnight. In the morning boil until juice jellies on a cold saucer, 10 to 15 minutes longer. Put the relish into sterilized glass jars.

Mrs. Appleyard thinks you very likely have rules for mustard pickle and piccalilli that you like just as well as you would hers. Besides, your church or community club has probably published a book with everybody's great-grandmother's favorite rules. She's just read over her own receipts and think they sound pretty much like everyone else's. It's made her rather hungry and she is going to look in the cellarway for some chutney and eat it with a toasted cheese sandwich.

AUTUMN
IN VERMONT

Autumn in Vermont

THERE is not, Mrs. Appleyard says, one autumn — there are many seasons, each with its own personality and special admirers. In August maple branches that are going to die in another year or two suddenly turn scarlet. They will be bare in September. If a whole tree, the kind Vermonters call a soft maple, changes, in August, from green to crimson and scarlet and the color of wild grapes, it is a sign that it is dying. It may live a few years longer but some spring it will be only a gray skeleton. Mrs. Appleyard is still burning logs from a tree to which this happened.

Her favorite foliage season is not the full burst of blazing color. She likes best the time when beech and birch leaves are still green among the reds and yellows of the maples, when there is still green on the maples themselves and when elms are great arches of gold. This is when she visits her favorite places. Along one road, most of which winds among fir and hemlock and balsam, there is a small hayfield, not more than half an acre in size. It is surrounded on three sides by hardwood trees — half a dozen kinds of maples, poplars, white birches, elms, beeches, ash trees. It is like a room with old tapestries on the walls. Color is more delicate here than out on the hills. Some of the maples turn a delicate pink. Others are like the sunny side of a peach or the color of an American beauty rose. An ash is olive green faintly touched with dull violet, elms pale lemon yellow.

Most people drive so fast that they pass it without knowing it is there but almost everyone slows down around the next curve. Here are the Worcester mountains, deep purple today, all of them — Hunger, Hogback Man, Worcester, Catamountain, Elmore. Vermont is the oldest part of the world and these are some of its oldest mountains. Behind them the sky is cloudless except for the fantastically twisted skeins of white that are vapor trails.

133

Once, on a day rather like this but before jets made vapor trails or rattled Mrs. Apple-yard's blue Canton by breaking the sound barrier, she came through a pass at the end of the range with her daughter Cicely. There was probably plenty of splendid color but she can't remember looking at it. She thinks they may well have been the last people to use this old road. Cicely drove her car, a Model A Ford Phaeton. It was high enough from the ground to clear jagged rocks, narrow enough to pass trees already growing out into the road and it had an uncanny ability to balance on the tops of ruts above seas of mud.

In the eighteenth century coaches used to have outriders who would at times inspect the road ahead and see if it were passable. Cicely, on this occasion, had an outwalker, Mrs. Appleyard. This guide, a sort of Green Mountain Sherpa, went ahead and shouted back warnings of bogs and rocks and trees. Once, after a muddy tussle, she removed a rather large, bad-tempered maple limb from the trail. Sometimes Cicely stopped the car and dismounted while they conferred on the best route. Occasionally they got dead branches and corduroyed a boggy place. A good deal of the time Cicely drove standing up on the seat so she could see over the hood. You can't do this in a Cadillac.

The Ford brought them through safely. The last Mrs. Appleyard knew about that car, its motor was still being used to saw lumber. She rather wishes she had it out on the lawn with petunias planted in it. Still perhaps it is happier keeping active. Like its driver and its outwalker, it always liked to go. This is one of the most damaging statements that Vermonters can make about women, who are supposed to prefer to stay at home and braid rugs.

It was certainly imprudent of men to invent the automobile, Mrs. Appleyard thought, as she mounted her Falcon and set off for Willoughby Lake one fine September morning. What woman who had a car would stay at home on a day like this?

The maples around the lake were at their peak of color that day but what Mrs. Appleyard remembers best is water. Sometimes it was a still green mirror for the flaming hills. Some-times it rippled blue and violet. Where the two mountains, Hore and Pisgah, almost touch each other, it shone black like polished iron. She remembers too the icy spring water running into a granite trough. She had a paper cupful to drink with her egg and lettuce sandwich.

A large car, with a license from a state that Mrs. Appleyard is too polite (or too cowardly) to name, stopped. A senior citizen (female), somewhat younger than Mrs. Appleyard, got out and approached the spring with a cup of repoussé silver in her hand. She filled it four times in rapid succession and drank as fast as she could swallow. Then she directed a young man in a broad-brimmed hat to fill five plastic gallon jugs. While he was doing so, she gave Mrs. Appleyard a synopsis of her life history.

"I've driven three thousand miles to get this water," she announced. "I'm going to keep it on ice and take it home to Algy — that's my husband. He and I were both born about a mile from here. When I used to go with my father to St. J., for trading, we always stopped here on the way home and let the horse rest and gave him a bucket of water and had a drink ourselves and filled a jug for Gramps. It helped his rheumatics. Algy lived next door. His father, Mr. Branston, he was the storekeeper, he was a great one for books.

I don't know how many times he read *David Harum*. And art, he loved art. He bought a whole portfolio of these Remington prints, you know — cowboys, bucking broncos, covered wagons and Algy — that's my husband — he got this idea he wanted to go west and be a cowboy."

Mrs. Branston filled her cup again and after a brief pause continued: "So he, Algy, helped Mr. Branston in the store till we'd saved a little and then we drove west in our Model T. It had a brass band on the radiator."

"Did he get to be a cowboy?" Mrs. Appleyard asked.

"Well, storekeeping was more his line. I guess riding his father's old Morgan mare wasn't much of a preparation. After he was bucked off the third time and broke his leg, he went behind the counter. Been there ever since. We've got a real nice little supermarket, if I do say so. I couldn't get Mr. Branston to come east. Now Rodney here, he's crazy about Vermont. I bought him a nice little farm yesterday. He wants to be a poet and raise Morgan horses. Might as well try it and get it out of his system, his father says. He can always go back in the store and while he's here, he'll have some water that's fit to drink . . . That's right, Rodney, put the jugs in the icebox . . . Well it was nice talking to you. Stop and see us if you get out our way."

Mrs. Appleyard promised she would and the Lincoln Continental rolled on into the wild blue yonder. Well, not just blue that day — vermilion, Tyrian purple, apricot, jade, russet, shocking pink, pumpkin color, cherry bronze — you name it, Willoughby Lake had it. Here, fifty miles north of Appleyard Center, a few yellow leaves were already beginning to fall. They twisted like butterflies through the still air. One lighted on a clump of chicory still, in spite of cold nights, bluer than the sky. There was thistledown in the air too. It felt frosty as Mrs. Appleyard turned south.

If frost comes tonight — she thought — maple leaves will shrivel and turn brown. It will be beech and birch season with brown-edged beech leaves and quivering gold disks on the birches. Hydrangeas will change from ivory to pink, to rusty tan. Zinnias will blacken but calendulas will still be a blaze of orange. The wild sunflowers will still hold up their sprays of sunshine, almost till larch season.

Then the larches would have their days of splendor, running through their color scale — blackish green, gray green, olive green, honey color, tawny gold, to the shade of a well-browned popover. At last the needles would fall, leaving the trees looking like discouraged brush heaps. In the fields around them steeple firs would be black against lion color. The sooner snow came and covered things up, the better Vermont would look.

It was a beautiful day for the Foliage Festival and Mrs. Appleyard received many ill-turned compliments on her management of the landscape. After a while she began to believe she really had arranged to have a great blue heron zoom up past the sunflowers with a goldfish in his beak and that she had drilled her five white-tailed deer to go bucketing across a green field, pausing to snatch red apples from an old tree and vanishing among flaming maples.

Her house was open to visitors, more open than she had expected. She was surprised when a young man appeared wearing the camlet cloak and a tall beaver hat. He found them in a closet on the third floor, he said.

He was speaking the truth — that's where Mrs. Appleyard keeps the cloak. It is an eighteenth century one of dark blue camlet — a sort of mohair — with a double caped collar and a lining of handwoven brown linen. It looks rather like one Washington wore when he crossed the Delaware. Its present wearer helped himself generously to sponge cake, fruitcake, oatmeal cookies and cheese biscuits and complained because he couldn't find a cocked hat to go with the cloak. He seemed to think Mrs. Appleyard's costume department was not well organized.

"I'll have things better arranged next year," she promised.

"What do you mean, better arranged?" asked her daughter Cicely who had rescued the hat and cloak and returned them to their usual places.

"I mean I'll have Roger Willard put a lock on the door to the third floor and I'll turn the key and put it in the secret drawer of my maple desk," said her mother with old-fashioned New England hospitality.

"They could still use ladders," said Cicely gloomily.

"I think on the whole they were rather well-behaved this time," said her mother. "No one climbed on the woodshed roof and rang the bell and I didn't hear anyone playing the bass drum."

"They were too busy catching your goldfish," said Cicely. "One little monster had five in a glass jar. He said to me, 'Your mother charges too much for these fish.' I asked him how much you charged. He said fifty cents apiece."

"I do hope he paid you," Mrs. Appleyard said. "How much is five thousand three hundred goldfish at fifty cents?"

Cicely advised her mother not to regard her pond as a gold mine operated for the benefit of the Appleyard Center Historical Society. No money seemed to be changing hands, she said.

Luckily the bowls with the silver donation for the society were generously filled. After she had put the money in the bank, Mrs. Appleyard was free to drive east and south and west. She decided — as usual — that the most beautiful view of all was within two miles of her own house.

She soaked her mind in enough color to last a year. Most of it is a rainbow blur to her now but a few things stand out. There was a tall spruce tree covered with woodbine to the very top so that its dark branches were completely covered with maroon and crimson leaves and dark blue berries. She remembers a single maple standing alone without a fallen leaf and every leaf like a flame. She still sees roads with rivers of red leaves along the edges. When it rains, she remembers, maple trunks and branches turn black and the leaves are brighter than ever. Then wind comes and there is a Paisley shawl of color under each tree.

She remembers a morning of thick silver mist. Suddenly a red-gold tree like a burning torch flashed out of the mist and seemed to burn it away. Across the valley she saw that the mountains were deep purple with snow on their crests. One late afternoon there were thunder clouds, black as night. Flashes danced among yellow leaves, making trees look like lightning and lightning like trees. She remembers an acre of white birches, the trunks etched with black, each tree with a halo of gold.

It is still officially autumn until December 20th. Mrs. Appleyard woke up weeks before that day and saw a strange light in her room. Even before she pulled up her shades she knew that her catamount-colored field was white now. Yes, there it was, with the blue shadows of white birches crossing it. She could see them through the starry sky of the frost picture — that crystal etching of a mountain glen with tall spruces and rocky cliffs along an icy river. It soon vanished but her own field shone white and blue till evening. Then, after the red sun slipped down, the sky was turquoise green behind clouds of purple and gold. The maples along the distant hilltop were fans of black lace.

In the store, men exchanged stories of old times, of thawing frozen pipes, of skidding fifty feet backwards down icy hills, of being stuck in drifts at 52° below zero.

And they call this autumn! thought Mrs. Appleyard. In my calendar winter's come — but then can spring be far behind?

In Vermont the answer is yes.

Emperor of the Garden

THAT'S WHAT the Chinese used to call pumpkins — when they had Emperors. Whether it is still a Chinese symbol of health and prosperity, Mrs. Appleyard does not know. Pumpkins are certainly a cheering sight in Vermont gardens after the early frost has turned cornstalks from green to straw color. She likes to see the globes of orange-gold among the corn and she always has a few seeds planted, partly for looks, partly for jack o'lanterns at Halloween. The big pumpkins are less good in flavor and texture than the less decorative small ones known as "pie punkins."

Mrs. Appleyard sometimes uses these for cooking but — this is a local scandal — it is known in Appleyard Center that at about Thanksgiving time she has sometimes been seen buying a can of Libby's pumpkin. When questioned about this practice — she was standing right beside a generous heap of pumpkins and squashes — she alleged that unless your own pumpkin is at exactly the right point of ripeness pumpkin is better out of a can and much less trouble.

In any event when you have acquired some stewed and strained pumpkin, no matter how you got it, your work has just begun. Mrs. Appleyard learned from her husband's mother that to make the best pumpkin pie the pumpkin should be slightly dried and caramelized. To do this she butters a big iron frying pan lightly, puts in two cups of stewed pumpkin and cooks it down to a cup and a half. She does it over medium heat on top of the stove, stirring it often and turning over the whole mass occasionally so that it all comes in contact with the pan. This browns the pumpkin slightly and brings out its natural sweetness. Drying it out in the oven does not give the same effect: it simply makes it crusty outside and leaves it still moist inside.

When your pumpkin is golden brown, thick and smooth, it is ready to use in various ways. Of course the first is

PUMPKIN PIE

FOR EIGHT

For two 8-inch pies or one 12-inch one

1½ cups cooked and browned pumpkin	½ teaspoon ginger
2 tablespoons flour	½ teaspoon salt
1 cup sugar	½ teaspoon nutmeg
3 cups rich milk	2 eggs
1 cup cream	2 tablespoons sugar ⎱ extra
1 teaspoon cinnamon	1 tablespoon flour ⎰

Put the pumpkin in a large bowl, sprinkle it with 2 tablespoons flour, stir thoroughly, stir in the sugar. Your pie shells should be ready, built up well around the edge and nicely fluted. Butter the bottom of a saucepan. Scald the milk in it, add cream and seasonings. Pour it over the pumpkin mixture. Stir. Add well-beaten eggs. Stir all together until mixture is well blended. Mix the extra flour and sugar, add a pinch of spice to it. Scatter it over the bottom crust of the pie shells. Fill shells with the mixture about ¾ inches deep. Moisten strips of gauze and put them around the edges of the pies to keep them from browning too fast. Bake 15 minutes at 450°, then reduce heat to 325° and bake about half an hour longer. Pies are done when they just shake in the middle or when a silver knife slipped into the middle comes out clean.

One of Mrs. Appleyard's grandsons is such a favorite of hers that she allows him to put whipped cream on his pie. She prefers hers plain with a piece of Vermont cheese alongside.

Perhaps you have some filling left. This is lucky because when your grandson says, "Is the pie all *gone?*" in a tone of despair, you say, "Yes, but I made you a pudding."

PUMPKIN PUDDING

FOR FOUR

1 cup pie filling	1 tablespoon spices (mixed)
2 eggs, well beaten	1 cup milk
½ cup sugar	

Butter a small casserole. Mix the above ingredients with a wire whisk until they are well blended and pour the mixture into the casserole. Roll 2 Montpelier crackers into fine crumbs and mix them with 2 tablespoons light brown sugar. Scatter over pumpkin mixture. Dot with butter. Bake at 350° for 10 minutes. Reduce heat to 325°. Bake about 20 minutes longer until a silver knife comes out clean from the center and crumbs are golden brown. Serve hot if you like. Mrs. Appleyard prefers it cold, offers whipped cream or thick sour cream with it, eats hers plain.

PUMPKIN SOUP

FOR SIX

At Christmas time Mrs. Appleyard's descendants asked for cranberry pie and mince pie so she preceded the turkey with this soup, which is a beautiful color as well as good to eat.

2 tablespoons butter	2 cups chicken stock
1 slice of onion, minced	2 cups milk
2 tablespoons flour	1 cup pumpkin, browned as for pie
¼ teaspoon nutmeg	1 egg yolk
½ teaspoon paprika	1 cup cream
½ teaspoon garlic powder	2 tablespoons sherry (optional)

Melt the butter. Cook the onion in it until onion is straw colored. Remove pan from heat. Shove onion aside and blend flour, mixed with spices, with the butter. Return to heat. Work in first the chicken stock then the milk. Cook until it bubbles around the edge, about 3 minutes. Stir in the pumpkin. Pour mixture into the top of a double boiler and cook it uncovered for 20 minutes, stirring occasionally. At serving time, beat the egg yolk and cream lightly together in a small bowl. Stir hot soup, a tablespoon at a time, into the mixture, about 4 tablespoons, then stir this mixture into the soup. Cover and let it cook until the soup is well heated. It should be the consistency of thick cream. If you use sherry, add it at the last minute. Serve the soup in bowls with paprika sprinkled over it. It will be the color of a frosted sugar-maple leaf. Toasted Montpelier crackers go well with it.

Mrs. Appleyard has just thought what the Chinese probably call pumpkins now. Since "garden" is a sentimental word, she thinks they are probably known as Commissars of the Tractor Patch. Their cultivators have probably conveniently forgotten that pumpkin seeds were first brought to China by Yankee sea captains, whose ancestors got them from Huron Indians, whose ancestors got them over a path through the wilderness that began in South America.

Small world, commissars!

Serious Business

DEALING with pumpkins in the autumn was a comparatively frivolous occupation. There were grim tasks ahead for the Vermont housewife. Men slaughtered the hogs but women had the responsibility for seeing that they were properly cut up and cured. Lard had to be tried out. Fat pork must be salted. The head must be made into head cheese and the feet jellied. The small intestines must be cleaned and made into sausage cases. This task was often assigned to children, thus giving some of them a lifelong prejudice against sausages. However, sausage meat was chopped up and seasoned just the same. Bacon was cured. So were shoulders and hams.

Mrs. Appleyard will spare you the details of most of these processes. She thinks you will feel sufficiently exhausted and grateful for living in the twentieth century if she just gives Miss Beecher's rule for curing hams. Miss Beecher got the formula from Mr. H. H., as mysterious a figure as the Mr. W. H. about whom Shakespeare aroused so much curiosity. Indeed Mr. H. H. is perhaps the more mysterious of the two. At least there are several possible Mr. W. H.'s and there are not even any guesses about Mr. H. H. The only thing we can feel sure of is that he was energetic, wise in his work and respected for it. After all, that's a good deal to know about anyone.

MR. H. H.'S RECEIPT FOR CURING HAMS

Take an ounce of saltpeter for each ham, and one pint of molasses to every pound of saltpeter.

Then take a quarter of a pound of common salt for every pint of molasses used.

Heat the mixture till it nearly boils and smear the *meat* side with it, keeping the mixture hot and rubbing it in well, especially around the bones and recesses.

Let the hams lie after this from four to seven days, according to the size of the hams.

Then place them in a salt pickle, strong enough to bear an egg, for three weeks. Then soak eight hours in fresh water.

Then hang in the kitchen, or other more convenient place to dry for a fortnight. Then smoke from three to five days, or until well smoked.

Then wrap in strong tar paper, tying it close.

Then tie them tight in bags of coarse unbleached cotton, stuffing in shavings, so that no part of the paper touches the cotton. Hang them near the roof in a garret, and they will never give you any trouble.

You might think that Mr. H. H. had told all but even he has not made the ham-curing quite so difficult as it really was. He is — Mrs. Appleyard thinks — pretty casual about the smoking process. Perhaps he did not wish to take sides in the fine old controversy about whether hams are better smoked with hickory sticks or corncobs. That may be why he does not say what fuel to use. Also he assumes, rather lightheartedly, that you have a place to smoke several hams at once. Some of the big eighteenth and nineteenth century kitchen chimneys did have places for smoking a few hams, but farms where many hams were smoked usually had a smokehouse. It might be in continuous use for weeks at hog-killing time. The fire had to be kept going night and day. Mrs. Appleyard remembers hearing one expert say that he never had a whole night's sleep for three weeks during ham-smoking season. He always visited the smokehouse several times a night to stoke the fire with corncobs so as to keep the smoke just right.

The kind of ham you cured yourself and hung in the garret was supposed to be improved by hanging there for at least a year. Some people thought two years was better and if you could serve a ham smoked by your great-grandfather it enhanced your social position. Mrs. Appleyard thinks a ham a year old is quite edible. Any resemblance between a Vermont cob-smoked ham and the kind that is well soaked — so that you pay for the largest amount of water and the least amount of ham — and that has been painted with a dab of synthetic smoke isn't even coincidental: it's just plain impossible.

(Relax, Mrs. Appleyard, you know perfectly well you can still get a cob-smoked ham from Harrington's in Richmond, Vermont.)

You cooked your own ham from the garret by putting it large end down in a big kettle and simmering it for hours — probably five or six. It was supposed to be done when it turned over in the kettle of its own accord. Most modern hams are tenderized (an unfavorite word of Mrs. Appleyard's). They can be baked in a slow oven without preliminary simmering.

The old-fashioned way to treat them was to let them cool in the water in which they were cooked and then peel off the tough outer skin. Modern hams have usually had this skin removed already.

BAKED HAM

1 ham, 8–10 pounds, cooked and skinned	1 teaspoon dry mustard
1 cup fine homemade bread crumbs	1 cup light brown sugar
whole cloves	

Basting Sauce:

½ cup fizzy cider	½ cup ginger ale
½ cup brown sugar	½ teaspoon ginger

Score the ham across diagonally in two directions to make a diamond pattern. Mix the crumbs, mustard, and sugar and rub them well into the fat. Push in cloves at the points of the diamonds.

Mix the basting sauce. Put the ham into a roasting pan on a rack and pour the sauce around it. Bake at 300°, basting several times, until the surface is glazed and brown, about an hour. Internal temperature should register 165°. If you serve it hot, remove it from the oven at least 15 minutes before you serve it. It will be easier to carve it neatly. Ham, either hot or cold, should be sliced thin.

When the ham was served hot, Mr. Appleyard liked with it — and why not? —

CHAMPAGNE SAUCE

2 tablespoons butter	2 cups hot clear Chicken
2 tablespoons flour	Stock (p. 71)
1 cup champagne	

Melt the butter, let it brown a little. Remove pan from fire, blend in flour. Return to low heat and stir for 2 minutes. Blend in hot stock gradually, stirring constantly. Cook 3 minutes. Let it come to the boil but not boil. If it is not perfectly smooth, strain it through a fine sieve, reheat to boiling point, add the champagne and serve.

Perhaps you think this is a waste of champagne. Mrs. Appleyard is inclined to agree with you. You can substitute white wine or you can add flour and stock to the juices in the pan. Or you can make

RAISIN SAUCE

To ½ cup of the juice in the pan add:

1 cup clear stock (p. 71)	1 cup seedless raisins
3 tablespoons vinegar	1 tablespoon Worcestershire sauce
¼ teaspoon cinnamon	½ teaspoon nutmeg
½ cup orange marmalade	

Mix all together. Cook slowly until the marmalade is melted. Serve in a separate bowl.

With the ham you might serve broccoli with melted butter and lemon juice and Corn Pudding (p. 105) or instead of the pudding you might prefer

RISOTTO
FOR EIGHT

1½ cups rice	½ pound mushroom caps, sliced
1½ cups chicken stock	2 tablespoons minced parsley
2 tablespoons butter	⅛ teaspoon ginger
1 small onion, diced	¼ teaspoon nutmeg
1 cup celery, diced	½ teaspoon paprika

Lightly butter an enamel iron frying pan in which the risotto will be served. Put in the rice and the chicken stock and cook over medium heat, stirring occasionally, until the rice has absorbed almost all the stock — about half an hour. Test the rice. If it is not tender, add another half cup of stock and cook until it is absorbed. While the rice is cooking, melt the butter in an iron frying pan and sauté the onion and celery for 3 minutes. Add the mushroom caps. Cook 5 minutes, stirring occasionally. Vegetables should be slightly *al dente*, not mushy. Add the minced parsley and seasonings. Add the mixture to the rice. Rinse out pan with ¼ cup stock and add it to the rice. Keep the rice warm until serving time. One advantage of a risotto is that it improves by standing. Reheat it at serving time. Be sure it does not stick to the pan.

If you like Mustard Sauce with ham either hot or cold there's a rule for it in *The Winter Kitchen* (p. 100).

Ultimately, Mrs. Appleyard hopes, you will have some thinly sliced delicious cold ham on hand. Good to serve with it is

CONVENT PIE (C.V.S.)

1 cup cream, scalded	1 tablespoon minced parsley
1 cup homemade white bread, diced	1 green pepper, seeded, chopped
4 tablespoons (½ stick) butter	3 eggs, well beaten
½ cup macaroni, freshly cooked	½ teaspoon salt
½ cup Vermont cheese, diced	2 tablespoons fine bread crumbs

Scald the cream and pour it over the diced bread and 3 tablespoons of the butter. Add the macaroni. Add the cheese, parsley, and green pepper. Stir in the beaten eggs and salt. Put in a well-buttered casserole, top with bread crumbs and dot with 1 tablespoon of butter. Bake at 375° till nicely browned — about 40 minutes.

Serve with Mushroom Sauce (p. 149) or Tomato Sauce (p. 153).

Mrs. Appleyard will just mention that it is not necessary to think of ham as an Easter dish just because your market tells you it's "traditional." If you like it, by all means have it but the "tradition" is one started by ham processors about twenty years ago. They probably thought it was only fair to stake out a claim to Easter since the turkey growers had somehow got a firm clutch on both Thanksgiving and Christmas. The traditional meat for Easter is the Paschal (Easter) lamb — spring lamb, in other words. If you had eaten salted, pickled or smoked meat all winter, lamb was a refreshing change.

Turkey is a comparatively new feature of Christmas dinner. In Mrs. Appleyard's youth, turkeys were grown especially for Thanksgiving and were hard to get at any other time. Roast goose was then the traditional Christmas dish. Perhaps it is because people find goose difficult to cook and carve that turkey has taken its place. Advice on how to roast a goose is in *The Winter Kitchen*, (p. 238). It assumes that you are dealing with a young goose. Since geese may live to be twenty or thirty years old, this assumption is not always justified. Mrs. Appleyard is acquainted with an elderly gander who bounces out of an elderberry bush, honking, and tries to bite her tires. The last time he did it, he waited till she had passed so she thought it was a car behind her, swung out and almost went into the brook. She suspects the gander of having heard she likes Goose Liver pâté (*W.K.*, p. 236). She wants it clearly understood that he is safe from her roaster.

A better buy than goose, if you'd like a change from turkey, is a

ROAST SUCKLING PIG

12-pound suckling pig   1 raw potato
Chestnut Stuffing (p. 148)   fizzy cider
                1 raw apple

Stuff the pig with Chestnut Stuffing or — if you prefer — use a regular poultry stuffing (Basic Stuffing, p. 148). Add sausage meat to either if you like. Tie the pig's front legs together, bend and put them backward. Tie the hind legs together, bring them forward. He can now be placed, lying down, on a rack in an open roaster. Open his mouth and keep it open with a raw potato. Insert meat thermometer in the hip. Be sure it does not touch the bone. Brush the pig with oil and rub lightly with flour seasoned with pinches of thyme and sage. Put into cold oven set at 300°. Roast it until thermometer registers 165°. This may take 5 hours or longer. After the thermometer reaches 120°, pour in a little fizzy cider and baste the pig with the juice in the pan. At serving time substitute a red apple for the potato in the pig's mouth. The eye sockets may be filled with whole raw cranberries or with hazel nuts. A wreath of watercress looks nice around his neck. Surround the platter with baked apples, with little heaps of potato balls with parsley and with heaps of Lima Beans with Mushrooms (*Winter Kitchen*, p. 68). Pass gravy made by blending 2 tablespoons of flour with 2 tablespoons of fat in the pan. Pour 2 cups of hot stock over this roux and blend it thoroughly. Season the flour with pinches of rosemary and sage. Simmer 5 minutes. Strain gravy if necessary and reheat it. Coleslaw (p. 116) goes well with roast pig.

For a drink to serve either with Baked Ham or Roast Pig you might like

APPLE CHAMPAGNE

You are supposed to have made and bottled this last year when Vermont McIntosh apples were crisp and tartly sweet. Use only clean, carefully picked fruit: no bruised wind-falls. There is probably a Vermont cider maker near you who will put your own apples through his press for a moderate fee. Arrange a time at his convenience and find out how many apples he will need to make 6 gallons of cider. Take 6 well-washed jugs with you.

You will also need a 5-gallon container, either a clean wooden keg with a bunghole or a glass carboy. Washing and transporting such items is a task suitable for men. Mrs. Appleyard has been a looker-on rather than a partaker of these activities. You must have a cool place to keep the keg or jug. Vermont cellars are usually cold enough but you may find a barn more convenient. By Veterans' Day it should be cold enough to keep your teeth chattering.

You will need also a large funnel, a pound each of white and light brown sugar. Put these through a triple sifter to mix them and get them free from lumps. Now pour cider into the jug or barrel. Do not fill it completely but leave space for the cider to fizz. Add the sugar. Do not put in bung or cork but cover the openings with a folded piece of sterilized cheese-cloth. Replace liquid from time to time from your extra supply of cider, keeping the champagne at the same level all the time. In about eight weeks it should stop working and be ready to bottle. You will need a syphon. Be sure sediment is well settled at the bottom of the jug. Syphon off only clear liquid. Put it into sterilized bottles. Cap them, label, and date.

Mrs. Appleyard thinks this is a good deal of trouble. She prefers real champagne or freshly made cider with just the faintest fizz to it. However, some of the best wives she knows encourage their husbands in such projects. She thinks they are right to do so. It may be the first step in getting their husbands to start cooking. She knows an earnest Vermont champagne maker who has now graduated to higher things and who turns out a very palatable Duckling Braisé à l'Orange. He serves Apple Champagne with it. Mrs. Appleyard speaks well of his 1963 pressing. By the way, ladies, before she passes on his rule for the duckling, Mrs. Appleyard pauses to inform you that the U.S. Government takes a fatherly interest in your wine making. It allows your husband to make 200 gallons and supplies him with forms to fill out. This will help keep him busy and happy at his work.

DUCKLING BRAISÉ À L'ORANGE
AUX BOULES D'OR (J.V.R.C.)

FOR FOUR

First fix a Mirepoix. This is a bed of vegetables, pork fat, herbs, and spices on which the duck rests. It can be varied somewhat according to what you have on hand.

MIREPOIX

2 ounces fat pork, diced	1 carrot, sliced
2 tablespoons diced celery	1 small onion, sliced
a few lettuce leaves	3 or 4 celery tops
2 tablespoons minced parsley	1 tablespoon chopped chives
1 bay leaf	2 cloves
¼ teaspoon cinnamon	¼ teaspoon thyme

Grease an iron enamel covered dish or an electric skillet lightly with pork fat. Spread the Mirepoix over the bottom of the pan. Brush the duckling with a little soft butter and lay it on the Mirepoix. If you use the skillet, set control at 200° or cook over very low heat, covered, for one hour. Then uncover, insert meat thermometer in second joint close to the body. Cook till thermometer registers 165°. This should be in about half an hour longer but time will depend on size and tenderness of the duck. It may take 2 hours altogether.

ORANGE SAUCE

Make this while the duck is cooking. It improves by standing.

1 tablespoon powdered orange rind   2 seedless oranges, sliced thin
½ cup orange juice, frozen   4 tablespoons currant jelly
1 cup Jellied Stock (p. 71)

Combine ingredients and simmer 10 minutes. Keep warm until needed.

BOULES D'OR
FOR FOUR

These are potato balls scooped out from sweet potato and steamed until they are soft but not mushy — about 20 minutes. Mrs. Appleyard is not very adept with potato balls so when she served the duckling, she substituted for the golden balls

SWEET POTATO PANCAKES
FOR FOUR

2 cups hot mashed sweet potato   4 tablespoons cream
2 tablespoons butter   flour with a pinch of nutmeg

Mix potato, butter, and cream. Let the mixture cool enough to handle. Form it into small flat cakes. Dip into flour lightly. Cook slowly in a large iron frying pan greased with butter over low heat. Turn only once. The first side should brown in 15 minutes, the second side in about 10 minutes. These can be done ahead of time and kept warm until needed. They also go well with ham or roast pork.

At serving time have a hot stainless steel platter ready. Set the duckling on it. Arrange the cooked orange slices around it and surround them with a ring of tiny green peas. Arrange the Boules d'Or or Pancakes neatly among the peas. Garnish the platter with watercress.

Strain the juice from the roaster into the pan containing the orange sauce. Boil it for a minute or two, skimming fat from the top. Serve it in a heated gravy boat.

Now all you need is an expert carver like J.V.R.C. Good appetite to you.

Stuffing Makes the Bird

ONE interesting thing about turkeys is how they ever got the name. They originated not in Turkey but in America. The first ones were taken to Europe from Mexico by the conquistadors not long after 1500. They might have taken a kind with blue heads. This is a very confusing idea to Mrs. Appleyard. Suppose in addition to broad-breasted or narrow you had to choose between red- or blue-headed! Of course she would choose red. That's the color her Pilgrim ancestors aimed at. If they shot more than they needed, they sold any extra ones for two cents a pound, thus founding the family fortune — if any.

It would be convenient to buy a Thanksgiving turkey for forty cents but Mrs. Appleyard realizes that she would have to roast it on a spit in front of the fire, being smoked herself while basting the bird. She turns happily to choosing between a gas oven and an electric roaster. In either she can cook the turkey peacefully by the low-temperature method and check its progress by a meat thermometer.

With this method, get your 20-pound turkey into the oven with the thermometer deep in the second joint, not touching the bone, by noon Wednesday. Brush the bird lightly with oil or melted butter. Have the oven at 200° F. By noon on Thanksgiving Day the thermometer should register 185° F. If it reaches that point earlier, the turkey can always be removed from the oven and be reheated for a few minutes just before serving time.

The juices in the pan will make wonderful gravy. On Wednesday, simmer the giblets and neck for 2 or 3 hours. Add the liver the last 20 minutes. Remove gristle from giblets. In a wooden bowl chop giblets, liver, and meat from the neck. When you make the gravy Thursday, use

4 tablespoons fat from the roaster	pepper, paprika, salt to taste
1 onion finely minced	pinch of nutmeg
giblets	2 cups stock from giblets
4 tablespoons flour	2 cups rich milk
2 tablespoons minced parsley	

Put fat in a big iron frying pan. Sauté onion and giblets over low heat till onion begins to brown. If mixture has absorbed all the fat, add another tablespoonful. Blend in flour and seasonings. Stir in the stock. Add the milk slowly. Keep stirring. The gravy can now rest — although you can't. At serving time reheat it. Pour into a warmed bowl. Sprinkle it with parsley.

BASIC STUFFING

Mrs. Appleyard wonders what Elder Brewster's wife stuffed turkey with. Not with bread made out of plaster of Paris and city air, she's quite sure. The poor ignorant Pilgrims did not know about retarding spoilage either. It's certainly a wonder they survived. Mrs. Appleyard recommends homemade bread, sliced thin, dried slowly in the oven and crumbled, not too fine. She allows about half a cup of bread crumbs for each pound of turkey.

For a 20-pound turkey

10 cups bread crumbs	salt to taste
3 onions, finely minced	2 cups Montpelier cracker crumbs, not too fine
½ pound butter, melted	3 eggs, lightly beaten
1 cup milk (part cream)	4 tablespoons Bell's seasoning
1 teaspoon pepper from the grinder	

This stuffing is rather on the dry side. If you like it moist, add more milk and another egg but remember that stuffing tends to moisten and swell during cooking because it absorbs juices from the meat. Leave some space for it to expand. Extra stuffing may be moistened with gravy, baked in a casserole, and served with cold turkey another day.

CHESTNUT STUFFING

This is Mrs. Appleyard's favorite, especially since she found out that you can buy chestnuts in cans all shelled and peeled. For a 20-pound turkey use Basic Stuffing. Reduce seasoning by half so that flavor of chestnuts will be detectable and delectable. Use 48 chestnuts. Break them into 4 or 5 pieces. If chestnuts are not available, try a pound of cashew nuts, left whole, or a pound of filberts and hazel nuts mixed.

OYSTER STUFFING

Mrs. Appleyard has a friend, some of whose family like plain stuffing, some of whom feel that Thanksgiving is illegal without oyster stuffing. She compromises by putting oyster stuffing in the breast and plain stuffing in the other end.

¼ cup juice from oysters	1 cup oysters, cut in small pieces
½ cup butter	4 cups homemade bread crumbs
1 onion minced	2 Montpelier crackers, rolled fine
½ cup celery, cut fine	pinch of thyme, pinch of nutmeg
1 egg beaten	

In a pan big enough to hold the mixture, heat oyster liquor. Add butter and as it melts, the onion, celery, oysters. Cook until butter froths. Remove from heat. With a pastry-blending fork, stir in bread and cracker crumbs, seasonings, beaten egg. If you like it very moist, add a little thick cream.

CORN STUFFING

For half the bread crumbs in the basic receipt, substitute cornmeal muffins, dried and crumbled.

MUSHROOM STUFFING

For the milk in the basic receipt, substitute Mushroom Sauce.

½ pound mushrooms, stems and all, cut fine
2 tablespoons butter

1 tablespoon flour
¼ teaspoon nutmeg
1 cup milk (part cream)

Sauté mushrooms in butter. Blend in flour and nutmeg. Blend in milk. Cook till it thickens. Add to stuffing.

But after all, you may ask, is the aim of the hostess to stuff the turkey or the guests? What else do you serve?

"Oh nothing much," says Mrs. Appleyard. "Just cream of squash soup with cheese biscuits, hors d'oeuvres too numerous to mention, whole cranberry sauce, candied sweet potatoes, mashed potato, Brussels sprouts in a ring of latticed beets, baby onions in cream and three kinds of pie — or would you prefer Baked Alaska? And don't forget to heat up the gravy. "Once," she recalls, "I served this menu to two young couples I hoped would get engaged. They did, only not the ones I'd planned for each other. Judging by their Christmas cards, I think the wives are now busy fixing turkey for eleven healthy, handsome children. Happy stuffing to you all."

The Melting Pot

WHEN Vermonters start braising ducklings, they have come a long way from the honest Anglo-Saxon attitude toward food that was the basis of Vermont cooking for its first hundred years. It changed during the early part of the twentieth century but it is the last thirty years that have made the most difference. The automobile and the airplane have affected food all through the United States. Maine lobsters turn up in California ready to bite the hand that boils them. Large red apples tasting like papier mâché arrive in Vermont. In exchange for turkey, maple syrup and butter, Vermont accepts margarine, TV dinners, pies thickened with cornstarch. Vermonters send Vermont cheese (postage paid) all over the country and make their own cheeseburgers with what Mrs. Appleyard describes as cheese-wax. They used to send out merino wool and potash and get back rum and molasses and window glass and guns as tall as a man and red velvet for a lady's basque.

Is it possible that Vermonters then were smarter than they are now?

Luckily there is a bright side to the picture. New Vermonters are being made. Like the rest of the United States, Vermont is a melting pot for people from other countries and for the ideas about food they bring with them. That Convent Pie, for instance, has an Italian background. The macaroni that goes into it was probably invented by the Chinese and the idea for it brought back to Italy by Marco Polo in 1295. From Italy also came the chestnuts that Mrs. Appleyard uses when she makes

MARRONS GLACES

She buys the chestnuts either canned or shelled, peeled, and dried from an Italian grocery.

1 pound shelled chestnuts	1 cup water
2 cups sugar	⅛ teaspoon cream of tartar

Dried nuts should be soaked overnight. Next morning put the nuts into a saucepan. Cover them with boiling water and simmer until they are tender, about 20 minutes for dried nuts, about 10 minutes for canned ones. Drain them. Put them on crumpled paper towels to dry. In the top of a double boiler with a tight-fitting cover, put the sugar, water and cream of tartar. Stir over low heat till sugar dissolves. Increase heat to medium. When syrup boils, cover pan and boil 5 minutes. Watch it — it must not boil over but must steam well to dissolve crystals from the sides of the pan. Uncover, put candy thermometer in place. Do not stir. Cook to 290°. During cooking use a slightly moistened pastry brush to wash down crystals from the sides of the pan. At 290°, transfer pan from direct heat to bottom of double boiler containing simmering water. If syrup starts to thicken too quickly, put the pan briefly over direct heat.

Now, using two forks, dip nuts into syrup. Put in only a few at a time. When they look clear, drain them over the pan for a few seconds and then put them to dry on a lightly buttered baking sheet. Pack in paper frills in a shallow box.

If you prefer, you may pack them into glass jars as you remove them from the syrup and when all the nuts are cooked add 3 tablespoons of brandy to the syrup and fill the jar with it. If you do not like brandy use a tablespoon of vanilla and two of water. The syrup as used for dipping needs dilution, otherwise you might find yourself with a jar of solid marron

brittle on your hands. This was not the idea. Either version, in Mrs. Appleyard's opinion, makes a delicious sauce for ice cream. Break each marron into several pieces when you use them in sauce.

From a Scottish neighbor Mrs. Appleyard learned to make what he politely called

VERMONT OATCAKE

For this to be at its best, you need flour ground out of whole oats. Mrs. Appleyard has a small electric grinder, intended for grinding coffee, that does the trick in 3 or 4 minutes. She has also made the flour by putting rolled oats through a Foley food mill. This makes a good oatcake but the other has more flavor.

½ cup butter
2 cups home-ground oat flour
⅓ cup cream

3 tablespoons Vermont honey
dissolved with 1 tablespoon warm
water or 4 tablespoons maple syrup

salt to taste, about ½ teaspoon

Butter should be at room temperature. Use a pastry-blending fork and mix it well into the oat flour. Add the honey (or syrup) mixed with the cream and salt. Butter 2 eight-inch pans well. Press the mixture into them, using well-buttered hands and a fork. Make creases to mark each pan of oatcake into 8 squares. Dot with a little extra butter. Bake at 325° till lightly browned — about 12 minutes. Let oatcake cool in the pans. Remove carefully with 2 spatulas: it's crumbly. Serve with soup or salad or afternoon tea. For use with tea, dot the squares with butter, put them on a baking sheet, slip them into a 325° oven for 4 or 5 minutes, and serve hot.

Some excellent Vermont cooking is of Lebanese origin. Here is a rule for

MAHLIMSA (A.S.)

LAMB STEW

olive oil
1 pound lamb from the forequarter
1 green pepper
1 large can of tomatoes
1 tablespoon fresh mint leaves

1 tablespoon minced parsley
½ teaspoon allspice
½ teaspoon cinnamon
1 bean garlic
salt and pepper to taste

An electric skillet or a heavy iron frying pan may be used. Oil the pan lightly with a little olive or Wesson oil. Trim most of the fat off the lamb and cut the meat into cubes. Put it into the pan over medium heat. Cover the pan but remove the cover every few minutes and stir the meat. If it sticks to the pan, add a little more oil. Seed and chop the green pepper. Cut up the tomatoes. Chop the mint and parsley. If you cannot get fresh mint and parsley use ½ teaspoon parsley flakes and 1 teaspoon mint flakes. When the meat has browned, add all the other ingredients. Cover the pan and simmer until the meat is tender — about an hour. Serve rice or baked potatoes with it or another Lebanese dish:

SPINACH PIES

Mrs. Appleyard used Parker House Roll dough (p. 8) after it had had its first rising to make these. She thinks it could also be done successfully with a package of hot roll mix.

Flour your hands and a pastry board and make balls of dough about 2 inches in diameter. Leave them on the board, covered with clean towels, and let them rise about half an hour.

In the meantime make your spinach filling. Wash and drain spinach, the kind that comes in a plastic bag. Place the washed spinach in a pan and sprinkle it with 1 tablespoon salt. Form the spinach into balls, squeeze the leaves together and discard the juice. Then chop the spinach and add the following ingredients.

1 medium onion, chopped fine	¼ cup olive or Wesson oil
½ green pepper, seeded, sliced thin	juice of 2 lemons
1 teaspoon allspice	1 teaspoon cinnamon
1 teaspoon ground cumin seed	1 teaspoon mint leaves, chopped
1 teaspoon minced parsley	salt and pepper to taste

Mix everything thoroughly with the spinach. Now pat out the balls of dough to make patties about 5 inches across. Place some of the spinach mixture in the center of each patty. Pick up 3 sides of the patty and pinch them together firmly. Place patties in a well greased 12 x 9 pan, 2 inches deep. Bake at 450° until puffed and lightly browned.

Also from Lebanon came this rule for

STUFFED GRAPE LEAVES
FOR SIX

The friend who told Mrs. Appleyard about this dish said that she must be sure it was really grape leaves she had; that some kinds of leaves were poisonous. Mrs. Appleyard knows this is so because she once knew a lady with a sense of color who garnished an autumn salad with poison ivy leaves. Fortunately they were recognized and the guests ate cornflakes. It is unlikely that Mrs. Appleyard will pick poison ivy instead of grape leaves. Poison ivy is scarce in her part of Vermont and besides there is a grape arbor nearby. She hopes you have one too.

Pick the biggest and best leaves. Wash them. Boil in water until they change color — about 5 minutes. Fish them out with a spoon with holes. Drain. Cut each leaf in half lengthwise, removing the thick center vein. Before you boil the leaves get ready this

Filling for Grape Leaves:

2 medium onions	1½ pounds lean lamb meat from forequarter,
2 tablespoons butter (extra)	put twice through the grinder
1 cup rice	1 teaspoon chopped fresh dill leaves
1 cup water	3 tablespoons butter
salt and pepper to taste	2 tablespoons lemon juice

Mince onions fine and cook them in the extra butter until they are pale yellow and transparent. Add rice and water and cook covered 10 minutes. Remove pan from fire, add lamb, seasoning, and dill. Cool slightly. Stir mixture well and knead it with your hands. Now make the mixture into small balls, using a heaping teaspoon of the mixture for each.

Place each ball on the dull side of a half grape leaf at the broad end of the leaf. Thus the shiny surface will be outside. Fold right and left flaps over the filling and roll the filled leaf into a sort of cigar shape. Now butter a frying pan or an electric skillet lightly, lay in the stuffed grape leaves. Add 3 tablespoons butter and 2 cups hot water. Lay an earthenware plate over the filled leaves to keep them in place while they cook. Cover the pan. Cook over medium heat for 35 to 40 minutes. Add lemon juice. Transfer the leaves to a hot platter and serve.

Perhaps it will be a relief to you to know that if you don't have grape leaves you can use boiled white cabbage leaves instead.

An Armenian friend gave Mrs. Appleyard this rule for

TOMATO SAUCE

6 tablespoons oil	2 tablespoons parsley, minced
4 tablespoons butter	2 onions, chopped
1 stalk celery, chopped	½ teaspoon each white pepper, red pepper
2 beans garlic, pressed	½ teaspoon powdered thyme
1 green pepper, seeded, chopped	1 teaspoon salt
¼ teaspoon cinnamon	4 tablespoons flour
⅛ teaspoon cloves	2 quarts peeled ripe tomatoes
2 carrots, sliced	2 tablespoons light brown sugar

Mrs. Appleyard makes this when the tomatoes in her garden are at their best and cans it for winter use. She says that unless tomatoes are really at their reddest and juiciest, canned tomatoes — 2 large cans — would be better.

Put olive (or Wesson) oil into a large frying pan and add butter and everything else except the tomatoes, flour, and sugar. Stir carefully over low heat until onions and green pepper are soft. Shove the vegetables to one side, remove pan from the heat and blend the flour into the hot fat. When it is well mixed, return pan to the fire and add 4 cups of hot water, slowly, stirring it in well. Add tomatoes, peeled and quartered, and the sugar. Mix well, set it, covered, on the lower rack of the oven at 300° and let it cook for an hour. Uncover it, stir it well from the bottom. Let it cook half an hour longer. Strain it through a fine strainer. Good with spaghetti or meat loaf or rice.

In Mrs. Appleyard's garden eggplant is likely to be frostbitten before it is ever ripe enough to cook, but once in a while she has had some. One of her friends who had been traveling in the south of France gave her this suggestion for serving it.

EGGPLANT WITH A SOUTHERN ACCENT
FOR SIX

Mrs. Appleyard made this in a big scarlet and ivory enameled iron frying pan.

1 large eggplant, peeled and sliced	¼ teaspoon basil
2 eggs	¼ teaspoon allspice
2 tablespoons water	½ teaspoon pepper from the grinder
1 cup Montpelier cracker crumbs	¼ cup olive oil
1 cup fine homemade bread crumbs	6 large tomato slices
½ teaspoon garlic powder	6 large onion slices

¼ pound Vermont cheese sliced

The best way to peel an eggplant is to put it over hot charcoal on a grill and let it get scorched and smoky. Having no charcoal, Mrs. Appleyard did it under the flame of her gas broiler for 3 or 4 minutes, turning it several times. The skin comes off as it does from tomatoes seared in a gas flame. Cut the eggplant into 6 slices about ⅜ of an inch thick. Beat eggs and water and pour mixture on a plate. Mix cracker and bread crumbs with seasonings and spread them on another plate. Dip the eggplant first in egg, then in crumbs, then in egg again. Put olive oil in the frying pan. Lay in eggplant slices. Cook over medium heat until well browned — about 15 minutes, turning them carefully. Use 2 pans if you do not have a pan large enough to hold them all. Drain them on brown paper. Keep them warm.

Now peel and cut the 6 slices of firm, almost ripe tomatoes. Dip them and the onion slices into seasoned crumbs and cook in olive oil until lightly browned on both sides. In your serving pan place eggplant slices, cover first with onion slices, then with tomato slices, then with cheese slices. Run the pan under the broiler until cheese melts and bubbles. Serve very hot.

With the Eggplant Mrs. Appleyard served

BROILED LAMB PATTIES

These come all ready to cook at one of Mrs. Appleyard's favorite shops but if you do not find them, your butcher will grind the meat from a forequarter of lamb and you can make it into cakes about the size of a hamburger.

A pound and a half of ground lamb makes 6 patties.

Broil them as far from the flame as your broiler will allow you to place them and with the door partly open. Put a meat thermometer into one of the patties and cook them to an internal temperature of 150° (medium rare) or 160° (well done). It will take about 15 minutes to brown the first side, a little less for the second — about 25 minutes in all. Serve with them Mint Jelly Sauce (p. 107–108).

With this combination of eggplant and lamb and mint Mrs. Appleyard served a salad that was supposed to be Greek, just the sort of thing Odysseus ate when he was traveling around the Mediterranean, no doubt.

RIPE OLIVE SALAD

FOR SIX

garlic mayonnaise	18 ripe olives, pitted
garden lettuce	2 pimentos, cut in strips
½ cucumber, sliced	1 cup cottage cheese
	⅓ cup sour cream

Make the mayonnaise in the blender (as on p. 122) but add 2 beans of peeled garlic. In a shallow bowl arrange the lettuce, the crinkly bronze kind if possible. Slice the cucumber very thin (as on p. 110), remove pits from the olives. Cut the pimentos into very thin strips. Mix cheese and sour cream and heap them in the center of the lettuce. Surround cheese with a ring first of olives, then of cucumber slices. Decorate cheese with pimento strips. Pass mayonnaise in a separate bowl.

Dinner on the Wing

MRS. APPLEYARD'S recollections of eating partridge go back to the time when she was a débutante. Dressed in rose and ivory brocade and ancestral lace, she was confronted by menus like this, handsomely inscribed on gilt-edged cards and mentioning a suitable wine for each course.

Oysters on the Halfshell

Radishes   Salted Almonds   Olives

Borscht Polonaise

Trout Rochambeau   Potatoes Noisettes

Sweetbreads au gratin   Flageolets sautés au tarragon

Filets Mignons aux Champignons

Fresh Asparagus Mousseline

Roman Punch

Roast Partridge, Bread Sauce   Chicory Salad

Ice Cream Chambord

Camembert Cheese   Crackers

Coffee

On the whole such meals were some of the least interesting Mrs. Appleyard has ever eaten, and she is sure her son Hugh's partridge was much better than the Edwardian ones.

Luckily no one was standing near the window in Hugh's house when the crash came. He thought at first it had been hit by a hunter's bullet but, when he looked at the shattered glass on the floor, in the middle of the heap was lying a dead ruffed grouse. It had flown straight through the glass, breaking its neck. After sweeping up the glass and boarding up the window, Hugh asked his mother how to cook the partridge.

Her shelf of cookbooks, dating from the reign of William IV, proved as confusing as an income tax blank. None of the experts seemed to know what they were cooking — a New England partridge (which is a grouse), a western grouse (which is a prairie chicken), or an English partridge, which comes with a metal tag on it saying so but not giving away the secret of how to cook it.

Some of the writers said the birds should merely fly through the oven. ("Not one with a glass door, I hope," said Hugh.) Others wanted them simmered for hours and then roasted. The cooks could not even agree about the color of the meat. Some said it was dark like duck. Others claimed it was white like chicken. They also said rattlesnake and rabbit and tuna fish were like chicken. Mrs. Appleyard feels that cooks should know what they are cooking.

"I'm going to drive down to River Bend and ask Mr. Colton, the Chief of Police," she said. "He'll just be coming off traffic duty when I get there. I'm sure he'll know about partridges."

In much less time than it would have taken to go through the rest of her cookbooks, Mrs. Appleyard was back with the Chief's instructions.

"The breast meat of a ruffed grouse, usually called a partridge though it's not one," she reported, "is ivory in color, more like guinea hen than chicken. Legs are dark and tough with not much on them — you discard them. Hang the bird by the neck in a cool place four or five days. Pluck and clean it; make a rather moist stuffing, perhaps with a little finely chopped celery and apple in it. You are supposed to have one bird apiece."

"How many picture windows does he think I have?" asked Hugh.

"Rub the birds well with butter inside before you stuff them," continued his mother. "Then put a lot of softened butter on the breasts and wrap them carefully in aluminum foil. Without the foil, Chief Colton says, they get as dry as old pine chips. Don't overcook them. Put them on a rack in a dripping pan and cook them at 325 degrees for about half an hour. Then unwrap them, put them on a fireproof serving platter and run them under the broiler for a minute or two to brown them. The Chief says you really ought to have wild cranberry sauce with them. He knows a bog —"

"They — I mean *it* — will be garnished with green grapes and like it," said Hugh firmly.

When the partridge was served four days later, Mrs. Appleyard tactfully supplied a good many breasts of chicken to keep it company. She also made Bread Sauce to go with both kinds of birds.

BREAD SAUCE

3 cups milk	1 small onion, stuck with 8 cloves
¼ teaspoon pepper from the grinder	½ cup dry bread crumbs rolled fine
⅛ teaspoon nutmeg	5 tablespoons butter
1 teaspoon salt	¾ cup coarse bread crumbs

Put the milk, seasonings, onion in the top of a double boiler. Add the ½ cup of fine bread crumbs. Cook over gently boiling water for 30 minutes. Remove onion. Add half the butter and stir well. Keep warm. In an iron pan, melt the rest of the butter over medium heat. Add the ¾ cup of coarse crumbs. Toss and stir till crumbs are brown. Put the sauce in a bowl — Mrs. Appleyard likes it in a bright red one — and sprinkle the crumbs over it. The sauce should be about the consistency of whipped cream.

Mrs. Appleyard is glad to report that when the partridge was equitably divided by Hugh among the assembled gourmets, her fragment was not like a pine chip.

From Minnesota by way of New Jersey, Mrs. Appleyard received a suggestion for cooking partridge which sounds restful for the cook and also delicious.

The writer says she browns the birds all over in butter, then cooks them in a pressure cooker. She did not say how long but Mrs. Appleyard assumes that, since the breast is white like chicken, the time might be about the same as for the breast of a small broiler. She uses, her friend wrote, only the breasts of the birds and for sauce adds sour cream to the juice left in the cooker. Mrs. Appleyard hereby warns all local partridge-grouse that if they fly through her windows, this is how she plans to treat them.

With them she means to serve

EGGPLANT WITH ALMONDS

FOR SIX

⅓ cup butter   1 bay leaf
1½ pounds eggplant, peeled, sliced   1 slice of onion
        ⅜ inch thick   pinch of nutmeg
1 cup light cream   ½ cup almonds, blanched, peeled and sliced

In a big iron enamel pan in which you will serve it, melt the butter and brown the slices of eggplant in it. Scald the cream with the bay leaf, onion, and nutmeg. Remove onion and bay leaf, pour cream over the eggplant and sprinkle with the blanched sliced almonds. Bake at 325° until eggplant is tender and almonds lightly browned — about 45 minutes.

She will also serve a tossed salad of many kinds of lettuce and for dessert avocado halves filled with lemon sherbet and sprinkled with crystallized ginger.

Now everything is settled till the partridges arrive.

Whose Game?

MRS. APPLEYARD is all in favor of rights for men. She feels they should be encouraged to go hunting in fine autumn weather and, as one of her friends puts it, "work off their rough." The more electronic the world gets, the more important it is, Mrs. Appleyard feels, for men to go shooting. She just wants it clearly understood that whatever game they bring home they must skin, clean, cook, and eat. She has had all she wants of rubbery fish, wild duck that have "just looked at the fire" and of six-point stags, who have toughened their muscles by bucketing around her estate, served straight from the incinerator. Give her a capon to roast and a good book to read while it's cooking and she will not dream of interfering with any man who has taken off his scarlet hunting hat and jacket and has donned his chef's cap and apron.

However, it happens now and then that some hunter says to her, "Could I get your ideas on how to cook — such and such?"

Of course he doesn't want to be told how but he will, generously, consider her ideas. Naturally he feels free to discard them. This is all right with Mrs. Appleyard.

WILD DUCK

Many duck hunters like — or say they like — duck almost raw. They preheat the oven to 500°, put in the duck without stuffing or garnish of any kind, and snatch it out 15 minutes later. That is their inalienable right but Mrs. Appleyard has had duck cooked in a less savage fashion and prefers it.

Allow half a duck per person to be served. Only the breast supplies any meat. Stuff the duck only with a stalk of celery, a slice or two of onion and a small apple, not peeled but cut in quarters. Do not salt the duck while it is cooking. Put it on a rack in an open roasting pan at 325° and roast it about 40 minutes. Baste it two or three times during cooking with the juice that runs into the pan. And don't forget to serve some currant jelly with the duck.

Mrs. Appleyard was so shocked when she last heard the price of wild rice that she has given up that delicacy. She still likes it better than ordinary rice but not about fifty times better. She says brown rice, cooked according to directions on the package, is really almost as good as wild rice. She thought of planting wild rice around her pond but decided that the ducks would eat it before she ever got any. At present they are enjoying her goldfish.

Duck, wild or tame, seems to harmonize with oranges, so you might like to serve with your duck some

ORANGE AND ONION SALAD

Peel seedless oranges down to the pulp and cut out the orange sections. Allow an orange for each person to be served and for four oranges one mild onion, sliced thin. Combine the two, cover them with French Dressing (p. 122). Put them in a bowl with sprays of watercress arranged around the fruit. Toss just before serving.

Green peas have always been considered the proper vegetable to go with duck. The Yor Garden tiny green peas, frozen, are as near your own peas as you are likely to get, especially if you cook them in the shortest possible time.

GREEN PEAS
FROZEN

Do not add any salt until after the peas are cooked. They are already lightly salted and when you taste them, you may decide you do not need to add more.

¼ cup water   1 package tiny green peas
2 tablespoons butter

Put the water in the pan and bring it to the boil. Put in the peas. Cover. Cook 3 minutes. Add the butter. Cook about 3 minutes longer. Taste them. They will probably not need any more cooking. Turn off the heat. Keep covered till serving time, then reheat very briefly.

PHEASANT

Mrs. Appleyard likes pheasants running around in their own feathers and honking among the wild apple trees a good deal better than she does on a platter. If you must cook one, she thinks you'd better split it and broil it by the slow broiling method. Allow one for each two persons to be served. Keep the pheasant as far from your flame as your broiler will allow. Brush it lightly with melted butter. Start it breast side down. Cook it 20 minutes, turn it. Brush it with butter from the pan. Cook until tender, about 15 minutes longer.

BROILED GROUSE

Broil this like the pheasant. Mrs. Appleyard's expert on grouse says it ought to be done in about 20 minutes.

For a vegetable to go with either grouse or pheasant Mrs. Appleyard likes

BROILED GREEN BEANS
FOR FOUR

After all, she has to do something with all those beans she cut on such fine long diagonals and froze with such swiftness and decision.

1 tablespoon butter (extra)	4 slices bread
1 cup light cream	2 tablespoons butter
3 medium onions, sliced thin	1 package frozen green beans, French cut
½ teaspoon curry powder	½ cup cheddar cheese, coarsely grated

Melt the extra butter in a pan (iron enamel) in which you can serve the beans. Add the cream and the onions and curry powder and simmer for half an hour. Crumble the bread and brown it lightly in the 2 tablespoons of butter. Cook the beans until almost done — 8 to 10 minutes — in the smallest amount of water possible. Stir them into the onions and cream. Add more cream if needed. Scatter on the browned bread crumbs and the grated cheese. Bake at 350° for ten minutes. Run the dish briefly under broiler till cheese bubbles.

GUINEA HEN

Guinea hens are not usually considered game. Yet when Mrs. Appleyard went out to lunch in the country one day she saw a whole tree full of rather lumpish-looking birds that were conversing in most unmusical tones. She commented on this to her hostess who immediately called her son who grabbed his gun and, with commendable briskness, shot two.

This is how his mother planned to cook them.

CASSEROLE OF GUINEA HEN WITH CREAM

2 guinea hens	½ cup hot milk
2 tablespoons melted butter	1 cup cream
4 thin slices larding pork	salt to taste
1 tablespoon butter (extra)	½ teaspoon nutmeg
1½ tablespoons flour	1 teaspoon paprika
½ teaspoon onion flakes	

Put the guinea hens, cleaned but not stuffed, in an iron enamel casserole. Brush them with melted butter. Have them breast up and lay the larding pork over the breasts.

Set the pan in a 375° oven. Cook for about 40 minutes. Turn birds twice during this time and baste them with juice in the dish.

While they are cooking, melt the tablespoon of butter and add flour. Remove pan from the fire, add the hot milk, blending well, and the cream and seasonings. Cook over low heat for 5 minutes. When birds are cooked to an internal temperature of 165°, remove the larding pork and all the fat from the casserole. Return birds to the pan. Pour the cream sauce over them. Keep warm until serving time. Reheat and serve.

Mrs. Appleyard was sorry to miss this but after all she was very well satisfied with her lunch, the main dish of which was

BROILED SQUABS

These are so delicious that they make other kinds of poultry (that's what pheasant and duck and grouse are, after all) seem rather indelicate. Mrs. Appleyard has a French cookbook that describes twenty different ways of cooking squabs. You may drench them with fine vintage wines, garnish them with white grapes, with green peppers, with ham and apricot fritters. If you would like to make Squabs New Yorkaise, Mrs. Appleyard can tell you how. If you have all day and plenty of truffles, veal, chestnuts, and mushrooms on hand, this seems a nice project in case a delegation from the U.N. drops in for supper.

There is another rule that suggests that you "shuffle them in a casserole." Mrs. Appleyard, who is not very good even at shuffling a pack of cards, at this point resigned from further research. She doesn't see how squabs can be better than they are plain broiled.

Squabs are supposed to be especially good broiled over charcoal but Mrs. Appleyard finds an electric grill satisfactory. Allow one squab for each person to be served. Split and flatten the squabs. Brush them lightly with melted butter. Do not salt them — or any other meat for that matter — during cooking. Salt only toughens cooking meat. Start them bone side toward the flame and cook about 8 minutes. Turn them, baste with butter in the pan and cook about 6 minutes longer. Do not overcook. Test for tenderness with the point of a small, very sharp French knife. If more cooking is needed, turn them, baste again and cook 2 or 3 minutes longer. Put squabs on a hot platter in a wreath of parsley. Season the juice in the pan with pepper and salt to taste and pour it over them. With a tossed salad of chicory, watercress, and endive, some homemade graham bread with sweet butter, some freshly picked peas with a little thick cream poured over them, who would yearn for Squabs New Yorkaise? Not Mrs. Appleyard.

When she was a bride in 1912, Mrs. Appleyard had not yet learned to boil water. Fortunately she had this French cookbook, which she used to read earnestly before ordering dinner, and a deputy chef who believed every word Mrs. Appleyard told her. In this innocent time, you could buy eight pigeons for two dollars. They were tough, for they were squabs no longer, and their meat was dark in color. However, Mrs. Appleyard gave Bridget such wise advice that she turned out a *plat du jour* that Mr. Appleyard said was "the best yet."

His wife was so pleased with this compliment that she forgot some of the things with which he was, perhaps, comparing the pigeons. This is how she and Bridget cooked them: Mrs. Appleyard sat in the parlor and featherstitched little garments for Cicely — in case she came — and Bridget did the less intellectual work in the winter kitchen.

POTTED PIGEONS WITH RICE CROQUETTES
FOR FOUR

4 tablespoons butter	½ teaspoon nutmeg
4 pigeons, ready for the oven	¼ teaspoon each of thyme and cinnamon
12 very small onions, peeled	2 cups Jellied Stock (p. 71)
2 tablespoons flour	½ cup red wine

1 pound button mushrooms

Melt the butter in a large frying pan and brown the birds all over in it. Transfer them to a large well-buttered casserole. Put the onions in among them. Mix the flour and seasonings and make a roux in the frying pan. Cook it 3 minutes over low heat, remove pan from the fire. Melt the jellied stock and blend it gradually into the roux. Add the wine. Cook the sauce 5 minutes and pour it over the pigeons. Cover the casserole tightly and bake in a slow oven (300°, Mrs. Appleyard thinks) until the pigeons are tender, about 4 hours.

In the meantime Mrs. Appleyard did some more featherstitching, made some calls (with calling cards), played the piano and rested. (What from?) Bridget sliced mushroom caps and put the stems chopped up with a little stock and water to simmer on the back of the stove. She also carried out ashes, polished a little silver, and made

RICE CROQUETTES

Deep-fat frying had no terrors for Bridget. After all, "The Mrs." had told her how. "Heat the fat," Mrs. Appleyard said. "Then cut a cube of bread from a slice an inch thick, just the soft part. Mr. Appleyard likes that last batch of bread you made, Bridget."

"Thank you'm. He's a lovely gentleman."

"Drop it in the fat," Mrs. Appleyard continued. "Count forty slowly and then if the bread is golden brown, the fat will be all right to fry your croquettes."

"Yes'm," said Bridget.

"Slide the croquettes in very gently. Use that spoon with the holes in it that belonged to Mr. Appleyard's grandmother. Put in two at a time."

"Yes'm."

"Don't forget to drain them on brown paper."

"No'm."

After this exertion Mrs. Appleyard rested. Bridget got right to work on the croquettes. They would be fried at the last minute but they would hold together better if they had been in the icebox a while, Mrs. Appleyard said. It was a fine modern box that held a hundred pounds of ice. The ice came first from the pond, then from the ice house. Mr. Appleyard brought it in and washed off the sawdust.

For the croquettes Bridget assembled

¾ cup rice	1 egg yolk (extra)
¾ cup boiling water	1 tablespoon water (extra)
1½ cups milk, scalded	1 cup fine bread crumbs
1½ tablespoons butter	lard for frying
3 egg yolks	1 glass raspberry and currant jelly

She then read her notes of Mrs. Appleyard's wisdom carefully.

Wash rice in several changes of water. Put it into boiling water in a deep saucepan. Cover tightly. Cook till rice has absorbed all the water. Add scalded milk. Fork rice over lightly. Cook over hot water until soft. Take from heat. Stir in butter. Cool 5 minutes. Stir in egg yolks. Spread mixture on platter to cool. Make balls the size of a golf ball. With your thumb, press a good hollow in the top of each ball. Chill. Later, heat fat. Roll balls in egg yolk beaten with water, then in crumbs, then in egg again. Test fat, fry croquettes golden brown, drain on brown paper. Keep warm. At serving time Bridget warms a big blue and white platter. She puts jelly in the hollow of each croquette.

For the time has come. The pigeons are tender, so are the onions. Bridget sautés the mushroom caps in butter. She adds them to the casserole, also pours in the stock from the mushrooms. She puts the pigeons and the onion on the hot platter, gets the sauce bubbling hard in the casserole and pours it over the pigeons, arranges the croquettes and sprays of parsley around them. She carries the platter proudly from the shining black and silver stove to the table. She also brings broccoli with hot lemon and butter sauce poured over it.

Mr. Appleyard's knife is well sharpened. He pours claret into the glasses and begins to carve the pigeons. Bridget hasn't a thing on her mind now except an Orange Marmalade Soufflé in the double boiler (p. 182) and a foamy rum and butter and Maple Syrup Sauce (p. 58) to go with it. Oh, and the coffee and the liqueurs and washing the dishes. Nothing else. A nice easy place. No children — yet. Her own bedroom with a fireplace. Good wages — six dollars a week. And she'd soon be a fancy cook and get seven, maybe, if Mrs. Appleyard gave her a good reference . . .

Blessings on you, Bridget, wherever you are. You will always have a good reference from Mrs. Appleyard.

In the meantime, lacking pigeons, you can cook Cornish Rock Hen, Guinea Hen, Duckling or even chickens the way Bridget did the pigeons.

Mrs. Appleyard and Bridget also learned to cook venison, for one of Mr. Appleyard's friends, Alan Thompkins, was a hunter and generous with the results. He always got his deer. Vermonters then spoke — and still do — as if each man had a deer with his name neatly tattooed on it just waiting to be shot. When deer season begins in Vermont, you can't get an appointment with a dentist, a doctor or a garage man. Carpenters lay aside their T-squares. Plumbers do not plumb. Lawyers stand on street corners with neon red caps on their heads. Merchants oil gunstocks. Pretty soon, if no one gives you a haunch of venison, you can buy it in the IGA store. Alan gave the instructions for cooking the venison to Mrs. Appleyard, who passed them on to Bridget and then began to make an embroidered jacket for Cicely to wear to her christening — in case the weather was warm. That Cicely might be a boy and be christened in frosty December did not occur to her. She happily embroidered sprays of pink rosebuds while Bridget dealt with a large haunch of venison. It had been hanging for three weeks and Alan Thompkins said it would be just right and he would come to dinner three days later with great pleasure. That would give them time, he said. So Bridget began to make the marinade according to his directions and three days later served

ROAST VENISON

8-pound roast of venison, boned and tied   ½ pound beef suet

Venison is a dry meat and needs larding. This may be done with a larding needle filled with strips of larding pork. Alan Thompkins preferred beef suet and he dropped in and taught Bridget an easier method. He took a well-scoured icepick, punched holes in the venison here and there and showed Bridget how to push bits of suet into the holes.

"You have a natural talent," he told her. "Be sure you put slices of suet on top too."

Bridget repeated this compliment to Mrs. Appleyard and added that Mr. Thompkins was a lovely gentleman. She then trotted amiably to her kitchen and began to make the marinade.

1 quart Zinfandel	1 tablespoon mixed herbs (thyme,
6 cloves	rosemary, tarragon)
1 teaspoon nutmeg	½ teaspoon allspice
3 onions, sliced thin	1 teaspoon cinnamon
5 beans garlic, peeled and sliced	3 carrots sliced
1 quart fizzy cider	1 bay leaf

Pour this mixture over the larded venison, which should be in a covered roaster. Let stand in a cool place two days. Turn the meat twice each day. The day it is to be served, pour off the marinade and save it. Brush the venison with a little oil and rub it with flour seasoned with pepper, nutmeg, thyme, sage, and paprika. Cover it with slices of beef suet. Put about a cup of the strained marinade in the pan. Replace it as it cooks away. Cook at 275° for about 4 hours. Allow 30 minutes to the pound. This is if it is liked slightly rare, like roast lamb cooked pink. Allow an extra half hour if you like it well done. Increase heat of oven during the last half hour. (Bridget, of course had no test for her oven except how it felt to her freckled pink cheek. She brisked up the fire at the end of the cooking by opening all the drafts and shaking out the ashes. Mrs. Appleyard now uses a meat thermometer, cooks venison to 150°, medium rare.)

Thicken the gravy by making a brown roux of butter and flour and blending in the hot juice from the pan. Add one glass of currant jelly. With the venison Bridget served Inside-Out Potatoes (*Summer Kitchen*, p. 42) and

BRUSSELS SPROUTS

FOR FOUR

1 pound Brussels sprouts	1 cup dried bread crumbs
4 tablespoons melted butter	1 tablespoon lemon juice
2 hard boiled eggs, chopped	

Like most members of the cabbage family, Brussels sprouts may contain cabbage worms so soak them 15 minutes in salted water. Remove any worms that have emerged to drink, drain and rinse the sprouts, steam until tender in an Italian folding steamer over boiling water, about 15 minutes.

Melt the butter and let it brown slightly. Add the bread crumbs, tossing them in the butter. Add the lemon juice and the chopped egg. Add more butter if necessary. Put the sprouts in a hot dish. Scatter the mixture over them.

COLLOPS OF VENISON

Mr. Thompkins was so pleased with Bridget's roast venison that the next time he got a deer he gave the Appleyards some collops cut from the tenderloin. Mrs. Appleyard had often read of medieval characters eating collops. She thought they must be something like dollops but as she did not know what dollops were either, collops continued to be mysterious. She was much surprised and pleased when Mr. Thompkins told her that collops were rather thick slices of meat.

If Bridget broiled them, he said, he would make the sauce, right at the table in a chafing dish — if Mrs. Appleyard had one. Naturally the Appleyards had a chafing dish. In 1912 no bride could have been legally married without one. Hers was Sheffield plate and copper. When Mrs. Appleyard thinks of the Welsh rabbit Mr. Appleyard used to cook in it on Bridget's night out, she wishes she had not grown tired of polishing it and had not given it to the church rummage sale.

While Bridget was broiling the collops, Mr. Thompkins made

CURRANT JELLY SAUCE

1 cup Burgundy   ¼ cup Jellied Stock (p. 71)
thin peel of 1 lemon   1 glass currant jelly
          ½ cup orange marmalade

Cook the Burgundy and the lemon peel cut in thin strips together for 5 minutes. Add the stock. Boil 1 minute. Add the jelly and the marmalade. Stir until they are thoroughly melted. Put in the broiled collops, two apiece, turn them over in the sauce and quickly remove them to slices of buttered toast on hot plates. Pour some of the sauce over each serving.

With the collops Bridget served lima beans which she had been keeping warm in butter and thick cream for a while and also

GLAZED SWEET POTATOES
FOR SIX

6 good-sized sweet potatoes   ½ cup water (hot)
½ cup butter   ¼ cup sherry
¾ cup light brown sugar   ½ cup peanuts, chopped

Sweet potatoes cook more quickly than white ones. Steam without peeling until a sharp knife can be pushed into one rather easily — about 25 minutes. They should not be mushy. To peel them, cool slightly, hold a potato on a fork while you peel off the skin. Cut them crosswise in ⅜-inch slices. Butter a shallow baking pan and put in the potato slices in one layer. Dot them generously with butter, sprinkle them with brown sugar. Pour hot water around them. Set the pan into a moderately hot oven — 375° — and bake until the syrup is quite thick and the potatoes tender, about half an hour. Baste 3 times with the syrup. Just before serving, tip pan and pour sherry into the syrup and baste potatoes again. Scatter

some coarsely chopped peanuts on each slice of potato, set pan back into the oven for 5 minutes.

NOTE: The sherry is optional. Vermonters sometimes use half a cup of maple syrup instead of the brown sugar and occasionally stir a little rum into the maple syrup. In this case omit the peanuts, for in their presence the delicate flavor of the maple syrup is not detectable.

VENISON MEAT LOAF

FOR EIGHT

It would be more impressive to call this galantine or *pâté maison*, but it would be meat loaf just the same. In Vermont in deer season you can often buy venison and the butcher will grind it for you.

¾ cup jellied soup stock	1 pound ground venison
1 teaspoon dried onion flakes	1 pound Vermont sausage meat
½ teaspoon dried garlic flakes	½ pound veal
1 teaspoon poultry seasoning	½ pound chicken livers
pinch of nutmeg	½ cup dried bread crumbs
6 slices homemade bread	2 tablespoons melted butter
2 eggs lightly beaten	6 strips beef suet
2 tablespoons brandy	

Get the butcher to grind veal, sausage meat, and chicken livers with the venison. Melt the jellied stock and add to it the onion, garlic, poultry seasoning, and nutmeg. Crumble the 6 slices of bread, pour the mixture over them, and let it stand until bread has absorbed the liquid. Stir it well with a pastry fork, add the beaten eggs and the brandy and mix well. Then work it thoroughly into the ground meat mixture. This is done most easily with your hands. Knead it well and put it into a large well buttered glass dish, or use two smaller ones if you like. Mix the dried bread crumbs with the melted butter and cover the top of the loaf. Lay on the strips of beef suet.

Bake at 350° until meat thermometer registers 165° — about an hour and a quarter. Serve with Mushroom Sauce (p. 149) or Tomato Sauce (p. 153). It is also good cold and slices well. It can be served with a tossed salad or used in sandwiches.

Half the amount given will make a loaf that will serve four generously. It should cook in about 50 minutes.

"It seems to me," said Mrs. Appleyard's daughter Cicely, who was kindly checking this manuscript, "that you are leaving your readers in terrible suspense. You've never said whether I got born."

Mrs. Appleyard is glad to put her readers' minds, if any (readers, she means), at ease. Cicely was born in daffodil time one fine sunny April morning. Mrs. Appleyard was up early for once and soon mother and child were both doing well. Mr. Appleyard stood the ordeal splendidly. The only casualty was Bridget, who fainted in the front hall five minutes before the baby arrived. The doctor went down and revived her and got back in time to make Cicely's acquaintance.

He said she was a fine specimen.

She was not a specimen to her mother: she was Cicely. That's why Mrs. Appleyard began to laugh as soon as she saw her daughter. They have been laughing in each other's company ever since. Mrs. Appleyard's readers will no doubt be glad to know that Cicely's feather-stitched petticoats and the rosebud-embroidered christening jacket fitted her perfectly.

The Right Apples

IF YOU take the right precautions, Mrs. Appleyard says, you can have perfect applesauce all the year round. This happy state of affairs used to be achieved by keeping barrels of Gravensteins, Greenings, Baldwins and russets in a cool dark cellar. They ripened at different times and by the time you finished with the russets it was time to think of strawberry shortcake.

Fortunately for those not thus equipped there are other methods. You may can applesauce in glass jars or package it and sharp-freeze it, keeping it frozen until you need it. This is the method she uses and she has found that it is the most popular fruit in her freezer, more so than raspberries, strawberries, blueberries or peaches — in that order.

Of course, she says, you must have the right apples. This remark ought to be unnecessary but, alas, there are cans of applesauce with expensive labels and prices that taste like nothing; there are packages of frozen applesauce that taste just like the package. You don't get anything better out of a freezer than you put into it. This message should be cross-stitched and hung over the freezer, she says.

She is not so narrow-minded, however, as to specify that the apples grow on her own trees. These sprangly-armed centenarians produce a crop only every other year, but luckily she has neighbors who have the mystic ability to produce apples every year. She even admits that excellent apples grow in other states, Massachusetts for one; New Hampshire for another. She likes apples best that are juicy, smooth in texture, firm in substance, sweet but with a delicate tartness. Vermont apples, in fact.

There are several good kinds. Mrs. Appleyard prefers the early ones for freezing: the golden Transparent, the Dutchess with pink candy stripes on its pale yellow silk, or the deep ruby Wealthy. Gravensteins are good too, she says, and without the white flesh and handsome red and green skin of the McIntosh, life would be bleak indeed. Crabapples with their sourness mellowed with plenty of sugar and spice also have their place in her affections.

Apples properly picked, not shaken from the tree, keep so well that people forget that a ripe apple fresh from the tree is better than one picked partly ripe, shipped and stored. This is true of oranges, strawberries and raspberries. It is vital in the case of peas and corn. Even the humble carrot is better freshly pulled out of the ground than it is sulking in a cellophane bag.

Once a visitor from Texas asked if he might pick an apple and eat it right from the tree. Mrs. Appleyard kept him company in this project one cool August evening, and she thinks his rapture was not ill-founded. So if you plan to put applesauce in your freezer, you are fortunate if you have a neighbor whose trees are hanging heavy with fruit, or if you know a local market where local fruit is sold.

This is how Mrs. Appleyard makes the applesauce she puts in her freezer.

CANDIED APPLESAUCE

12 Vermont apples	1 clove
2 cups water	⅛ teaspoon nutmeg
1 cup sugar	¼ teaspoon cinnamon
thin yellow peel of half a lemon, cut fine	

Mrs. Appleyard often makes this sauce with just sugar and water. What she is trying to suggest is that with good apples you should go easy on the seasoning.

Wash the apples carefully to remove any possible residue of spray. Peel them. Put the peel — much of the flavor of the apple is in it — on to boil in the water while you quarter the apples, remove seeds and pips and slice the apples about a quarter inch thick. Now strain the liquid off the skins, measure it and add enough to make 2 cups. Add the sugar and seasonings and stir until dissolved. Drop in the apple slices and cook them until they are transparent. Remove them with a skimmer to a pan big enough to hold all the sauce, set in a larger one containing cold water. Keep doing this until all the apples are cooked. If necessary, add more syrup made with half a cup of sugar to a cup of water. If at the end you have too much syrup, as you may if your fruit is very juicy, cook it down to a cupful and pour it over the fruit. When it is cool, the fruit will be almost jellied.

If you can't resist the temptation to eat it right away — and why should you? — serve it with ice cream, sour cream or (best) thick Vermont cream. Good cheddar cheese made from whole Vermont milk goes well with it too.

If you can it, simply pack it in sterilized jars with new rubber rings. Put the jars on a rack in a tightly covered kettle, add hot water, steam them long enough to seal them tightly. This amount of apples will make only about three pints, so double it to make the process worthwhile.

If the applesauce is to be frozen, Mrs. Appleyard usually omits the seasoning and she makes it in small quantities. She puts it in plastic bags protected by square pasteboard containers. She says it is important to cool the pan of sauce thoroughly (adding ice cubes to the water in the outer pan), to package it quickly, and to have your freezer well below zero. She says the freezer compartments in refrigerators do not always produce this temperature. If yours does not, better do a large batch, cool it well and take it to the locker plant for sharp-freezing.

When you eat it next winter you will remember the first buds on the apple trees, the little red knobs among jade green leaves, the trees piled with snowy blossoms flushed with pink, and the sound of bees making apple blossom honey, the first hard, sour green globes, the branches bending under the weight of topaz and ruby fruit, while a charm of goldfinches flies by, the bare tree with apples the pickers never reached, against the hunter's moon.

It's all in the package, Mrs. Appleyard says, and isn't it lucky, she adds, that some people like apples that are large, handsome, thick-skinned and flavored like sawdust?

She thinks Vermonters are rather like Vermont apples. They wear well. They have a basic solid goodness lightened by a sharp tang — and there aren't enough of them to go around.

Apples were on hand all winter in Vermont cellars. How you used them was a matter of temperament. Those of an extravagant nature would bite into the best-looking apple, just as it came from the tree. This practice was frowned upon by the best farmers and housekeepers. They always chose to eat first apples with bruised spots on their striped pink and white sides. This could go on until spring.

It was said of one prosperous family that "the Barringtons always ate rotten apples."

Their poorer neighbors would laugh and say, "Those rich folks! Wouldn't you think they'd throw 'em away?"

They overlooked the fact that the Barringtons got rich — and stayed so — by not throwing things away. For instance there was the homespun sheet. It was spun out of the finest merino wool by Mrs. Barrington before she married. We might think it was meant for a blanket but Vermont beds in wintertime were made up not with the linen sheets, which she had also woven, but with ivory-colored sheets of wool. Linen was too cold for winter. After you had put a stone jug full of hot water at the bottom of the bed and then, just before you got into it, had passed a brass warming pan full of hot coals between the sheets, you could go to sleep without much danger of freezing before morning. Of course you had a feather bed and several quilts and a blue and white coverlet over you.

Each of the homespun sheets was made of two widths from the loom, seamed together. It was along this seam that the first signs of wear came after a few years. Mrs. Barrington carefully ripped the two widths apart, sewed what had been the outer edges together and blanket-stitched them along the edge. After five or six years the sheet showed wear along the seam again. Mr. Barrington needed a new nightshirt so Mrs. Barrington made him one. She dyed it a cheerful bright red with cochineal to make it warmer. After about three years it had one or two thin places, so she made it over for him into an undershirt.

This lasted until their oldest son started courting one of the Appleyard girls. He also planted the corn that spring and he asked his mother for something to put on the scarecrow. She gave him the undershirt. This had such a satisfactorily terrifying effect on the crows that it was still being used when the Barrington-Appleyard wedding took place. By that time the undershirt had faded to an agreeable shade of dusty pink.

The Barrington's youngest child, Phoebe, was six years old that autumn and needed a new dress to go to school, so — Mrs. Appleyard is not inventing this — Mrs. Barrington made Phoebe a pretty pink dress. Can you possibly guess out of what?

Naturally during these years Mrs. Barrington cut the spots out of many a bruised apple and used the remainder in various ways. She cut them in pieces, ran heavy thread through them with a big needle and hung them from the rafters to dry. She baked them in a reflecting oven before the open fire. She baked them in the brick oven, scattering them with sugar, grated lemon peel, and cinnamon. She peeled and cored them, simmered them — hanging the kettle on a crane over the fire — with water until they were tender. Then she took out the apples, "threw in three or four cups of nice brown sugar," let the syrup boil up, skimmed it until clear, put back the apples, let them boil for five minutes, served them for tea with thick cream.

Here are her directions for

BREAD AND APPLE PUDDING

Peel tart apples, grate them in a baking dish. Grate in as much stale bread. Beat up 2 eggs in a pint or so of milk and make it quite sweet with sugar and flavor with rose water or grated lemon or orange peel. Mix well into the apple and bread crumbs. Bake it and eat it hot as pudding for dinner or, as an article for the tea table, cold, with cream. If you have quinces, grate in one third quince, adding extra sugar, and it is a great improvement.

She also peeled fruit, put it in a stone jar with a small mouth, scattered sugar and raw rice between layers, covered the top of the jar with bread dough. She set the jar in the brick oven and let it stay all night. Quinces or peaches could be added. This was a healthful dish for children. They loved it, she said. In those far-off times, Mrs. Appleyard wonders, did children really like healthful dishes?

In her spare time Mrs. Barrington made jelly of apples and wild grapes. The favorite dish, however, was

APPLE PANDOWDY
FOR TEN

There is an old song about Pandowdy. Mrs. Appleyard remembers only a few lines.

> ... the turkey's in the pan
> and the dowdy's on the fire
> and we're all getting ready for Cousin Jedediah
> and Nehemiah
> and Hezekiah.

CHORUS
Oh won't we have a jolly time,
Oh won't we have a jolly time,
Oh won't we have a jolly time,
We'll all take tea!

Tea of course was a real climax. The Revolution being over, tea was no longer being thrown into Boston Harbor and you could drink it without fear of being considered disloyal to your colony. Since "Fire" and "Jedediah" are rhymed, Mrs. Appleyard thinks that these verses must have been sung no farther south than Boston. They would sound all right in Vermont too. Her rule for Apple Pandowdy came from the Appleyard side of the family.

½ pound butter
 3 cups soft light brown sugar
¼ teaspoon each cinnamon and nutmeg
⅛ teaspoon cloves

piece of thin lemon peel 1 inch square, cut fine
3 pounds Dutchess or other tart apples, pared and cut in eighths

Crust:

2 cups flour
4 teaspoons baking powder

3 tablespoons butter
¾ cup rich milk

Melt half the butter in a large graniteware milk pan or some other fairly deep fireproof dish. Add 2 cups of the sugar (real sugar, *not* brownulated) and mix well. Stir in the seasonings. Put in the pieces of apple and the rest of the butter in small bits among them. Put the dish in the oven at 450° and bake the mixture until the apples start to soften and the syrup starts to bubble up among them — about 10 minutes. In the meantime make your biscuit dough. Sift the flour and baking powder together 3 times into a bowl, cut the butter in with a pastry blender until it is in very small lumps. Cut in the milk. Toss the dough on a very lightly floured board. Knead it briefly and pat it out about ¾ of an inch thick. Take small lumps of it and put them over the bubbling apples, leaving little spaces between them. Return the pan to the oven and bake until the top is puffed and well browned, about half an hour. Reduce the heat to 400° if they seem to be browning too fast. Never put on the crust until the syrup is really bubbling. It's the heat underneath that makes the biscuit crust rise. You may use packaged biscuit mix if you like but it should be enriched with extra butter, Mrs. Appleyard says, and by the time you've done that, it's not much more trouble to make your own mixture.

Peach Pandowdy is good too. For 10 people use 18 peaches and use the same amounts of butter and sugar as in the Apple Pandowdy. No spices, about 3 drops of almond extract. Otherwise use the same method as for the Apple Pandowdy. If Cousin Jedediah drops in to tea he'll probably be delighted.

Thick cream, Hard Sauce (*Winter Kitchen*, p. 130), or vanilla ice cream all go well with Pandowdy.

CIDER APPLE JELLY

Take good tart apples — Wealthies if you can get them because of the red color of their skins. (McIntosh will do, Mrs. Appleyard says.) Wash them but do not peel or core them. Cut them into quarters. Cover them with sweet cider made that day if possible. It must not have started to work at all. (Pasteurized cider will not do.) Boil the apples in the cider until they are very soft. Put them in a jelly bag and let the juice drip through. Do not press the bag. Measure the juice. To each pint add a pound of sugar warmed in a shallow pan in the oven for a few minutes. Bring the liquid to the boil and boil it until it jellies on a cold saucer — from 20 minutes to half an hour. Skim it carefully, put it in sterilized glasses. Let it cool slightly. Cover the glasses with paraffin. Cover, label, and date them.

BOILED CIDER

Someone asked Mrs. Appleyard to tell her how to boil cider. No one had told Mrs. Appleyard how, so she poured a gallon of cider, made the day before by one of her neighbors, into a two-gallon kettle and cooked it down to about 2 quarts. It was then a dark, rather adhesive liquid, pleasantly tart in flavor. It can be used in making mince pie meat or you can add it to mince pie meat you buy. A tablespoonful or two gives extra body and flavor to hot spiced cider. When you are frying apple rings to go with sausage, you can glaze them with a little boiled cider and when you bake apples you can add a little to the filling. You can, in fact, use it in many apple dishes to intensify the flavor.

CIDER APPLESAUCE

4 quarts apples, peeled, cored and quartered
2 quarts cider

Cook over low heat until the apples are tender. Measure. Add ¾ cup of warmed sugar for each cup of cooked fruit. Cook, stirring carefully from the bottom until the juice is quite thick. This is a dark golden brown in color. It is good as a relish with roast pork, ham, or sausage. It may also serve as a dessert with thick cream.

DEEP DISH APPLE PIE

First the pastry. (This is enough for the tops of 2 deep-dish pies, perhaps with some left over to make cheese straws or some little turnovers another day.)

4 cups all-purpose flour, sifted 3 times and measured

Use what is left over for flouring your pastry board and rolling pin. You may need a little extra flour for rolling but use as little as possible.

salt to taste	1 cup lard, very cold
1 cup butter, very cold	1 cup ice water

Use a large wooden chopping bowl, a chopping knife, and a spatula. They should be chilled while you are sifting the flour and salt. Any bowl from Mrs. Appleyard's pantry in autumn is automatically chilled.

Put the flour, butter, and lard into the bowl and chop them until the butter and lard are in pieces the size of the end of your little finger tip. Add half a cup of ice water, all at once. Work it well into the flour with the chopper. Add the rest of the water, work it in. You now have your paste. Never touch it with your hands but only with the chopper and spatula. Flour your pastry board lightly, put the paste on it. Flour your rolling pin. Roll the paste out into an oblong 12 x 5 inches.

Cut it into 3 pieces. Lay end pieces on top of the middle one. Turn the board 90 degrees. Roll the paste out again, never touching it with your hands and repeat the cutting into thirds, laying the end pieces on the middle one and giving the board a 90-degree turn until you have gone through the whole process 7 times. Unless you prefer to do your own arithmetic, you may take Mrs. Appleyard's word for it that you now have 2187 layers of paste with cold air trapped in it. Now cut the paste in 3 pieces, wrap each one in wax paper. Rinse your hands in cold water and shape each piece of paste into a ball. This is the nearest you come to touching it with your hands. Put the paste into the refrigerator to chill for at least 4 hours before you bake your pie or pies.

For one deep-dish pie to be made in a 9-inch Pyrex dish

⅔ cup granulated sugar	12 McIntosh apples, washed,
¼ teaspoon nutmeg	pared, cored and sliced
⅛ teaspoon cinnamon	¼ cup butter
juice and grated rind of 1 lemon	

Mix the sugar and spices. Grease the dish lightly with paper from a stick of butter. Put in a layer of apple slices. Sprinkle it with spiced sugar, dot it with butter. Sprinkle with lemon juice and rind. Repeat until the dish is full. Heap the apples slightly toward the center of the dish.

Now roll out a circle of pastry that will be slightly larger than the dish. Moisten the edge of the dish a little. Put on the pastry circle, press it down lightly, and trim it neatly. Of the trimmings make a twisted ribbon of pastry and lay it all the way around the dish quite close to the edge. Cut openings for steam to escape with your shears. Mrs. Appleyard likes to make bowknots out of the last scraps of paste to decorate the top of the pie. You don't tie them. You just lay on two loops and two ends in an appropriate position and, where they join, lay on a small strip to hold them together. Chill the pie in the refrigerator until your oven is ready at 450°. Bake it at that heat for 10 minutes, reduce the heat to 350°, and bake till it is puffed and delicately browned — about 35 minutes longer. Serve it warm with hard sauce, ice cream or thick cream. A piece of Vermont cheese is pretty nearly a necessity with it.

Vermont Cheese

IT WILL probably not surprise anyone to hear that Mrs. Appleyard feels strongly about cheese. *"Processed Cheese!"* is something she hisses when she feels in a profane mood. In calmer moments she admits that it has certain virtues: no one is likely to be tempted to eat too much of it and any that is consumed leaves real cheese for those who appreciate it. She can talk herself into quite a mellow mood by such statements, though of course she doesn't really mean a word of them.

Fortunately, honest, time-ripened cheese is still made in Vermont, but no one makes Mrs. Appleyard's favorite kind. She happened to read about how Roquefort cheese was discovered. During a thunder storm, a French shepherd took shelter in a cave and began to eat his lunch of bread and ewe's milk cheese. Seeing his sheep frightened by the storm, he hurried out to herd them to a safe place. Weeks later he came back to the cave, which had a strange smell. You guessed it — the cheese had turned to Roquefort.

Mrs. Appleyard happened to have on hand cream cheese she had made herself and freshly baked bread. She quickly combined them, wrapped them in waxpaper and put the package in her cellar, which is as much like a cave as anything nearer than Smuggler's Notch.

"I will forget it," she said and conscientiously did so until one of her daughters asked her if anything had died in the cellar.

Mrs. Appleyard remembered her experiment. She wished she had made more. It was a little like Camembert, a little like Liederkranz but with its own secret flavor too. She realized too late that if she had kept some of the cheese for a culture, her cellar might now be as famous as the caves of Roquefort but the assembled gourmets left not a crumb. She tried it again but it was never the same. Yet the ingredients are simple enough. All you need is about twelve quarts of milk from some perfect Guernseys who have just had all the green grass they want, June grass, eaten under a blue sky with great Gainsborough clouds sailing over it and plenty of bobolinks singing as they fly. Put the evening's milk, still warm, in pans on the back of the stove. You need a wood-burning stove and you must be baking bread in the oven. Next morning the cream will have risen and will be quite thick above the clabbered milk. If it has not clabbered let it stand until it does. Skim off the cream.

Beat it to amalgamate it well, but not enough to make whipped cream of it. Use a wire whisk, not an eggbeater. Put it into a bag made of four thicknesses of sterilized cheese-cloth. Hang the bag among the apple blossoms where the shade will dapple it. The blossoms were still pink, Mrs. Appleyard remembers, and there were scarlet buds already opening among the leaves.

Did this pink and gold and chrysoprase shade give the cheese its warm gold color? Well, frankly, no. That came from the June grass. You can color cheese, Mrs. Appleyard has read, by boiling marigolds or grated carrots in the milk. No doubt you could also add U.S. certified color but not with the idea of pleasing Mrs. Appleyard, thank you.

In about two days no more liquid will drip from the bag. It should feel almost dry. Now all you need do is scrape every bit of it out of the bag, stir it well with a fork, put it into a Sandwich glass dish, chill it and eat it with enormous dark red strawberries and sugar.

Mrs. Appleyard does not really advise trying to make Camembert-Liederkranz out of it. Perhaps if the old cheese factory at Appleyard Center had not fallen down before she came there and happily took up the hobby of keeping buildings in a more or less erect position, she might have been tempted to be a cheese maker. Yet on the whole it may be better for the village to smell of apple blossoms, lilacs, new mown hay, crushed mint and wood smoke, each in its season. However, if anyone succeeds in making Appletree Camembert, please let Mrs. Appleyard know. She'll be right along to sample it.

The best cheese for cooking, she thinks, is natural cheddar. Cheese souffle, cheese fondue, cheese biscuits are all delicious made with rather mild cheddar. Dry cheddar, grated, is fine for topping casseroles and to serve with onion soup. Aged cheddar is excellent eaten with toasted Montpelier crackers. Perhaps Mrs. Appleyard's favorite cheese dish is Welsh Rabbit as Mr. Appleyard used to make it. Calling it a "rarebit" is as out of place as putting tomato soup, flour or milk into it. It is, Mr. Appleyard used to state firmly, a rabbit in the same sense that a Cape Cod turkey is codfish and a Bombay duck is a very dead fish, so dry that it splinters.

WELSH RABBIT

Here is how to make a Welsh Rabbit for six.

2 tablespoons butter	½ teaspoon salt
1 cup beer	¼ teaspoon cayenne
2 teaspoons Worcestershire sauce	2 pounds mild soft cheddar cheese
2 teaspoons dry mustard	cut into small pieces
2 egg yolks, lightly beaten	

Mr. Appleyard used a silver chafing dish, but an electric skillet is a good substitute. The chief thing to remember is that cheese dislikes high heat or long cooking. It shows its resentment by getting tough and stringy. Melt the butter. Pour in the beer and bring it quickly to a boil. Add the seasonings. Reduce heat. Add the cheese. Stir well so that the small cubes into which you have cut it will melt quickly. Your assistant — you must have one — is toasting English muffins. She also beats the egg yolks in a small bowl and presents them at the right moment. You add a good dollop of melted cheese to the eggs and beat them together with a fork. Add the mixture to the contents of the skillet. Stir well until it thickens. The muffins are ready, hot and buttery.

Dunk one into the rabbit. It will emerge veiled in ambrosia and gold, dripping, pungent, and succulent, ready to go on a hot plate and receive a final spoonful of rabbit. Beer foams in tall glasses. Major Grey's chutney circulates around the table.

Mrs. Appleyard says: "After all there's nothing better than Vermont cheddar."
Nobody contradicts.

CHEESE MAKERS

Up in South Troy, Kraft makes Cracker Barrel cheddar. Cheddar cheese is also made at Cabot, at Plymouth by John Coolidge, by Crowley at Healdville and by Stanley Wisell at East Wallingford. Cottage cheese is made at Cabot, Burlington, and St. Albans. Economou Cheese Company at Hinesburg makes Greek Aspro and Italian Ricardo. Economou and Richmond Co-op Creamery both make Mozzarella. Colby, like cheddar but more porous and crumbly, is made at Bellows Falls by Coolidge, Crowley.

Please Pass the Cheese

CHEESE is not only one of the oldest foods used by man but it is also one of the most versatile. Mrs. Appleyard says you can serve it at every course in a meal and still not find it monotonous. It can be among the hors d'oeuvres, appear in the soup, serve as the main course in a quiche or a soufflé, go along companionably with the salad and be served with crackers and fruit for dessert. Then toward ten o'clock on a cold night if you toss a Cheese Fondue together, you still find customers.

Naturally you are not limited to one kind of cheese. You may feel in a mood for Roquefort or Danish Blue one day and for Camembert or Liederkranz the next. You may put cream cheese in chocolate frosting and top your casserole with Gruyère. You can use cheese in biscuits, in puffs, in sauce, in croquettes, in turnovers, and still tomorrow find a good way to serve it that you've never tried before.

Vermonters are lucky, Mrs. Appleyard thinks, in having their own cheddar cheese available and varying with the season and even with the day on which it was made. It is never really exactly the same as the last pressing — you can taste grass blown into silver waves in one batch, red clover in another, ripe corn in a third.

CHEESE FRENCH TOAST
FOR TWO

½ cup heavy cream   ¼ teaspoon nutmeg
½ cup Vermont cheddar cheese, grated   2 eggs, well beaten
⅛ teaspoon pepper   6 triangles of bread

Mix the cream, the cheese grated rather coarsely, and the seasonings and cook over hot water a few minutes, stirring, until the cheese melts. Cool by setting pan into cold water. Beat the eggs with a wire whisk and beat them into the mixture. Grease a baking sheet well with butter. Dip slices of bread into the cheese mixture one at a time, coating both sides. Place them on the baking sheet and bake at 375° until they are light brown and bubbly, about 15 minutes. Serve very hot with a tossed salad.

GARLIC CHEESE MUFFINS
FOR FOUR

Another luncheon dish begins with a whole head of garlic. If you don't really like garlic, read no further.

1 whole head of garlic   1 teaspoon dry mustard
2 tablespoons butter   1 teaspoon paprika
1 pound cheddar cheese, cubed   1 tablespoon Worcestershire sauce
1 egg, beaten

Peel and crush the garlic beans and toss the pulp lightly in the butter for 2 minutes. Melt cheese over hot water, add the garlic and other seasonings. Beat the egg in a small bowl, add gradually 3 tablespoons of the melted cheese, beating it in with a wire whisk. Pour it back into the cheese mixture and cook till it thickens.

Have English muffins split, toasted, and buttered ready on very hot plates. Pour the sauce over. Serve with chutney and salad.

CHEESE OMELET (E.R.K.)

For each person allow

butter   salt to taste
2 eggs   pepper from the grinder
1 slice of well-aged cheddar

Do this in an iron enamel pan in which you will serve it. Customers must wait while you do it.

Melt butter in the frying pan. Have broiler lighted.

Add about half a teaspoon of water for each egg. Beat with a fork just enough to blend yolks and whites and salt and pepper. Pour eggs into the pan and let it cook about 2 or 3 minutes, picking up thick part with a fork and letting the liquid part run underneath. When it is cooked about half as much as it would be for an omelet, remove from burner, lay slices of cheese over it and run the pan briefly under the broiler for another 2 or 3 minutes — until the cheese melts and the omelet puffs up around it. Serve at once. It will collapse soon but will still taste good.

Baking powder biscuits, split, buttered and toasted under the broiler are good with this omelet.

TOASTED CHEESE SANDWICHES — OPEN
FOR SIX

Toast 6 slices homemade bread on one side only. Spread untoasted sides of the bread lightly with mayonnaise. Mix

4 tablespoons soft butter	1 tablespoon liquid from chutney
few grains cayenne	2 cups coarsely grated cheddar
½ teaspoon garlic powder	1 teaspoon mustard
	1 slice onion, crushed

Spread this on the bread. Lay slices on broiler pan and cook under broiler till cheese bubbles — about 3 minutes.

CHEESE SANDWICHES — SHUT
FOR ONE

1st method:

Spread one side each of 2 slices of homemade bread with soft butter. These buttered sides are for the outside of the sandwich. No seasoning. Fill the sandwich generously with well-aged Vermont cheddar. Press firmly together. Toast under broiler first on one side, then on the other, until well browned and the cheese is melted, about 3 minutes to a side. Add a little extra butter to the second side if necessary.

Serve with a tossed salad and chutney.

2nd method:

Use an iron frying pan. Melt ½ teaspoon of butter in it. Lay in the sandwich generously filled with Vermont cheddar cheese. Turn heat as low as possible. Put another ½ tablespoon of butter on top of the sandwich. It should brown on the first side in about 5 minutes. Turn it with 2 spatulas. The second side will brown in about 4 minutes. It is done when cheese starts to melt and run out into the pan. Mrs. Appleyard made about 365 of these last year. She has one for supper when she's asked out to lunch; makes an extra one for a friend who drops in, using a second frying pan, generally succeeds in scorching one: that's hers — healthful charcoal granules and all. For more than two, she advises using the first method. She thinks her Tomato Conserve (*Winter Kitchen*, p. 142) goes well with them.

With soup or salad she sometimes serves

QUICK CHEESE STRAWS
MAKES TWELVE

1 cup grated cheese   1 teaspoon garlic powder (optional)
1 teaspoon paprika   1 package pastry mix

Mix the cheese, rather finely grated, and the seasonings. Make pastry according to directions on the package and roll it out into an oblong 8 x 12 inches. Sprinkle it with the cheese, fold it over, roll it out again, sprinkle again with cheese; fold over, roll out and sprinkle with cheese once more. Cut in 12 strips.   Lay on baking sheet. Bake at 400° until delicately brown and crisp — about 10 minutes.

CHEESE BISCUITS (M.O'M.)

Mrs. Appleyard used to mix these with her hands. Now she uses an electric mixer and finds the task much easier.

2 cups flour   ¼ teaspoon baking powder
1 teaspoon dry mustard   ½ pound butter
1 teaspoon paprika   1 teaspoon Worcestershire sauce
½ pound grated mild cheddar, about 2 cups

Have cheese and butter at room temperature. Sift flour with mustard, paprika, and baking powder 3 times. Cream butter in mixer, add Worcestershire sauce, cream in the cheese. Add the flour and keep beating until mixture is well blended. On a pastry cloth or very lightly floured board, make a long roll of the dough, 1¾ inches in diameter. Wrap it in waxed paper and chill it at least 2 hours. It may be chilled overnight if that is more convenient.

When you bake the biscuits, heat the oven to 325°. Slice off circles from the roll, ⅛ inch thick. Make into small balls. Flatten them slightly. They should be about one inch across. They will spread, so allow space between them. Keep 2 pans going. Bake them 8 minutes. Do not overbake. They should not brown except slightly on the bottom. This rule makes about 4 dozen and a few over that were tried by sympathetic passersby — "just to see if they were all right."

Of course it's a good deal easier to pass an

INTERNATIONAL CHEESE TRAY

Split and butter Montpelier crackers and bake them at 350° until they are a delicate tan — about 20 minutes. Put them in a dish in the center of a big tray and arrange around them dishes containing: Roquefort (French), Stilton with Port Wine (English), Edam (Dutch), Camembert (French), Liederkranz (German-American), Crowley (American) cheese and a suitable number of cheese knives.

CHEESE QUICHE

FOR SIX

A quiche is, roughly speaking, an open-faced custard pie that may have various ingredients in it besides the basic mixture of eggs and cream. A real French quiche is served in a pastry that stands alone. Americans are less adventurous and usually serve the quiche in the dish in which it was baked. Line a dish with packaged pastry — unless you are in a mood to make it Mrs. Appleyard's way (p. 174) — cover the pastry with chef's foil. Weight it down with dry beans. Bake it 8 minutes at 400°.

Now make the filling:

6 slices bacon	2 cups light cream
¼ cup chopped chives	1 cup Vermont cheddar, coarsely grated
4 eggs	nutmeg, cayenne, pepper, salt to taste

Cook the bacon in a 350° oven until crisp but not overcooked. Discard beans. Scatter bacon in small pieces over the bottom of the cooked pastry shell. Sprinkle chives over the bacon. Beat the eggs and the cream together. Stir in the cheese and the seasonings and add to shell. Bake at 400° for 10 minutes. Reduce heat to 325° and bake until a silver knife will come clean from the middle — about 25 minutes longer. Bacon and chives will come to the top which should be puffed and golden brown.

Variations:

Instead of cheese use a large mild onion sliced very thin and sautéed in butter until yellow and transparent. Spread the slices of onion over the bacon. Add a pinch of marjoram to the seasonings.

Substitute for the cheese a cup of mushroom caps, sliced thin and tossed in butter for 3 minutes with a little minced onion.

Substitute 4 tablespoons Roquefort cheese and two 3-ounce packages of cream cheese for the cheddar cheese. Mash them together with a pastry-blending fork and blend cream and beaten eggs into the cheese. Omit the bacon. Sprinkle pastry with minced chives and parsley.

CHEESE SOUFFLÉ
FOR SIX

½ cup butter	1½ cups milk
6 tablespoons flour	½ cup cream
1 teaspoon paprika	2 cups (scant) grated Cheddar
pepper and salt to taste	1 tablespoon butter (extra)

6 eggs, separated

Make a roux of the butter and the seasoned flour. Cook over low heat 3 minutes, remove from heat, blend in the milk smoothly. Cook over low heat till smooth and thick, add the cream and the cheese. Cook until the cheese melts. Cool slightly. Heat oven to 350°. Put the extra tablespoon of butter in a 2-quart straight-sided casserole and set it in the oven. Add beaten egg yolks to the cheese mixture. Beat egg whites so stiff that they stick to the bowl. Fold them gently into the cheese mixture and fill the casserole. Butter should be hot but not brown.

Start casserole on lower shelf of the oven. After 20 minutes move it *gently* to the upper shelf. If it browns too fast, reduce heat to 325°. Bake until it ceases to make any sound of hissing and bubbling. Listen! You must hear *nothing*. It takes nearly 50 minutes to reach this happy silence. Customers must wait for it.

Sometimes soufflé lovers put collars of buttered brown paper around the dish to give it extra height. Mrs. Appleyard is not deft enough in removing this to have it help her much but don't let that stop you from trying it.

A young friend who was using her rule was just about to put a soufflé in the oven when the telephone rang. Her guests had a flat tire and would be at least an hour late for lunch. This bride certainly deserves an honorary Cordon Bleu. She hastily put the soufflé into the refrigerator. When the guests called to say that they would be there in about an hour she made some mystic calculations and got the soufflé into the oven and out again so that it was done at exactly the right moment, says she always makes it ahead of time now. Mrs. Appleyard has not mustered up enough courage to try this yet but she's still planning to.

Instead of cheese you may use a cup and a quarter of finely minced ham or chicken or puréed spinach or finely flaked flounder in the soufflé. Most people seem to like cheese best. Tiny baking powder biscuits spread with a mixture of mayonnaise and Underwood's deviled ham and run briefly under the broiler go well with it. So do freshly picked green peas from the garden or a salad of several kinds of lettuce, tossed with French dressing and garlic croutons. Chutney harmonizes well with it, so does Tomato Conserve. Mrs. Appleyard will not continue: this conversation is making her too hungry.

CHEESE RING

On a hot day a cheese ring that is cold makes a good main course for luncheon. Serve a salad and Parker House Rolls (p. 8) with it.

2 tablespoons gelatin	½ pound Danish Blue cheese
½ cup cold water	½ teaspoon onion powder
9 ounces (3 packages) cream cheese	1 cup heavy cream

Soak gelatin in cold water in a small saucepan. Place it over hot water, stir occasionally till gelatin dissolves. Lightly oil a ring mold. Mash together the cream cheese and the Danish Blue, add onion powder. Whip cream. Mix it into the cheese. Add the gelatin. Pour mixture into the mold. Chill at least 2 hours. Serve surrounded by oak leaf lettuce. Decorate platter with radish roses and stuffed olives and carrots in matchstick pieces. Pass mayonnaise.

If you are still interested in cheese, you will find in *The Summer Kitchen:* Cheese and Chutney appetizers, Cheese Cubes, Cheese Soup, Surprise Cheese Cake. In *The Winter Kitchen*, Cheese Balls, Glazed Strawberry Cheesecake, Cheese Croquettes, and Cheese Fondue are mentioned. Mrs. Appleyard hopes this will keep you out of mischief — such as toying with wheat protein derivatives — at least temporarily.

Fireplaces in the Hills

SOONER OR LATER everyone in Vermont cooks outdoors. Many a scorched frankfurter, carbonized hamburger and well-blackened marshmallow has Mrs. Appleyard received and briskly concealed in the handiest patch of goldenrod. After some years of this, she worked out a system — not foolproof, that's impossible, but one that turns out rather palatable meals. The Appleyards have built stone fireplaces on strategic Vermont hills within a radius of fifty miles from Appleyard Center. Since expeditions to them are made on brilliant days of clear blue and gold, the fireplaces all face northwest to take advantage of the breeze that brings such weather. The chef packs a griddle and an open grill, dry wood of a suitable length, kindling, charcoal (if there's a man who knows how to use it), potatoes, a casserole or two, already cooked, needing only warming. There is also a big wooden bowl and a bag of greens to toss in it. French dressing lurks in a screw-top jar. There are French-fried onion rings. (These — this is Mrs. Appleyard's secret — come in a can.) There is a gallon thermos jug of Appleyard Center punch and whatever is going to be cooked when the man in charge of the fire says it's just right.

It may be Vermont sausage to cook on the griddle with a thermos of batter for griddle cakes. It may be steaks of Gaspé salmon to broil on the grill or large numbers of chicken legs, also to be broiled. On great occasions it is a steak, a noble New York sirloin, at least two inches thick and of suitable acreage. There are ashes left in the fireplace from last time and in these Mrs. Appleyard buries the potatoes. They are all ready, of uniform, medium size, washed, pricked in several places and wrapped in foil. They should be done in about 50 minutes. The steak will probably take about 16 minutes, including turning, for a 2-inch one, longer for a thicker one. A long-handled steak turner is a great help but two pancake turners will do. Never use a fork: it may pierce the meat and waste the juice. Before you begin to broil the steak, set the casseroles and the onion rings to heat on the griddle at the back of the fireplace. Toss sliced mushroom caps in butter for 5 minutes in an iron frying pan and set them aside to keep warm. Get someone to toss the salad greens till each leaf is well coated.

When the fire is just right — glowing coals, no flames, no smoke — put the steak on the hot grill. Cook it one minute. Turn it. Cook one minute. Turn it again. Cook 7 minutes. Turn it. Cook until done as you like it (about 5 minutes for Mrs. Appleyard). Dig out the potatoes. Put the steak on a well-and-tree aluminum platter or a wooden plank with a metal holder. Have a sharp knife ready. Fate cannot harm you: you have dined this day.

That is, you will have dined when you have added mushrooms and sliced tomatoes and onion rings to your plate and sampled what is in the casseroles. Sometimes it is candied sweet potatoes with chopped peanuts and a dash of brandy. It may be baked corn with green and red peppers or French-cut green beans topped with garlic croutons. There's the salad too and something for dessert to fill any possible chinks, just an apple pandowdy heating on the griddle. With hard sauce. And Vermont cheese.

Mrs. Appleyard has described these dishes elsewhere. She here takes up the crucial question about steak. *How do you know when it's done?* She used to have a very sharp knife at hand, cut into the steak just before the last turning and then estimate the remaining cooking time. This is still a possible way to deal with the crisis. One of the best steaks she ever cooked was done this way. It was for a birthday party of Mr. Appleyard's. It was four inches thick, weighed over five pounds and took, including the turning, a little over forty-five minutes to cook. He pronounced it perfect — what else could he say? — but those were forty-five tense moments.

Now Mrs. Appleyard depends for broiling, as she does for roasting, on a meat thermometer. She admits that this guide to perfection looks a bit unromantic at an Appleyard fireplace in — say — Middlesex with Couching Lion bluer than the sky. Or in Jeffersonville with the roar of the great falls and its foam drifting into the smoke of the fire. Or on a hill in the kingdom where the words on the gate are *Haec semper meminisse juvabit.* Yes, unromantic but as soothing to the nerves as maidenhair fern or water running over dark rocks under thick green moss or birch trunks pink after rain. Please try it — indoors or out.

Sear your steak one minute. Turn it, sear it one minute on the other side. Turn it. Insert the thermometer. Be sure it does not touch the bone. Watch it. When it registers

130°, turn the steak again. Cook to 145° for rare, 150° for medium, 155° for well done. Mrs. Appleyard realizes that in a large group there are usually people who like steak well done. She supposes it is possible to have two steaks — and two thermometers.

She also says that she buys a steak two days ahead and keeps it on a rack in a covered roaster in a cool pantry. Writing this has made her so hungry that she's going to get one and start this ripening process. She won't go fifty miles to cook it — just drive through her covered bridge to her fireplace on the hill. Drop in when you see the smoke signal. The steak will be rare.

Vermont cooking, Mrs. Appleyard reflected, has changed since the days the Appleyards came up over the Lightning Ridge Road with strings of frozen beans hanging from the sides of the ox sledge. Yet the best Vermont cooking has not changed fundamentally. Like the best Danish or French or English cooking, it always was — and it still is — based on the use of the best materials: cream, eggs and butter, freshly picked fruits and vegetables. Whether you are making coffee cake or a cheese soufflé or broiling a steak, you need the same sauce with them: it's called care — care for your materials, for your tools, and for your family and friends. And, to bring out the flavor, you don't season it with monosodium glutamate or anything synthetic.

"I suppose it's a secret," said the bride who had stayed to help Mrs. Appleyard wash the dishes.

"Why no," said Mrs. Appleyard. "Almost everyone has some on hand and you don't need much. I'd say about a teaspoonful to a pound of care."

"Oh," said the bride. "You must mean love."

Yes — that's what she meant.

HOW TO
AND HOW NOT TO

TOOLS OF THE TRADE

GLOSSARY

INDEX

How To and How Not To

O N GLANCING through her published works on cooking, Mrs. Appleyard notices that she has devoted a good deal of space to telling you what not to do. These are the remarks to which you should pay strict attention for they are based on sad experience. Almost everything embarrassing that can happen to a cook seems to have happened to Mrs. Appleyard. She says "almost," for who knows what calamity is hanging over that stew she is making with one hand while she is writing this with the other?

She has it labeled in her confidential receipt book "Perfect Stew." She wishes she had been more modest. Such effrontery may well earn its just reward.

At this point in her reflections an astrologically minded friend called her on the telephone.

"This is a fortunate day for you Gemini people," she said. "Mercury is in the ascendant. It's a lucky day for creative enterprises."

Mrs. Appleyard was delighted. She had seen Mercury the evening before, not far from a shining fingernail of a new moon. He looked rather impersonal but all the time he was taking an interest in her!

So rise, Mercury, ascend, blast off, have a wonderful time! Mrs. Appleyard thanks you for keeping her stew simmering just right.

In the meantime she is listing various cooking processes alphabetically and revealing some of their dangers as well as their special excellence.

Au gratin. We usually think of things cooked in a rich cream sauce topped with buttered crumbs and perhaps cheese as something done "au gratin." Actually the "gratin" is the grating of stale bread used for the topping. You don't really need to grate it; you may roll it if you prefer. Mrs. Appleyard is likely to brown the crumbs in butter before she puts them

189

on top of the casserole. Then she puts the dish in the oven or over low heat until the sauce just starts to bubble. At this moment it used to be necessary to brown the upper surface with a salamander (q.v.). Now you can slip the dish briefly under your gas or electric broiler. Watch it! Charcoal is better served in some other form.

Batter. A batter is something you beat. What you beat it with depends somewhat on your equipment, somewhat on what you are making. Wire whisks, electric mixers, blenders, rotary eggbeaters all have their virtues. What you are beating is a combination of eggs, flour, milk, and seasonings. You may be making a batter for fritters, for a pound cake, for pancakes or a soufflé, or for something to dip veal cutlets in: these batters are all cousins. Making any particular sort of batter is described in its own place.

Blanch. Originally blanch meant to whiten or bleach. It was the term for whitening almonds by removing their brown skins. You still blanch almonds by pouring boiling water over them and letting them stand a few minutes until the skins loosen. Blanching, as the term is now used, is pouring hot brine on vegetables before freezing. Mrs. Appleyard thinks this is a bad thing to do. See page 125.

Boiling. There is more to boiling than you might think. Vegetables and fish should be boiled. Meat should be simmered. Water cooks away faster in Appleyard Center than it does at sea level. It disappears even a little faster than usual when the barometer is falling, just before snow or thunder. That's when you scorch the beets. When you are making sauce in the top of a double boiler, what you want underneath is hot rather than boiling water. Boiling syrup soon starts to scorch when the bubbles become volcanically large. Always use a candy thermometer and check the temperature often.

Bouquet. This is used in making soup and stock. You tie together sprigs of parsley, thyme, summer savory, tarragon, basil and marjoram, a leaf of sage, a bay leaf, a stalk of celery. When the soup is done, you fish out the bouquet. This is easy to do in summer if you have your own herb garden. You can pick your own herbs and dry them for winter use. Mrs. Appleyard knows that herbs can also be bought in glass bottles. That's what she does.

Braising is one of the best ways of cooking the less tender cuts of meat. Put seasoned flour in a paper bag. Shake the meat in it, brown the meat in hot fat, turning it often for a few minutes. Add a small amount of water and cook it over very low heat in a tightly covered pot. An electric skillet is perfect for braising. Follow the temperature schedule suggested in the directions on the skillet handle.

Broiling. Mrs. Appleyard used to broil things in a most complicated way, turning them often, allowing for the time used in turning, starting them near the flame to sear them, finishing them farther away from it. They generally turned out all right but it was nervous work. Since the invention of the meat thermometer, things are more peaceful. She turns the meat only once, keeps it at least three inches from the flame all the time, obeys the thermometer's advice. She says that you still need to know your own thermometer and your own broiler, that you still have to be able to estimate the time you will need and that — as in the case of soufflé and baked potatoes — the customers must wait for the steak, not the steak for the customers.

Browning in Fat. When you flour meat and brown it for braising, remember that different fats brown at different temperatures. Butter browns more quickly than oil, beef fat, chicken fat or lard. Watch it, especially if you undertake to brown flour in fat to make gravy. Mrs. Appleyard is not much in favor of this process, which has to be done just right. If you brown flour too long, your sauce will be gray rather than brown. The brown color of gravy should come naturally, she thinks, from the meat and the juices in the pan. If it isn't brown enough she has been known (or rather until this moment it's been her secret and she *hasn't* been known) to add some caramelized (scorched) sugar or — easier still — a little instant coffee dissolved in hot water. A teaspoonful works wonders.

Corning. Why is pickling beef called corning? Mrs. Appleyard has just learned and can't wait to tell. Corn, in England, was the grain of wheat; in Scotland, the grain of oats. Then there was barleycorn, so useful in making malt liquors that it was personified under the name of John Barleycorn; of such a convenient length that a barley corn was used as a measure of length — about a quarter of an inch.

When gunpowder was invented, it was formed into grains which came to be called corns. Gunpowder contained saltpeter. So did the brine for pickling beef. The English language, which never likes to leave a word with one meaning when it might as well have five, transferred the idea of corns from gunpowder to beef. It tells how to corn beef on page 40.

Cornstarch. Mrs. Appleyard never mentions this preparation except to tell you not to use it. She will say why right here and then try to forget the whole thing. Anything — pie, custard, fruit, sauce or soup — into which you put cornstarch is going to taste of it and also have its unattractive, slightly glutinous texture. If you wish to eat corn, eat it as corn. It is, in its own place and season, a noble vegetable. Excellent corn comes out of the freezer and out of cans. Mrs. Appleyard suggests elsewhere in this book a number of ways of using corn but she hopes you will not insert its flavor into an innocent unsuspecting apple pie or a delicate custard.

Yes — cornstarch thickens liquids more easily and quickly than flour does: you may perhaps save five seconds and two twists of the wrist by using it. *Yes* — cornstarch thickens custards more cheaply than eggs. So would candle wax. *Yes* — cornstarch quickly thickens the sauce of baking fruit. It also makes it both sticky and slippery, gives it a sinister luster and spoils its flavor. If you feel you must thicken your pie filling, do so with arrowroot flour or with instant tapioca, both of which are tasteless. Arrowroot is good to have on hand. The Indians used it to heal wounds caused by poisoned arrows. As for cornstarch, Mrs. Appleyard would be in favor of giving it back to the Indians except that she thinks it would be a mean thing to do.

Never buy cornstarch. Never think you ought to use up that package your husband's great-aunt left on the pantry shelf. Enough cornstarch and corn syrup lurk in things you buy without adding any yourself.

Frying is a process often used because it is supposed to be simple. It does not always result in something gourmets come miles to get. There was more indiscriminate frying in Vermont fifty years ago than there is today. Mrs. Appleyard remembers how a neighbor, who used to serve meals for large numbers of campers, once described her methods of cooking steaks for fifty people. She was going to serve them at five o'clock. It was then two-thirty.

She pointed to a large clean metal barrel and proudly announced that the steaks were all ready. Fascinated though horrified, Mrs. Appleyard asked how she fixed them.

"Well," was the reply. "I get fifty nice fresh round steaks and pound them good with a mallet. Then I put plenty of good lard in my spider, heat it good and cook them *real* good till they're nice and brown outside and cooked good all through. Then I pack them in the barrel, there's a big pan in the bottom to catch the gravy. I keep pouring the juice in the frying pan over them. When I finished I put a big round dish on top of them and all my flatirons on it and I wadded in newspaper. Yes, that's an old horse blanket my grandmother wove I've got the barrel covered with. Comes in real handy. You'd be surprised how good and hot they'll come out."

Mrs. Appleyard expressed surprise at the ingenuity of the method and admired the white, red and three shades of indigo of the blanket. She said she felt sure the steaks would be hot. She did not mention that she was also sure that they would be tasteless, tough, and greasy.

She thinks a big improvement was made when meat markets started grinding tough meat into hamburgers and women began panbroiling them or cooking them on a lightly greased griddle. Panfrying ought to be done with the smallest amount of fat possible. Add more fat to the pan if necessary but have only enough to keep the meat from sticking. The pan may be fairly hot at first. Sear the meat on both sides, then cover the pan and turn the heat as low as it will go. After a few minutes turn the meat over. Cook it a minute or two on the other side.

It is very difficult to give precise directions for frying. The size of your pan, the amount of meat in it, the temperature produced by your burner will all vary. A meat thermometer can be helpful. One method that Mrs. Appleyard has seen used effectively is to brown the meat quickly on top of the stove and then transfer it to the oven set at 200°, and leave it there until the meat thermometer registers the correct temperature. Breaded veal cutlet takes kindly to this treatment.

Mrs. Appleyard, as you may have guessed, prefers butter for frying because of its flavor. It browns more quickly than oil or lard, takes more careful watching than other fats but she feels it is worth the extra trouble.

Remember that in panfrying it is the heat of the pan that is doing the cooking. The fat is to keep the food from sticking. Different foods need different amounts. Chicken livers, for instance, need a good deal. So do fried eggs. In both cases the fat should be spooned over them while they are cooking. In the case of hash, where a glazed brown crust is the object in view, the meat and potatoes are tossed in plenty of fat for a few minutes until they have absorbed most of the fat. Long, slow cooking over a very low flame follows. Griddle cakes need only brief cooking and the smallest amount of fat possible. If you have a big iron frying pan, seasoned by years of contact with the best butter, you may need no extra fat at all. One of Mrs. Appleyard's neighbors simply wipes such a surface with a raw potato. Sautéing is a form of panfrying (see p. 196).

A word of advice from Mrs. Appleyard on deep-fat frying: DON'T.

You can burn yourself severely. It's dangerous to small children. It's a fire hazard. It takes practice and while you are practicing you are piling up cholesterol in the family arteries. It is true that using modern electrical equipment is safer than the old-fashioned open kettle and that on the average the product is better than it used to be, but it can still turn out food too brown outside and half cooked inside or greasy all through from having soaked fat.

Mrs. Appleyard's advice is to let Howard Johnson's do it. They know exactly how. You can take things home with you. Above the counter is a price list. One of the remarks on it is "Fr. Fr. to go." Mrs. Appleyard brooded on this several times while she was eating a perfectly cooked hamburger.

Why she wondered, should they say Far Far to go? Of course there are Howard Johnson's restaurants everywhere but it seems an odd way of welcoming us.

Then someone came in and ordered French Fries to go. All became clear.

Now when she is feeling in a mood of desperate dissipation, she murmurs happily, "Far far to go." She takes some insulated bags from her pedigreed collection, she drives along some of the loveliest roads — she knows at least six different routes — and comes home with a good supply of French-fried potatoes and ice cream. Since she is going to freeze the potatoes, she asks for them unsalted. She packages them neatly, dates and labels them. At serving time she puts them briefly into a very hot oven. You'd never know they had traveled all those miles.

Mrs. Appleyard has been asked several times for rules for doughnuts. She replied with her grandmother's rule (p. 60), honestly admitting that the shadow of a doughnut she has fried herself has never crossed her plate. She also reveals (on p. 44) how her mother-in-law made fried pies. So far as she is concerned, such sports are for those who like to live dangerously. She would rather relax with her feet up and her hair standing on end reading a little sadism by John Collier.

Gill. Every now and then some writer of cookbooks who has been speaking sensibly of cups and pints suddenly advises you to put a gill of brandy into a fruitcake or a gill of rum into a rather moderate amount of eggnog. A gill is half a cup.

Glaze. This is clear meat stock cooked down until it forms a strong jelly. It is useful in making aspics, meat gravy, in stock for basting meat, in soups and sauces. The term is also used when we speak of cheesecake with a fruit glaze. Cake is sometimes said to be glazed with boiled icing.

Labels. A sight often seen in the local supermarket is a figure in a blue coat with a mink collar, a hat that almost matches and velvet boots topped with fur. This fur is man-made, very likely from cornstarch, and it doesn't even pretend to match anything. This costume belongs to Mrs. Appleyard and she is reading the label on a can or a package or a loaf of bread. Pretty soon she heaves a slight sigh, returns the package to the shelf and buys some raw materials. Get into the habit of reading labels, she says. It's a great economy and your food will taste better than it would with all those interesting chemicals added to it.

Lard. To lard a piece of meat is to insert strips of fat in it with a larding needle. A simpler method is to punch holes in the meat — dry meat such as venison or veal — with an ice-pick and then punch fat into the holes. Salt pork is generally used for larding but bacon or beef suet may also be used. This process, which Miss Parloa calls simple and describes in a whole page of practical prose, makes Mrs. Appleyard feel that it's very restful to have broiled chicken for dinner.

Margarine is to many people an acceptable spread for bread or rolls. It is not, however, interchangeable with butter in cooking. Any receipt that prescribes "butter or margarine" is necessarily inaccurate. They have different textures, different melting and browning points, different flavors: they must be used differently. For instance, in a frying pan, margarine hisses and disappears before it has cooked anything but itself. It is much more sensible — if you do not use butter — to use Wesson oil or safflower oil. Olive oil, if you like the flavor, is good. Corn oil, in Mrs. Appleyard's opinion, tastes too strongly of corn. She has never yet tasted a cake made with any kind of oil where she could not tell that it was not made with butter.

In her faraway youth, there was an unspeakable substance on the market called cooking butter. When a pound of sweet, freshly churned butter cost thirty-five cents, you could buy a pound of cooking butter for twenty-five. Only what could you do with it? If you put it into a frying pan, a sauceboat or a mixing bowl, you could ruin a good many dollars' worth of food, even in those innocent days when a dollar was worth a hundred cents. It wasn't really an economy.

Mrs. Appleyard was brought up with the idea that if you had two grades of butter, you should put the good one into your cake and on your vegetables and the bad one on the table where people could avoid it. Of course this meant you really had just one grade — the best. Compared to old-fashioned cooking butter, margarine is a delicious substance but Mrs. Appleyard thinks you should put it on the table in plain sight and cook with the best butter.

If your motive is economy, you will find that this method works splendidly. No one will eat much margarine so the meal will cost less than you thought. However, economy is not Mrs. Appleyard's main motive in entertaining: she doubts if it's yours either. She just thinks people ought to know what they are doing and she is afraid that magazines that so glibly recommend "butter or margarine," as if they were the same thing, do so because they like to have those succulent advertisements displayed in their pages. Please forgive this slight tinge of skepticism. If you do not mind sacrificing flavor and texture, most receipts can be adjusted to the use of margarine. Only not by Mrs. Appleyard.

Among the economists are also those who cook with salt butter instead of sweet. Butter costs about eighty cents a pound. You can buy five pounds of salt for twenty-two cents. So when you buy salt butter you pay at the rate of eighty cents a pound for the salt in it and for the extra water held in the butter by the salt. That's high for water, even for Vermont water from your own spring — which is worth whatever it costs.

Mrs. Appleyard will now cease her attack of haggling — it was brought on by a letter accusing her of extravagance. She will go about her business, which is a batch of oatmeal lace cookies (half a pound of butter) in case you'd like to know.

Marinade is a combination of wine, vinegar, herbs, and spices in which meat or fish are left standing before they are cooked. Marinating is the name of this process. Materials for salad or hors d'oeuvres may be marinated also.

Pastry Bag. Mrs. Appleyard knows how to make one — you begin by sewing a triangle of cloth into a bag shaped like a dunces' cap — but she thinks you'd better buy one. She herself prefers a metal cylinder with a plunger, invented since dunce's caps went out of style, thank goodness. She says the cylinder is easier to use than the bag and easier to clean. Directions come with it.

Pudding Bag. You are supposed to make this too out of a strong piece of linen. Don't! Use a brown-bread steamer or any can of suitable size with a tight-fitting cover that overlaps the edge of the container. Butter the can well, fill it two-thirds full, and set it on a rack in a tightly covered kettle over a steady source of heat that will keep the water boiling. Replace the water occasionally with more boiling — not cold — water. Several rules for steaming things will be found elsewhere in the book.

Render. Another term for *Try Out* (q.v.).

Roasting. This term is correctly applied only to meat cooked by radiant heat and turned frequently during the process. If you cook beef in a rotisserie, you are really roasting it as your ancestors did when they cooked it on a spit in front of the fire. When you put it in the oven on a rack in an open pan with hot air circulating around it, you are baking it. This is the nearest most of us can come to roasting, though if you have the time, strength and an oven above counter level with a broiler with enough space under it, you can roast meat under the broiler, leaving the door partly open and turning the meat often. A meat thermometer is an absolute necessity for this method, which Mrs. Appleyard does not recommend unless you like to act as your own turnspit.

For many years Mrs. Appleyard thought roasts had to be seared first at a high temperature, then cooked more slowly. If they were basted often during the cooking and if oven temperature and time were correctly estimated, this was a good method. Since meat thermometers became readily available, she has taken to the slow method. She puts the roast on a rack in an open pan, with the oven at 250°, inserts the meat thermometer and leaves it alone. During the last few minutes she bastes it with any fat in the pan and raises the heat enough to brown it a little. This is the most restful way of cooking a Sunday roast invented since brick ovens went out of style. Put it in before you go to church, stay as long as you like talking to the neighbors. All will be well.

Roux. A roux is a thickening for soups and sauces and soufflés. It is made by cooking equal amounts of fat and flour together. First melt the fat. In Mrs. Appleyard's case, for a white sauce this will usually be butter. (For gravy to go with meat where she wishes the gravy to have a brown color she uses whatever fat is in the pan — chicken, beef, or lamb for instance.) In either case she uses a heavy pan, iron or iron enamel, not aluminum, and melts the fat until it bubbles slightly. Then she removes the pan from the fire and sprinkles in seasoned flour slowly until it is well blended with the fat. Now she puts the pan back over very low heat and adds the liquid, stirring all the time until the mixture thickens and begins to bubble. White sauce, which is the basis for many dishes, is improved in flavor by being left cooking over hot water for at least a quarter of an hour. Longer cooking does no harm. If it seems too thick, extra liquid can always be added.

These are the quantities of thickening she uses:

For a thin soup to which real cream and egg yolks will be added later for thickening: 1 tablespoon flour, 1 tablespoon butter to a cup of liquid.

For a thicker soup when cream is not available: 1½ tablespoons flour, 1½ tablespoons butter to a cup of liquid.

THICK WHITE SAUCE, used in casseroles: 2 tablespoons flour, 2 tablespoons butter to each cup of liquid.

THICKEST — for soufflés: 3 tablespoons flour, 3 tablespoons butter for each cup of liquid.

The liquid may be milk, stock, or in the case of pan gravies, water.

In making a brown gravy, brown a little chopped celery, some finely minced onion, a few slices of carrot, some herbs, a mushroom or two, in the fat right in the pan in which the meat was cooked. Then strain and measure the correct amount of fat (1½ tablespoons to a cup of liquid) into a clean thick-bottomed pan. Work in the flour (1½ tablespoons to a cup of liquid) and cook the roux very slowly until it is browned to the color you like. This needs watching. Then work in the liquid slowly, stirring constantly. Make at least 2 cups of gravy. You can always use it later in soup or hash.

Mrs. Appleyard *almost* always turns out a smooth sauce, either white or brown, by these methods. When fate is against her, as happens to most of us, she is not too proud to admit that she detects a lump or two. It might happen to you. Strain it through a fine sieve into a double boiler and relax. Lately she uses Pillsbury's Instant Flour, has not seen a lump for weeks.

NOTE: There are situations — a pot roast or smothered chicken, for instance, where the sauce seems too thin. Estimate the amount of liquid. For 2 cups allow 2 tablespoons of flour. Season it. Put it into a cup, make a depression in the middle of the flour. Run *cold* water slowly into it, stirring it with a fork. Use twice as much water as flour. Remove meat to a hot platter. Strain thickening through a fine sieve into gravy in the pan. Increase the heat and cook it 5 minutes, stirring thoroughly. Let it stand a few minutes longer over low heat. This cooking will do away with the raw taste of flour.

Sauter means to leap or jump. When mushrooms, for instance, are sautéed, they are tossed in a little butter over rather brisk heat. The butter is well heated before the mushrooms are put in. A little oil added to it makes the food brown more quickly. You may move the mushrooms with a spoon and a fork or change their position by moving the pan up and down and sidewise. This is much more professional and impressive. Mrs. Appleyard is not very good at it. She relies upon the humble fork and spoon. She uses an iron frying pan but heavy stainless steel, iron enamel, or Teflon may be used. After you have removed the mushrooms you can easily make sauce to go with them. Add a little more butter, make a roux (see above) and work in stock or light cream or both.

Whatever you *sauter* will leave some useful fat and flavor in the pan. Rinse it out with hot water and add to stew, gravy, or soup stock.

Simmer. Water at sea level boils at 212°. It begins to simmer; that is, an occasional bubble comes to the surface at a lower temperature — about 185°. Meat simmered is more tender than if it is boiled. It takes knowledge of your stove to keep things simmering. An asbestos mat placed over the burner is a help. So is a French gadget consisting of two thicknesses of metal with holes in both and an air space between. It has a heat-proof handle. Your oven, if you can count on its maintaining an even heat, may be used for simmering. Set it at 200° and set your pan, already simmering, into it.

Lamb and beef are both badly toughened by being boiled. Poultry will stand rather higher temperatures but it too is better cooked just below the boiling point. If you are simmering something and it gets too near to the boiling point, you can always calm it down by adding a little cold water.

There is a theory, based on nostalgia, that you could simmer soup or stew on the back of a coal or wood range and calmly forget it. If you did forget it, the stew sometimes stopped cooking entirely because the fire went out or — when wood or coal was added — the kettle started to boil and the meat grew tough. Actually, when you have learned how, it is easier and more certain to simmer something by gas or electricity.

Try Out. This is such a commonplace term in Mrs. Appleyard's vocabulary that she was much surprised when someone asked her to explain it. As early as 1582, this was an expression for extracting fat by heat. Eskimos get oil out of blubber this way. When Captain Ahab was hunting for Moby Dick, he had to pause occasionally and his crew melted whale blubber and got the whale oil out of it. Honeycomb is tried out by heat and thus separated from the honey. Mrs. Appleyard tries out cubes of beef suet in an iron frying pan — that is, she melts the fat out over low heat. No other kind of fat is so good for browning hash. Having had a careful Vermont upbringing, she keeps the resulting cracklings.

She intends to use these golden-brown nuggets in various ways in spite of a rather depressing remark in her dictionary. It says cracklings are food for dogs.

"Lucky dogs!" she remarks as she scatters cracklings on her bowl of chowder.

Unmolding Jelly. Have a pan of water at 100° F. This will feel barely warm to your fingers. The water must be deep enough to come just to the top of the mold. Leave a tin mold in half a minute. A glass or earthenware one takes longer — about a minute. *Watch your timer*. Remove the mold from the water. Wipe it carefully. Uncover it. Put the plate or platter on which the jelly is to be served over the top of the mold. Center it exactly. Turn both mold and platter the other way up. Set the platter on the table. Be a little patient. The jelly will probably slip out by itself. If it does not do so with a slight squelching flump within five minutes, put a clean dish towel into hot water. Wring it out dry and lay it on top of the mold. This should break the seal between jelly and mold and you should hear that satisfying sound that means the jelly is at last resting on the platter, that it is beautifully embossed with grapes or an ear of corn or George Washington's profile and that you can now reveal it.

Mrs. Appleyard, who has what she hopes is just the average number of catastrophes in various types of cooking, suggests that you get your artwork out of the mold and into the refrigerator well before your guests arrive. There is nothing more nerve-racking than to have them find you with tomato aspic running down your arms. Please don't ask Mrs. Appleyard how she knows this.

Tools of the Trade

Mrs. APPLEYARD went to a bride's kitchen shower recently. As a result she is rather apprehensive about what the young couple is going to have to eat. There were three electric can openers but no spatula, an electric mixer but no sharp knives, enough casseroles for a family of twenty-six, a pressure cooker but no double boiler. Mrs. Appleyard tried to imagine menus suitable to this equipment. Her reason quailed before this task.

Well, anyway, she thought, they can have salad, for there were six salad bowls.

To equip her small winter apartment she recently chose, among about a century-and-a-half's accumulation of kitchen tools, things she considers really essential. She usually cooks for one person, one with whose tastes she is fairly familiar, but she can take care of four easily, six with a little ingenuity.

Here is a list of what she uses:

KNIVES

In a *plastic tray divided into four compartments* she keeps knives.

Stainless steel knives are convenient because you do not have to scour them, but when you really want to cut something you need French steel:

1 *small stainless steel paring knife*

1 *fairly large French steel knife* (blade at least six inches long). Use this for cutting meat and vegetables, also for chopping herbs, onions, garlic, and celery on a board. You hold the tip of the knife in one hand, the back of the blade near the handle with the other and mince the herbs by pressing down on them with the knife, scraping them together, and repeating this till they are the size you like. Mrs. Appleyard learned this by watching Dione Lucas on TV. Julia Child now does it with equal skill.

199

1 *old-fashioned chopping knife*, to be used with *a wooden bowl.*

1 *grapefruit knife*, the curved kind.

1 *carving knife*, French steel.

1 *bread and cake knife.* Mrs. Appleyard's treasure is a Christy knife, the kind where the blade is a series of curves. One with a sawtoothed edge will do.

1 *knife with a rounded end for spreading butter.*

With knives she includes, in the next compartment, anything with a blade.

2 *sizes of rubber scrapers.* These are one of the best inventions of the twentieth century. It's impossible to get the batter out of a mixing bowl so thoroughly with anything else.

Spatulas and pancake turners. On the whole the twentieth century has improved these. Almost any kind you buy is all right. Have at least two, one with holes in it, one without.

FORKS

1 *carving fork*, something large and strong enough for a strong man who is carving a turkey.

1 *large pastry-blending fork with curved tines.*

1 *medium-sized fork* with which — in company with a spatula or a spoon — you can manipulate things while they are cooking.

1 *asparagus tongs.* Not really a fork but at times it takes the place of both fork and spoon. It is, for instance, helpful in turning over steak or chops where, with a fork, you may pierce the meat and let the juice out.

SPOONS

1 *large spoon*, 2-tablespoon size, for serving vegetables.

1 *large spoon with holes in it* for removing meat and vegetables and leaving the juice behind.

1 *large wooden spoon* for tossing salad and for blending sauces.

1 *tablespoon* for measuring and stirring.

1 *teaspoon* for measuring and tasting.

1 *large ladle* for soup or punch.

1 *set of measuring spoons*, if you like, but it's not really necessary. You can learn to measure half or quarter teaspoons accurately with a teaspoon and a knife.

MEASURING CUPS

2 *measuring cups* each holding 2 cups. Keep one for wet ingredients and one for dry. Mrs. Appleyard uses an aluminum cup for wet ingredients and glass for dry ones. Also 1 holding 1 cup.

STRAINERS and SIFTERS

1 *colander* or a *large-size sieve* for draining washed lettuce and other vegetables.

1 *medium-sized fine-meshed sieve*, used in making purées or in straining gravy or soup.

1 *tea strainer*, also fine mesh.

1 *triple flour sifter*, 1-cup size. Modern flour is advertised not to need sifting but if you are going to combine spices and baking powder with it, you need a sifter.

1 *large sifter*, 3-cup size if you have room for it, not really necessary.

CONTAINERS WITH TIGHT LIDS

1 *5-pound container* for flour

1 *5-pound container* for sugar

1 *cracker box*

1 *cooky jar*

1 *tea canister*

Even if you use tea bags keep them away from the air. Keep coffee in its original container, in your refrigerator.

GADGETS

A gadget was originally a small tool used on ships. Now people have enough gadgets to stuff a ship's galley so full that you couldn't make plum duff in it. Mrs. Appleyard disciplined herself and chose only the most useful ones — to her anyway.

Grater. Out of half a dozen she chose a small flat one with different sizes of teeth, small for lemon peel or onion, larger for cheese or bread.

Knife sharpener. The handiest kind goes on a door casing. Pull the knife through the slot in it a few times and the knife comes out magically sharp. This is for women: men like to use a steel.

Ice-cream scoop. A good kind is the Zeroll. It is said to contain liquid that carries the warmth of your hand to the edge of the scoop. This sounds peculiar but anyway it works.

Jar opener. This is one of Vermont's best products. It is adjustable; it clamps onto lids of jars and bottles of many sizes and exerts such powerful leverage that even the most stubborn lids come off. Warming the lid by letting hot water run over it also helps.

Potato peeler. A sharp-edged double parer that takes off a thin peel and does not cut the operator.

THERMOMETERS

1. *Oven thermometer.* An inexpensive device that spies on the oven and lets you know if it's telling the truth.

2. *Candy thermometer.* Never try to make candy or to cook maple syrup for sugar on snow without this.

3. *Meat thermometer*, also used for fish. Mrs. Appleyard considers this an essential tool. She prefers the kind with a flat round disk and a sturdy metal shank. Remember when using it not to have the point touch bones or fat.

Can opener. The wall kind saves blood and tears.

Corkscrew. Imagine how embarrassed you will be when someone brings you a bottle of champagne and you can't open it! Get a *good corkscrew*. There is a kind that fits over the bottle neck that is powerful yet gentle with the cork. Recommended for cooks with a heart condition.

Timer. Many stoves have no timing devices. Even if yours does have one, you may — like Mrs. Appleyard — find it handy to carry a timer into another room with you. This is especially true if you have the habit of writing books and need to be aroused from your happy trance. It's pretty helpful even if you are just reading a book. Many a cake has been saved from carbonization by this intelligent device.

Clock. The kitchen is a good place for an electric clock but there is no reason for not using your great-grandmother's, the one with the little mahogany steeples and the gold eagle on the black glass door.

PANS AND KETTLES

It is not necessary to have large numbers of expensive saucepans. At one time Mrs. Appleyard turned out meals with only two pans. One was a 9-inch frying pan. The other was a double boiler. If she had to choose just one pan, it would be the frying pan. You can bake in it: such things as spoon bread, johnny cake, Yorkshire pudding. You can roast meat in it one day and make hash in it the next. If you have a cover for it — and you should have — you can simmer chicken in it. After the chicken is tender, you may — if you like — make a chicken pie with biscuits on top and bake it right in the pan. Another day you can bake apples in it or apple pandowdy or pineapple upside-down cake. In season Tomatoes Provençale may appear in it or patties of butternut squash. It is all things to all women. However, if you have space you'll find uses for more than one.

So have: 1 *small iron frying pan* about 5 inches across. Use it for tossing a little onion or a few mushrooms in butter, for cooking one perfect poached egg, for warming small amounts of vegetables or gravy.

1 *9-inch iron frying pan*. This size is the most versatile.

1 *12-inch iron frying pan*. This size is the best for use as a pancake griddle or for pandowdy for several people.

When you get a new iron pan, read the directions that come with it for seasoning it and follow them exactly. An iron pan, properly seasoned — oiled and slowly heated — is easy to take care of. Usually it can be cleaned simply by wiping it out with a paper towel or by rinsing it in very hot water. Set it over a barely warm burner or in a warm oven to dry. The older it gets, the better it will be.

Don't think Mrs. Appleyard has not been inquisitive enough to try pans of heavy aluminum, stainless steel, copper lined with tin, American, Dutch and Swedish enameled iron and, the latest thing, Teflon. She has a handsome selection to choose from and she chose her grandmother's iron pan.

She also inherited *iron popover pans*, which are good for baking popovers, muffins, individual fruit cakes, or clover leaf rolls. If you use frozen rolls, popover pans are fine for those too.

Black iron dripping pans are, to Mrs. Appleyard, worth their weight in uranium. They are oblong in shape and come in various widths and lengths. A useful size is 9 x 15. With a rack it makes a good roasting pan for meat. It supplies a perfect surface for oatmeal or sugar cookies. You probably know that snow melts more quickly under a black cloth than a white one. Did you also know that cookies bake more quickly on black iron than on aluminum? Isn't the world interesting?

Square aluminum pan for baking brownies: 8 x 8 is the best size.

Saucepans. Mrs. Appleyard does not advise you to make Hollandaise sauce in an iron frying pan. You need a deeper pan for sauce, soup, and vegetables, especially frozen ones. There is a small square pan with a rack and a cover that holds one package of frozen peas, takes only quarter of a cup of water and cooks them, if you add a lump of butter, in almost less time than it has taken to write this. She also keeps two larger pans within reach, a 1½-quart and a two-quart size.

Double boiler. You can always improvise one by setting a small pan over a larger one of simmering water. A cover is necessary. A real double boiler is more restful, Mrs. Appleyard says. She uses it for soup, for sauces — all kinds — to keep mashed potato hot, and to make Orange Marmalade Soufflé. She feels that it earns its keep. Her favorite is made of Dutch iron enamel.

Steamer. For cooking potatoes for several people or for cooking spinach or making chowder, a deep kettle holding a gallon is necessary. Mrs. Appleyard finds the bottom of her steamer useful for such purposes. She uses the top part for steaming potatoes in their skins, for steaming brown bread and puddings — blueberry to celebrate the Battle of Bennington, plum puddings for Christmas. If she wants to marinate a pot roast or make a small batch of chutney, she uses the kettle: the top fits both sections. She also steams certain vegetables in it.

Angel cake pan. Mrs. Appleyard cannot lead a completely happy life without a tube pan, the kind where the tube and the circle attached to it are removable. You can make angel cake, sponge cake or cheese cake in it and also jellied salads and pâté in aspic, though salads and aspics are easier to do in a straight-sided spring-form mold. However, you can manage with a tube pan.

BOWLS

A wooden salad bowl without any plastic finish. The 9-inch size will do for a small family. Toss salad greens in it. Use it for chopping hash and mixing turkey stuffing. Wash it well with mild suds, rub it smooth with a little steel wool. Of course a big Vermont salad bowl with plastic finish looks handsome with an arrangement of fruit or vegetables in it. So, incidentally, do bowls of silver, early Delft or Chinese porcelain. However, as they used to say in the nineteenth century: "The pony in the stable does the most work" or — in the early twentieth century: "The Ford always gets you there."

Mrs. Appleyard knows the contemporary version of this adage but she will not imperil foreign relations by making it. She just says you need an ordinary wooden bowl for everyday use.

Mixing Bowls. She likes best her old-fashioned brown Vermont pottery bowls. Favorites too are a big one flecked with blue that has had a "time crack" in it for sixty years and a big yellow one with a chip out of the rim. However, she has equipped her apartment with a modern set. They are opaque glass of several sizes, white inside, various colors outside. When mixing cakes, cookies or salads or soufflés, she always finds the size she needs.

Why anyone who can get glass bowls, iron enamel or pottery ones would buy plastic is a mystery to her. Glass, a material much in vogue with ancient Phoenicians and Egyptians, is still the best for many cooking purposes. Yes, you can break it, though with modern Pyrex you have to be pretty strong to do it. Plastic, meeting hot water, especially in a dishwasher, bulges into strangely distorted shapes. It absorbs the flavor of onions and the color of orange juice: both are hard to remove. It's fine for squeeze bottles and for jugs containing liquid bleach.

Mrs. Appleyard has seen a very cozy piggy bank made out of a Clorox jug. It's a nice size in case your child is a millionaire. She even, with a certain amount of ingenuity and little more energy than it takes to chop elm wood, sawed off the top of a jug and made a container in which to soak silverware in hot suds. This is a help in dishwashing but so was her grandmother's ironstone jug embossed with sheaves of wheat.

PLATES AND PLATTERS

Your best china ones should not be used in cooking or shoved into the refrigerator. They are only for serving. You need, when you are cooking, materials that are both fire- and frost-proof: stainless steel, enameled iron, Pyrex glass, or Teflon can stand both heat and cold, though Pyrex and Teflon should not meet extreme changes of temperature too quickly.

Mrs. Appleyard likes a platter on which she can both cook and serve. Her favorite is a *stainless steel well-and-tree platter*, 12 inches long. You can broil a steak on it and serve it right from the platter with all its own gravy. You can use the platter as you would an oak plank, cooking steak or fish till it is almost done, then arranging mashed potato or rice or polenta around the edge of the platter and small heaps of vegetables around the meat, some dots of butter — a minute or two under the broiler, and your whole meal is ready to serve. There are endless combinations you can use, some of which are described under Planked Dishes (see Index).

Perhaps it sounds a little fussy to say that you should have one or two steel or Pyrex plates at hand while you are cooking, one to hold materials, another to lay your tools on. If you prefer to keep wiping what you have stirred or cut up off your counter, it's all right with Mrs. Appleyard.

BOARDS

A good-sized *pastry board*. This is not absolutely necessary, you can roll pastry right out on your counter. Mrs. Appleyard however is miserable without the board, just habit probably.

A small *cutting board*. Nine inches square is a good size. Cut cheese on it, mince parsley, onions, garlic on it. Use it when you cut bread for croutons or celery for salad or when you slice hard-boiled eggs. It takes only seconds to rinse it off and it's ready for the next thing.

PASTRY FRAME

This is a great convenience if you make pastry often. It includes, besides the stretched pastry cloth, a cover for your *rolling pin*, which is certainly an essential if you do any baking.

ELECTRICAL APPLIANCES

The tools listed above as necessities can almost all be bought for less than you might spend for one expensive electrical appliance. Before you buy one, be sure it is what you really want and that you have space near an outlet where it can stand permanently. If it is not easy to get at, you probably won't use it much.

Beaters. Mrs. Appleyard did not bring her big electric mixer to her apartment. She did not have enough counter space for it. Instead she bought a small *electric hand beater* and finds she prefers it since it can be used in a bowl of any size and can be stored in a small space. Incidentally she also keeps at hand a *French wire whisk* and a *rotary eggbeater*. They proved lifesavers once when the current went off while she was mixing a sponge cake electrically.

Blender. Mrs. Appleyard regards a blender as a necessity. She makes soups and sauces in it, she purées vegetables with it. She uses it to make mayonnaise. This fearsome task used to take half an hour or more while you poured in oil, drop by drop, and wondered if it would ever thicken. Sometimes it didn't so you took some more egg yolks and started all over again. You can make mayonnaise in a blender in 65 seconds. The rule is on page 122.

Broiler. These used to be quite expensive but they are so no longer. A small one, besides broiling things, takes the place of a toaster, makes better toast than most toasters. Of course you do have to watch it but even the most automatic toaster cannot always be left to itself either.

Skillet. If Mrs. Appleyard had to choose only one electrical device it would be this modern version of the skillet on three legs that used to stand over hot coals in ancient fire places. Don't try to tell her that nothing has improved in cooking utensils. Without scorching your face or getting ashes in your dinner, you can simmer things for hours in an electric skillet. You can also boil things or — with the addition of a rack — even cook a small pot roast. That stew Mrs. Appleyard was making the other day really turned out to be perfect, as she had brashly labeled the receipt in her notebook. She makes chowder in the skillet and the temperature is so well controlled that she uses it for smothered chicken, cheese fondue or lobster Newburg. In a less exotic mood you can pan-broil frankfurters or hamburgers in it or make pancakes or French toast. It is fully immersible as well as versatile. Blessings upon the head of the friend who gave it to Mrs. Appleyard for Christmas.

Roaster. For a large family this is a good appliance, especially if your stove has only one oven. Using a roaster is rather a special skill but it gives good results if properly operated.

If you want your meat roasted, rather than steamed, you should set the cover of the roaster slightly ajar. When you have done this a tortoiseshell cat may come along and knock it off and glass is breakable . . . Let us turn to happier things.

Juicer. This extraordinary device can take four carrots that seem carved out of wood and in four seconds make them into juice so health-giving that Mrs. Appleyard positively enjoys sitting here and writing about it. Perhaps you think she had lobster thermidor for lunch.

She had carrot juice.

Probably the juicer is too specialized a device for most people but if you have one and a vegetable garden, you have a wonderful and easy way of making delicious combinations of vegetable juices. Cold soups in summer and hot ones in winter are both improved by the addition of these juices. They may be added to stew or gravy. Mrs. Appleyard can hardly wait until it's time to go into her garden and pick materials for a V-10 cocktail: tiny carrots, peas in the pod, green beans, young onions — tops and all — parsley, radishes, three kinds of lettuce and one beet. She doesn't grow lemons but she adds a slice or two. If you have a juicer and try this, she says that she really means one medium-sized beet to a pint of juice. The rather flat taste of beets is strangely prominent in combination with other vegetables. She likes to put one in for color but one is enough. This juice can be frozen for winter use. Mrs. Appleyard wishes she had made more.

Heating Tray. You will probably use this only for company but it's a great help then for keeping coffee, casseroles and dishes of vegetables hot but not too hot. A small one for your coffeepot and a larger one for other dishes is a good combination.

Other Trays. All trays need not be electrified. You will occasionally need to carry collections of things — cups, plates, silver — from one place to another. You can save both steps and possible breakage by using a tray. Any sturdy one will do. If you like a painted one, get one with a heat-, water- and alcohol-proof finish. Mrs. Appleyard once had a habit of painting and finishing trays herself. One day recently, she went out to tea and politely commented on the tray her hostess was using.

After laughing as heartily as any lady permits herself to do on Beacon Hill, the owner of the tray announced: "You painted it. In 1920."

"I *thought* it was an antique," said one of the younger guests.

It was an antique in a good state of preservation. Mrs. Appleyard wishes she had one like it. However, she gets along all right with one of modern stainless pewter.

CASSEROLES

An electric casserole might have been added to the list of electric appliances but Mrs. Appleyard feels that if you have a skillet, you can get on all right with ordinary ones. You should have at least two, one that holds a quart and a half and a larger one. There are good casseroles of many materials, each with its virtues. *Heavy copper*, heavily tinned, distributes the heat best but the tin wears off and has to be replaced. You know that fine old greenish patina that comes on copper and brass and bronze? Bare copper quickly produces it and it is not an ingredient you had better add to the — doubtless — interesting variety in your casserole already.

Glass casseroles or glass lined with Teflon are lighter in weight than copper and easier to keep clean. They are also comparatively inexpensive, can be replaced if broken.

Perhaps Mrs. Appleyard thinks too much about lightness and weight of utensils. She hopes you are so young and strong that you don't know what she's talking about.

Enameled iron. Though heavy to handle, these have many advantages. You can sauté onion in them and indeed do most of your preliminary cooking right over a low flame. They distribute heat evenly and are rather easy to clean. However, the enamel can be chipped and cracked if you really put your mind on it — or rather off it. Mrs. Appleyard would not like to have you see what happened to the bottom of her double boiler one day when she was making a miniature rocking chair.

Pottery. Lightest in weight, good distributors and holders of heat, are old brown bowls of Vermont pottery and tortoiseshell glazed dishes of nineteenth century Bennington. It wasn't always made at Bennington though it had the name. Many potteries made such dishes. They were more fragile than they looked but that didn't matter because when one got broken, you bought a new one, twenty-five cents for a medium-sized dish, fifty cents for a larger one. Mrs. Appleyard's now all have time cracks and she has given up cooking in them, uses them for big bunches of zinnias and calendulas. They don't leak yet.

French casseroles are almost as light in weight as old Bennington dishes, they distribute heat well, and can be replaced when broken. Mrs. Appleyard's favorite is straight-sided, holds two quarts. It is perfect for soufflés and for scalloped fish or macaroni and cheese.

Not precisely casseroles, since casseroles are deep and these are shallow, are *enameled iron dishes* with covers, a sort of compromise between casseroles and frying pans. They are useful for making things au gratin. They sometimes have long handles or each may have two short projecting handles. They can be used to cook over direct heat and to slip under the broiler to brown buttery crumbs. They come in attractive colors and look well on the table at serving time.

A word about the contents of casseroles: a casserole presents a situation extraordinary on this planet. You may get something better out of it than you put in. It is true that you can take leftovers not interesting in themselves, and by the addition of well-made sauce and seasonings, turn out something palatable. But don't press your luck. A casserole in itself is not a source of magic, either black or white. A casserole should not contain everything in the ice chest but the ice cubes and trays. It should not be an anonymous mush of this and that, doused with canned soup and monosodium glutamate. It should have a main theme: that is, one detectable substance — chicken, beef, mushrooms, fish, for instance — and whatever else is in it should be there because of harmony of texture and flavor. The simplest casseroles, such as a dish of spaghetti with real cheese and cream in the sauce, are often the best.

If you do any cooking at all, you need some *holders.* The best kind covers the back of your hand as well as the palm. Have at least two of the padded mitten type to use when you take pans out of the oven. Almost any cook burns herself slightly sooner or later. Mrs. Appleyard's daughter Cicely taught her this technique for dealing with minor burns. Don't wait! Press the burned place at once against the frosted coils of your refrigerator. Hold it there till the spot begins to hurt from cold rather than from heat. As Cicely said, it won't hurt you again.

WASHING UP

Let's face it — it will have to be done and it's easier if you have a system and equipment that suits your temperament.

One spring — on her mud-time ventilation tour — Mrs. Appleyard made more than twenty visits. In some of the houses the dishes were washed in private by thinly disguised princesses — or anyway countesses — of great beauty and distinction but in most cases the hostess herself was involved in the task, so Mrs. Appleyard was too.

She says there are about as many systems as there are people. There are the pure-hot-running-water addicts and the suds lovers who use enough soap for a TV commercial. There are dishcloth users and those who have brushes at the end of a rubber hose. Some hostesses have electric dishwashers with such delicate digestions that things must be practically completely washed before they are ever stacked into the racks. Filling a dishwasher is an art in itself and there's a different art for each dishwasher.

There are characters who dry dishes, even out of a dishwasher — and there are others who feel that dish towels are so unsanitary that they don't use them except as calendars. (Frequently, if you are checking the date, you find it's a last year's calendar.) There are stackers and non-stackers of plates. There are casual rinsers and those who pour boiling water over racks of clean dishes. Some hostesses snatch your plate and wash it almost before you have eaten the last bean. Others say, "Let's leave them to soak." Some follow this method so conscientiously that they soon practice what Mrs. Appleyard calls the puddle system — everything in the sink at once, dried on whatever is handy.

Whatever the system, the volunteer assistant should accept it and not offer any ideas. It's too late now. You can probably be most useful if you learn where things belong. Mrs. Appleyard is a mine of fascinating information about where china is kept from Vermont to Virginia. She knows where to put blue Canton and Dedham pottery in one house and that lovely old Dresden we get out for company in another. Five hundred miles from her desk she knows where the Paul Revere bowl is kept and the Swedish stainless steel forks too. She moves north a little and recognizes presents she gave to a friend forty years ago and an ancestral chip off a green Minton plate. She travels a few miles more and sees another friend's great-grandmother's Chinese export porcelain. They eat off plastic. Mrs. Appleyard knows where it belongs and where the Hester Bateman saltcellars go.

With so much experience, Mrs. Appleyard ought to have valuable advice to offer about dishwashing. She says it's a case of the more she sees, the less she knows. She will state a few principles and mention the minimum equipment to get dishes clean and say no more. She has spent many happy and congenial hours washing dishes in various places. She rather doubts if washing them alone is anyone's favorite sport. Certainly if you do them alone you have a right to follow your own method.

What you need most to get dishes clean, she says, whether you have a dishwasher or not, is a double sink. One side for very hot soapsuds, the other for rinsing. She prefers to rinse under running hot water but she knows you cannot always do this. You can get some of the advantages of a double sink by using *two large dish pans* and setting them in a single sink. Use one for suds, the other for rinsing water. If your dish drainer is at your right, put your pan of suds at the left of the sink, dishes to be washed to the left of that, pan of rinsing water at the right side of the sink. On the left of the sink set a *jug full of hot suds*. In this put your table silver to soak while you are washing glasses. If you do not have a suitable jug, a sawed-off Clorox jug will do. On the counter at your right should be a *rubber dish tray* that will drain into your sink and a *dish drainer* that fits the tray.

This arrangement makes a sort of assembly line. The dishes to be washed start at the left and end up clean at the right. Of course if the necessary space for the dish drainer is at the left of your sink, you reverse the arrangement.

Not being one of the dishcloth school of thinkers, Mrs. Appleyard has a lot of *plastic sponges*. She likes best the kind attached to a handle but she has others for various uses. She uses blue ones to wipe up things spilled on the floor; admits, when questioned that this color scheme could be reversed without wrecking the economy.

She also has a bristly *vegetable brush* and — in spite of the harsh-voiced career woman on TV who keeps telling her how to fry an egg and clean the pan — she uses S.O.S. soap pads to scour anything that needs it. She says they must be good to resist the irritation caused by this advertising. Where are you, Mrs. Berg?

The kind of dishwashing Mrs. Appleyard is talking about should perhaps be described as country style. It implies that you have a good but not indefinitely plentiful supply of hot water.

Wash and rinse the glasses when your water is the hottest. Put them to drain. Stacking plates with food on them is against the Appleyard code. She does not wish to worry about food on the backs of plates. It's a great help if someone is drying the glasses with an *Irish linen* glass towel while you are starting the plates. If you are alone, dry and polish the glasses at this point and put them away.

Now do the plates: wash, rinse well, in running water for the final rinse anyway. Clean, well-rinsed plates need almost no drying.

While they are draining and drying, pour the hot suds off your silver ware. Wash in fresh very hot suds, rinse, drain and dry. The best cloth for drying silver is *cotton flannel*. It does not scratch and it polishes as you rub. Except for removing egg stains — surprisingly it's the white, not the yolk that tarnishes — you seldom need to polish silver washed in this way. Put it away. By this time the plates should be dry. Remove any stray water drops from them and put them away.

If you have many dishes, you will of course have to replace both suds and hot rinsing water at intervals. For a small number of dishes, you will probably need to replace the suds only when you start on the kitchen tools. Use plenty of suds, rinse the pieces well, stack them in the drainer. They should not need drying. If you have iron things that do need it, set them in a slightly warm oven.

Really that wasn't much work, and Mrs. Appleyard who has just made candied grapefruit peel and eaten lunch (grilled cheese sandwich, a cup of her own V-10 soup, and applesauce made last September) is going to relax and read *Richard III* by Shakespeare. (Please don't tell her it's by someone else. She's in no mood to argue.) The dishes are all washed, by the way.

And now, Mrs. Appleyard says, she thinks she has prepared for every emergency in small-time cooking and dishwashing. Yes, she knows that's impossible.

Please be sure to let her know what absolutely vital thing she's left out.

Glossary

Ashcakes are a mixture of scalded cornmeal and maple sugar made into small round cakes and put on the hearth in front of the open fire. You covered them with hot ashes which you brushed off before you ate the cakes. Mrs. Appleyard plans to stick to her ancestral iron frying pan.

Baps are slightly sweet yeast-raised rolls.

Bishop is neither a church dignitary nor a chessman. It is a sweet drink made of wine, oranges, lemons, and sugar. In the eighteenth century it was port, mulled and spiced. In the nineteenth century it was a smocked dress with long full sleeves. Mrs. Appleyard had one. She's glad she does not have to cook or play chess in those sleeves.

Blancmange. Chaucer used this term for any kind of food that was white in color. Luckily for him he never had to eat blancmange with cornstarch in it.

Blanquette is not, as one might think, a blanket. It's a dish of chicken or veal in a rich white sauce.

Bloaters are herring smoked by a process that leaves them only half dried. The thoroughly dried ones are red herring.

Bouchées are tiny cakes of mouthful size and also very small cream puffs.

Bounce is a cordial made by pouring whiskey over fresh fruit. Cherry Bounce is the best-known kind but oranges, peaches, or raspberries, or a combination of fruits may be used. Mrs. Appleyard found no mention of it in English cookbooks. Perhaps Americans invented this energy-producing fluid.

Brawn is now a term for meat in aspic jelly. It used to mean the flesh of the wild boar. Chaucer and Milton, both of whom mentioned it, would be surprised to find it in a pretty mold in company with hard-boiled eggs and tomato flowers and with radish roses around it. A roast peacock with its tail on would look more natural.

211

Bubble-and-Squeak is a mixture of meat and cabbage fried together. The name is supposed to describe how it sounds while it's cooking.

Burgoo is oatmeal mush. It is made like Hasty Pudding (q.v.).

Café au Lait is equal amounts of hot drip coffee and scalding — not boiling — milk. It is also the name for the color of this mixture.

Calves'-Foot Jelly. Quivering jellies are often mentioned in descriptions of luxurious eighteenth and early nineteenth century meals. In one of the favorites the jellying substance was supplied by cooking two or three calves' feet for several days. Mrs. Appleyard's grandmother used to make this jelly and send it around to invalids in the neighborhood. It was appropriately made in a pottery mold with a pattern of grapes and vine leaves. Since what she jellied was about a pint and a half of sherry, it is perhaps not surprising that the invalids usually sat up and took notice.

Canapés. These items to provoke the appetite were a novelty in 1880. Americans began to go to France after the Civil War and French ideas about food began to penetrate American cooking, which had always been — and still is — basically of English origin.

Carbonado is a sixteenth century term for slashing meat or fish across and broiling it over hot coals. Those gentlemen in tall white caps who scorch steak over outdoor grills are unconsciously fixing carbonado. A character in *The Winter's Tale* yearned for toads carbonadoed. Beef simmered in beer is also carbonadoed. Mrs. Appleyard will settle for what she considers a well-cooked hamburger (*Summer Kitchen*, p. 30).

Carrageen. Irish sea moss used in making blancmange.

Caudle. A warm sweet spiced gruel mixed with wine or ale, served to invalids and to their visitors.

Charlotte. Mrs. Appleyard has tried in vain to find out for whom Apple Charlotte — a mixture of applesauce and bread crumbs — and Charlotte Russe, a mold of lady fingers and whipped cream, were named. If you know, please don't keep it a secret. In exchange Mrs. Appleyard will give you a rule for a nourishing dessert that starts with ten eggs.

Chartreuse is the liqueur made by the monks of the Grande Chartreuse near Grenoble and also for an elaborate sort of game pie with truffles in it.

Chowder. Not all early cooking terms were English. Chowder came from France by way of Canada. A chowder is any dish made in a chaudière, a deep kettle. So when New Englanders say of a New York mixture of clams and tomatoes, "That isn't chowder," they are wrong. It is chowder, whether you happen to like it or not, and so is chowder beer, made by boiling black spruce in water and mixing it with molasses.

Cobbler. In England this is a summer drink made of wine, sugar, lemon and pounded ice or a winter punch of ale, spirits, sugar, and spice. In the United States a cobbler is more usually a fruit dessert baked with a topping of either shortcake dough or batter.

Cocket. Mrs. Appleyard thought this might be something made out of a young rooster. Actually it means a second-rate loaf of bread. So they had it even in the Middle Ages. There's one thing to be said for cocket: probably nothing was put into it "to retard spoilage." When it got moldy, you could throw it away.

Corinths are currants — small seedless grapes from Greece or the Levant. One of the old kitchen tasks used to be picking them over, discarding the bad ones and removing stems, sticks and stones. When a fruitcake was in view, raisins also had to be seeded and citron cut into small dice. Ah! — those good old sticky days!

Court Bouillon. An easily made broth for cooking fish (p. 30).

Dingbats. A hot breakfast muffin made with graham flour.

Dodgers. There is a rule for this form of scalded johnny cake in *The Summer Kitchen* on page 89.

Dripping is the fat that falls from roasting meat. This is an English fifteenth century term for what Americans less concisely call fat-in-the-pan.

Duff. In the north of England *dough* was sometimes pronounced to rhyme with *rough*. Duff was dough, a dough pudding boiled in a bag. With raisins in it, it was called plum duff and was considered a delicacy on English and American sailing ships.

Dumplings are biscuit dough steamed or baked, either with meat or fruit. Apple dumplings may be made in various ways. Mrs. Appleyard's method is on page 46.

Eggs. Of the numerous mysterious terms involved in cooking eggs, Mrs. Appleyard mentions only a few. For instance there are *Eggs Brouillés*. This is a dressy term for *Scrambled Eggs*. What in Vermont are now usually called scrambled eggs are called poached in some of the old cookbooks and what are often called *Poached Eggs* are also known as *Dropped Eggs*. They are slid gently from a saucer into simmering, not boiling water, cooked till the white is set and served on hot buttered toast. Mrs. Appleyard knows a much more frightening way to do this but she feels she should spare your nerves. Did you ever make a *Shirred Egg?* Shirring is also a sewing term: it means gathering up material with accurately spaced small stitches. Shirring eggs is easier. You just bake them in shallow individual earthen dishes with buttered crumbs and cream. If you like to feel French, you may call them *Oeufs sur le Plat*. Since Appleyard Center produces delicious eggs, the brown kind that are her favorites, various ways of using them are mentioned throughout the book.

Farina is finely ground meal, usually wheat, but the term may be applied to meal made of other grains. The form in which it is now commonly met with is Cream of Wheat.

Firkin. Butter, when Mrs. Appleyard first started keeping house about half a century ago, still could be bought in firkins, which are small wooden tubs. They held half a kilderkin, which is the fourth part of a tun. Is that clear? Well, anyway it was a lot of butter. She thinks it was at least twenty-five pounds. It had sometimes "turned" — a polite way of saying it was rancid — before you even bought it. If a young bride mentioned this to her dairyman, he patiently shrugged off the remark and said, "June was a long time ago. Use plenty of soda."

This is why so many old rules for cooking include large amounts of soda. As modern butter is almost invariably in good condition, soda prescribed in baking is usually unnecessary. It should not be used unless there is sour milk or molasses in the receipt. It then combines with acid and acts as a leavening agent. Even then a better result is often obtained by using only a pinch of soda and substituting baking powder for the leavening. The receipts in this book have been adjusted for good butter.

Mrs. Appleyard bought only one firkin. She has since been buying butter by the pound.

Flan. A flan is a tart made out of pastry, preferably made with butter.

Fool may be apple, Damson, blueberry or gooseberry and perhaps others. This combination of whipped cream, fruit, and custard — troublesome to make, insipid to eat — seems well named to Mrs. Appleyard.

Frumenty is hulled wheat boiled and seasoned with sugar and spice.

Galantine. Chaucer spelled it galauntyne. It used to be a sauce for fish or fowl. Later it became the term for a cold paté of white meat of chicken.

Gallimaufry means a ridiculous medley. It also means a hash or hodgepodge or a ragout. It was a way of expressing sturdy English suspicion of French cooking.

Glacé. There are many words of French origin in old American cookbooks but most of them came into England with William the Conqueror or with French refugees in the seventeenth and eighteenth centuries. Later they traveled across the Atlantic in English ships. Glacé, however, is a different kind of word, brought back from France in the nineteenth century by American travelers. It means frozen, therefore iced, therefore glazed as with ice (icing) and after a while ice cream — as in meringue glacé à la crème or bombe glacée.

Goulash. It's handy to have a lot of names for stew. Call it goulash for a change.

Grunt is a combination of dumplings and fruit.

Haggis is made of a sheep's heart, lungs, and liver, minced with suet, oatmeal, onions, and seasonings. The proper way to cook it is to boil it in the sheep's stomach. There are feeble spirits who cook it in a pudding bag. Mrs. Appleyard did so when she was testing a receipt for a magazine. Perhaps that is why she found it so uninteresting that you are in no danger of having any if you drop in for lunch.

Hardtack means ship's biscuit or sometimes ship's food in general.

Haricot. In 1653 a ragout (q.v.) of mutton was also called a haricot. At present it is a kind of French bean. Why? Littré says the ragout gave its name to the vegetable. Just one of the problems that keep writers about cooking mentally alert. (Briefly.)

Hasty Pudding. Cornmeal mush made by stirring about a quart of cornmeal into three quarts of rapidly boiling water. When the wooden pudding stick, with which you stirred it, would stand up straight, it was "Lawful Pudding" — thick enough so you could legally feed it to your apprentices. Fried Hasty Pudding was a favorite Vermont dish.

Head Cheese is made by simmering a pig's head and feet for many hours with herbs and spices. The final result is a sort of aspic with small pieces of meat in it. It is usual now to chill it in a mold. The colonial fashion was to put it into a strong linen bag, set the bag into a bowl, and lay a heavy stone on it.

Hedgehog. If we decided to make this now in Vermont we'd probably call it a porcupine. A melon-shaped mold was filled with cooked fruit in jelly. When you got it out of the mold, you covered it with whipped cream and stuck it all over with sliced blanched almonds.

Hodgepodge or *Hotchpotch* both mean casual mixtures of a variety of ingredients. Probably both are cousins of the *Hot Pot* which is a sort of casserole in which you may find tongue, kidneys, oysters, onions, and other vegetables. Some of the receipts sound good. If Mrs. Appleyard gets around to trying one, she thinks she'll make it in a bean pot.

Hoe Cake. You need a broad-bladed hoe if you are going to cook johnny cake on it.

Hominy is the nineteenth century term for hulled corn. The term may be applied to all the grinds of hominy. *Samp* or *Big Hominy* was the coarsest and the finest was about the texture of coarse granulated sugar. When Mrs. Appleyard first came to Vermont, the hulled corn man used to come to the door once a week. What he offered was a dipper full of white and yellow kernels made by soaking the corn in soda, removing the hulls by repeated rinsings and then cooking it. Mr. Appleyard said it was an acquired taste. He ate it with thick cream and lots of dry, granulated maple sugar. These substances have an alleviating effect on a number of things but not — so far as Mrs. Appleyard was concerned — on hulled corn. She feels differently about finely ground hominy, says it makes the best spoon bread.

Honeycomb Tripe. Mrs. Appleyard tried valiantly but she never learned to like this either. Tripe is made from the second stomach of ruminants. It has a hexagonal pattern rather like honeycomb. The English brought both tripe and honeycomb to New England. They did not bring honeybees till 1638. This was a happy surprise to the Indians because what they called the white man's fly, like other immigrants, preferred the wide open spaces to their hives. Pretty soon Indians were expertly tracking bees to hollow trees and enjoying the honey. This is one time we did something good for the Indians.

Of course it was an accident.

Isinglass. About 1528 it was discovered that you did not really need to cook calves' feet for several days to make wine jelly. The air bladders of certain fresh-water fish had the jellying property strongly developed. The Russian sturgeon's air bladder made the best isinglass, a term said to be derived from the German word for it. It came in thin sheets and you broke off a suitable amount. Cookbooks did not guess any more closely than that for you. A lot of the romance and sense of peril vanished when you were told to take a pint of water and an envelope full of gelatin and feel quite sure you could jelly something. It took American know-how about three centuries to catch on and make American isinglass and almost another century before they called it Jello.

The mica, also called isinglass, through which the fire in the airtight stove used to glow so cheeringly, was not suitable for jellying anything, no matter what the cook told you. That was just her technical sense of humor.

Jerusalem Artichoke is a complicated name for a simple North American vegetable. It is the root of a sunflower. A sunflower is also a girasole and someone — no one knows who — decided that it must mean they came from Jerusalem. The English, always logical, call a soup made from them Palestine soup. Mrs. Appleyard has some growing back of her woodshed. There are suggestions for using them on page 67.

Johnny Cake is another name of mystery. Perhaps it comes from Journey Cake and New Englanders dropped the *r* and made it Jonny Cake. Perhaps it was originally Shawnee Cake. In old cookbooks it is sometimes Jonne Cake. In Rhode Island where the best cornmeal was grown and slowly ground to keep it white, it was usually called Jonny Cake. It could be made on a journey and baked on a board in front of the fire. It can still be made without this equipment (see p. 63).

Jumbles or *Jumbals* are crisp, rich sugar cookies. The classic kind was cut with a doughnut cutter and had a hole in the middle. Good-natured cooks baked the resulting small circles too and they were the perquisites of children whose noses brought them to the kitchen at the right time.

Junket was originally a basket made of rushes for carrying fish. Then it was a cream cheese made in such a basket. Later, about 1460, it was a dish of curds, sweetened and flavored, with a layer of thick cream on top. In Mrs. Appleyard's childhood it was a slippery white substance made of milk by using rennet from a calf's stomach and sweetened with sugar and vanilla. She and her brother called it slippy-go-down and declined it, he with bellows of wrath, she with large silent tears. She kept a supply of tears on hand for rice pudding, cornstarch pudding, turnips and parsnips. Why she was allowed to grow up, she is not able to understand.

Junket has also some cheerful associations. In the eighteenth century you might call any dainty kickshaw a junket. In America a junket was any outing at which eating and drinking were the chief entertainment. In winter in Vermont there were kitchen junkets. You took the board off the trestles, leaned it against the wall, set the trestles in the woodshed and shoved the chairs back against the wall. The fiddler played "Money Musk" and "The Devil's Dream" and "Portland Fancy." Some children were big enough to dance with their grandparents. The small ones, some clutching kittens, wandered among the dancers. So did their dogs. Later there was hot spiced cider and doughnuts. This was the kind of junket Mrs. Appleyard likes to think about.

Kedgeree. This dish originated in India where it is made with rice, onions, spices, eggs, and split pulse. To make pulse you have to have esculent leguminous plants. Mrs. Appleyard is delighted to be, quite suddenly, in a position to tell you that these are beans and lentils. (Please don't ask her how to split pulse.) In England and also in the colonies, they mixed leftover fish with rice, eggs, and spices and called it kedgeree soon after the Pilgrims arrived. It was supposed to be served very hot.

Ketchup, also spelled Catsup and in 1711 catchup. It probably comes from a Chinese word meaning the brine of pickled fish. Tomato ketchup is the best-loved kind in America but it may be made of mushrooms or walnuts or cranberries. Vermonters made Apple Ketchup.

Kickshaw. As early as 1597 the English began to express their contempt for the fussiness of French cooking. *Kickshaw* was the English way of saying *quelque chose*, meaning something — you aren't sure just what. Now a big hunk of tough mutton and an ancient cabbage, boiled in lots of water: you knew exactly what *that* was. In fact you had known for hours. It might not taste better than kickshaws but it had a basic straightforwardness that made it natural to eat it and feel morally superior. The Puritans brought this attitude to America. Perhaps it's time we outgrew it.

Kipper. This is a fish, usually a herring, rubbed repeatedly with salt and dried in the open air or in smoke. English kippers go well for breakfast with American hominy and Scotch marmalade, the kind made of Seville oranges.

Larder. We now think of the larder as being our whole store of provisions wherever we keep them. Its name originally meant the place where bacon, salt pork, and lard were kept.

Lobscouse. This was the marine version of the Boiled Dinner. Sailors mixed salt horse, as they called salt beef, with potatoes, onions, and any other vegetables available. When it had boiled several hours, they crumbled ship's biscuit into it. In 1706 this was considered a delicacy.

Macédoine is the French name for a mixture of fruit or vegetables embedded in jelly. So that was a macédoine you took to the church supper — and a delicious one if Mrs. Appleyard's experience is worth anything.

Marzipan or *Marchpane.* Some people think this name means March Bread because it was used to cheer people up in that long month of mud and wind. However, at New Year's Queen Elizabeth's chief cook always gave her an elaborate Marchpane, sometimes made in the shape of a palace, so it seems to have been eaten at other seasons. The traveled sophisticate who had been to Italy started to call it Marzipan about 1494 but among the simple characters who pounded up the almonds to make it, the old name hung on for quite a while. It was made originally of almonds and white of egg and sweetened with honey. Later sugar was used to sweeten it. Not until the twentieth century was it discovered that you could make it of cornstarch and Elmer's Glue All and flavor it with imitation almond. We are an ingenious people. Just give us time and some fish flour and we'll soon make delicious beefsteak. In the meantime, if you would like to make Marzipan, the rule is in *The Winter Kitchen* (p. 113).

Mead. This is a very old drink. Beowulf praised it. Another name for it is metheglin. Honey and water are fermented and the mixture is ready when it makes the head of the man who drinks it hum like a hive. Making it is simple: just track some bees to a hollow tree. Or would you rather have what Americans called metheglin in 1890? It was sarsaparilla soda. Probably few heads hummed.

Muffineer. Like a salt shaker only much bigger, for dredging things with sugar, usually made of silver.

Mull. To mull is to make ale or beer or wine into a hot drink with sugar and spice and beaten egg yolks. The English were doing this before 1607. Vermonters began to do so as soon as they got to Vermont and their hens began to lay. *The Winter Kitchen* (p. 113).

Nasturtiums. Nasturtium seeds may be pickled and used instead of capers in Caper Sauce or Tartar Sauce. Soak them in salted water for a day. Drain and rinse. Put them in a jar, fill it up with hot cider vinegar. Seal tightly. The flowers may be used in sandwiches.

Osmazome. This is what makes a roast of beef smell so good when it's cooking. It is said to be soluble in alcohol. Mrs. Appleyard thought of inventing an aerosol spray flavored with it to have around the kitchen but she's busy just now baking a meat loaf which has a pretty good osmazome anyway. Anyone who would like the idea is welcome to it. Just send her a couple of cans in return.

Pampelmoose or *Pampelmouse*. English versions for the French name for a grapefruit. Pampelmouse is what Mrs. Appleyard calls a grapefruit if it annoys her for any reason such as squirting her in the eye. *Shaddock* is another name for grapefruit.

Pandowdy. This combination of fruit and biscuit dough is not unlike a slump, a grunt or a cobbler. Probably all the names imply that the dessert is rather casually constructed without the nervous strain involved in making meringues and custards. Mrs. Appleyard's version of pandowdy is on page 172.

Pasty. A square of pastry filled with chopped meat, folded into a triangle and baked.

Pâté maison. An optimistic term for meat loaf.

Pemmican. We learned from the Indians to dry and pound lean meat and form it with melted fat into small cakes. It kept well and was a condensed form of food useful to explorers and soldiers.

Pièce de résistance. The main item in a meal such as a roast — the thing you really get your teeth into.

Pikelets. These are something like crumpets but a little larger. They are baked on a griddle.

Pilchards. Shakespeare knew these fish, a sort of small herring.

Pilgarlic is not — as one might think in our time of shortcuts — a convenient form of instant garlic. It is a sixteenth century term for a bald-headed man.

Pilau or *Pilaff* is an oriental dish of rice cooked with lamb, chicken, or fish with spices and raisins.

Pompion. This was how you spelled pumpkin in 1545.

Portable Soup. A strong broth of beef and vegetables, strained, jellied, dried and cut in squares. Mrs. Appleyard tells how to make it on page 71.

Posset. Hot milk with sugar and spice curdled with wine. In medieval England it was considered good for a cold. A posset cup is really a small covered bowl standing in a deep saucer. Posset was sometimes sweetened, thickened with brown-bread crumbs, and eaten with a spoon. The wine used might be "sherris sack" (dry sherry) or a combination of ingredients such as beer, whiskey, and brandy. Beaten eggs and spices creep in and out of it. Just which version cures a cold best is a question still undergoing statistical studies. You had to have a cold to be sure of getting some.

Powdered Soup. Powdering up dried herbs and spices for soup is an invention at least a century old. Make your own next summer (*see Bouquet*, p. 190).

Quahogs or *Quahaugs*. The Narraganset Indian name for the round clams which many New Englanders think make the best chowder.

Quenelles are balls of pounded, seasoned fish poached in a court bouillon (p. 30).

Ragout. A highly seasoned meat and vegetable stew, often made with mutton. To *ragouter* is literally to revive the taste of something. Mrs. Appleyard's study of old cookbooks has led her to believe that it was often necessary to conceal the taste of something. She rather thinks a ragout was one way of doing it.

Ratafia. A cordial flavored with almonds or peach kernels or small cakes flavored with the cordial.

Ratatouille. A stew of vegetables including tomatoes, eggplant and onions cooked in olive oil.

Rattle Ran (or Rand). This is a cut of beef often used for corned beef.

Rechauffé is the elegant way of describing warmed-over meat. *Miroton* is another name for it. How well you do it is more important than the name.

Rissoles are rounds of pastry with a croquette mixture of meat or fish rolled up in the pastry. They are fried in deep fat, not exactly a dish for calorie counters.

Risotto. A stew of rice, chicken and onions.

Rye 'n Injun. The combination of ground rye and cornmeal used in many Vermont dishes. Graham flour might also be combined with them in steamed or baked Brown Bread (see p. 19).

Salamander. This was a circular iron plate with a long handle. You heated it red-hot and put it over a pudding to brown it. "If you have not a salamander," says Miss Parloa, "the fire shovel can be heated and used in the same way; but the shovel is not improved by the operation." Mrs. Appleyard rather wonders if the pudding was. Another kind of salamander was "an iron poker heated red hot for lighting a pipe, gun powder, etc." Our ancestors certainly liked to live dangerously.

Saleratus. In the early part of the last century this was an impure bicarbonate of potash used in baking. Later the name was transferred to bicarbonate of soda, which is still, often needlessly, sometimes harmfully, prescribed for cooking. It should never be used in vegetables because it destroys vitamins as well as flavor. Mrs. Appleyard says if you want your peas and asparagus to look like a billiard table, you had better put in some harmless artificial green coloring. Soda is used with cream of tartar as baking powder. You can make this combination yourself but the manufacturers really do a better job than most individuals can.

Salmi is a ragout (q.v.) of partly cooked game stewed with wine, herbs, spices, and thickened with bread crumbs.

Sallet was the early Vermont name for salad. No one had heard of olive oil in Appleyard Center in 1912. Lettuce was still eaten with vinegar and sugar. Mrs. Appleyard thought it was probably nice if you liked it.

Salsify is also called oyster plant. It is the esculent root of the purple goatsbeard. It tastes more like parsnips than it does like oysters.

Salpicon is a mixture of minced meat or fish with mushrooms or truffles. Serve it with a rich sauce in pastry shells.

Samovar. The Russians, ever inventive, use this tea urn in which water is heated by plunging a hot metal cylinder into it.

Sass. "What did you have for garden sass?" means what vegetable did you have with your meat? There is also just sass, which may mean applesauce or stewed blueberries.

Savouries. This is the English term for appetizers or hors d'oeuvres; only the English, a hardy race, eat them at the end of the meal instead of beforehand, sometimes as well as beforehand. They include Angels on Horseback which are oysters and bacon on toast, Welsh rabbit, anchovies and sardines and various clever little arrangements of whatever is left in the Fridge. This word, if nothing else, would keep Mrs. Appleyard from eating any.

Scrag or *Scrag end* is the lean and inferior end of a neck of mutton. Perhaps after this is served, a few savouries might work wonders.

Scones are not very different from baking powder biscuit but they are baked on a griddle instead of in the oven. A griddle, in northern England and Scotland, is often called a girdle. Vermonters sometimes call it that too.

Scrapple. You have to have a pig's head to make this correctly. Mrs. Appleyard gives a less terrifying version on page 62–63.

Scrod. There seems to be some misunderstanding of this term. Lately Mrs. Appleyard has heard it used as merely another name for a young cod. She was brought up to believe that it might be either a cod or a haddock, weighing perhaps two pounds, split down the back and broiled. Plenty of butter was put on it while it was broiling and more melted butter was served with it. The last she knew, you could get it at the Parker House in Boston. When she bought it to cook it at home, she used to order "a haddock scrodded."

Shrub. This word may originally be the Arabic *shurb*, which means a drink. In the eighteenth century it was made of lemon, sugar, and rum. In Vermont it usually means Raspberry Shrub (see p. 115). It is sometimes spelled *Srub*.

Sippet. A small piece of toasted or fried bread to dip into soup or gravy. Cleaning your plate with a sippet was a tribute to your hostess's cooking. Let's all use sippets!

Skilly. A thin watery gruel with oatmeal in it. Prisoners were fed on it.

Slump, like grunt, is a combination of sweetened fruit — blueberries, raspberries or peaches — and dumplings.

Sole. A delicious flat fish found in European and English waters. Our American flounder is a fairly acceptable substitute for it.

Soufflé à la poêle. This was a breakfast dish in the nineteenth century. It's a sort of omelet.

Soup Maigre or meagre (French soupe maigre). A thin soup of vegetables or fish; no meat.

Souse. An eagle soused when he swooped down on a hare but in cooking, to souse meat or fish is to plunge it into some sort of pickle. Sometimes the beginning of the process was to powder the meat with saltpeter. The liquid used might be vinegar but a sheep's head was sometimes soused in ale.

The term was so well known that a minister once prayed: "Souse us in the powdering tub of Thy mercy that we may be tripes fit for the heavenly table."

His congregation understood him perfectly.

Spider. A spider, like a skillet, has legs and a long handle. It may also be called a trivet or a griddle.

Spoon Meat. This is a mixture of meat and vegetables, thicker than soup, thinner than stew. It was an advantage in pioneer days in Vermont to serve something that could be eaten with a spoon. If a spoon broke — as pewter ones often did — you simply tossed the pieces into the pan in which you melted up the pewter. When your husband felt in the mood, he got out his bullet mold and the spoon mold, made bullets for himself and made you half a dozen spoons.

Forks were more difficult to come by. They had to be made of steel or silver to be strong enough to eat with. The early ones had only two tines. That is why many Vermonters ate peas with their knives. It was, if done with dexterity, a perfectly neat process, Mrs. Appleyard says, for she used to enjoy watching it at church suppers fifty years ago. Women, conventional creatures, dominated by etiquette books, fussed around with forks but there were always some strong silent men who tucked their napkins into their collars and got to work with spoons and knives, with energy and dispatch, and with apparent satisfaction.

Succotash. This is the English way of pronouncing the word misickquatash, meaning a combination of beans and young corn (see p. 126).

Sweet or *Sweets.* In England the sweet is what we call dessert. Sweets are candy. Dessert is crackers and cheese or nuts and raisins eaten after the ladies have left the room and the men — in English nineteenth century novels anyway — are circulating old port around the table. Probably now they all have a good time in the butler's pantry together washing up the dishes.

Stock. Liquor made by boiling bones and meat, usually with vegetables, herbs, and spices, as a foundation for soups and sauces. See page 71.

Switchel. A cooling drink of molasses, vinegar, and water, sometimes with rum added, served to haymakers (see p. 116).

Taffy is the early English and also the American name for what the English now call toffee.

Timbale is a finely chopped mixture of fish or meat cooked in a mold of a special shape.

Tipsy Cake. A cake soaked with wine or brandy or rum, stuck with almonds and served with custard.

Trifle is rather like tipsy cake (see p. 65).

Toad-in-the-Hole. Toads have an undeserved reputation — the list of unpleasant epithets containing the word toad is a long one. One of the few good things associated with toads is this dish, a sort of Yorkshire pudding with sausages baked in the batter.

Trivet. A trivet is a three-footed stand on which a cooking pot could be set over hot coals in the fire place. Later the contents of the pot could be kept warm beside the fire. The modern use of a trivet is to act as a support for a very hot dish so that its heat will not injure the table on which it stands. It was very important for the blacksmith who made your trivet to get the legs all the same length and the top even. When he did so things went well because everything was all right — as right as a trivet, in fact.

Uncle Toby is the name for a jug made in the shape of a stout man in eighteenth century costume. It is also the name for a potent English punch. Perhaps the jug and the punch both are named for Tristram Shandy's Uncle Toby. He was not a water drinker "except fortuitously upon some advanced posts, where better liquor was not to be had." It was in the nineteenth century that Mrs. Appleyard heard an Englishman say of water, "What! Drink that stuff! Look what it does to your boots!"

No water ever goes into Mrs. Appleyard's Toby jug — just carrot juice.

Vinaigrette. A sauce for fish. It is rather like French Dressing (see p. 122).

Vol-au-Vent. A pie of pastry so light it will "fly in the wind." The contents, chicken or seafood in a rich cream sauce, keep it on the ground.

Wassail. A spiced liquor in which healths were drunk in England at Christmas time. Any excuse was good enough; they even went to orchards and drank the health of apple trees. Mrs. Appleyard wishes she had known about this ceremony earlier. Her apple trees need all the encouragement they can get.

Yeast. Mrs. Appleyard has about eighteen rules for making yeast, all different. She uses yeast cakes.

NOTE: Most of the information about these cooking terms came from the *Oxford English Dictionary*.

Index